BACH PERSPECTIVES

VOLUME 1

BACH PERSPECTIVES

VOLUME ONE

Published by the University of Nebraska Press in
association with the American Bach Society

Bach
Perspectives

Edited by Russell Stinson

VOLUME ONE

University of Nebraska Press

Lincoln and London 1995

ISSN 1072-1924
ISBN 0-8032-1042-6

CONTENTS

v

PREFACE

Bach Perspectives, to be issued as a serial, aims to develop and publish new studies on Johann Sebastian Bach. Each volume will include critical essays and commentaries on Bach's music as well as reviews of recent publications. In order to reflect the breadth and diversity of present-day Bach scholarship, the series will focus not only on the composer's life and works but also on the social and cultural context of his music; in addition, it will include occasional essays on the music of his contemporaries.

Sponsored by the American Bach Society, *Bach Perspectives* represents a "coming of age" for American Bach research. While its origins date back to the middle of the last century in Germany, Bach scholarship did not begin to flourish in this country until the 1940s, stimulated in large part by the German-trained scholars who immigrated here during the previous decade. One of the first to publish in English was Hans Theodore David, who received his doctorate in Berlin in 1928, left Germany in 1933 for Holland, and settled in America in 1936. In 1945, G. Schirmer brought out his monograph *J. S. Bach's "Musical Offering": History, Interpretation, and Analysis.* The same year W. W. Norton published *The Bach Reader*, which David edited in collaboration with Arthur Mendel.

The increasing role that Bach research came to play in American scholarly and academic life over the next several decades can be seen in the founding, in 1972, of an American chapter of the Neue Bachgesellschaft. Its first publication projects, including Robert L. Marshall's facsimile edition *Johann Sebastian Bach, Fantasia per il Cembalo*, BWV 906 (1976) and Gerhard Herz's *Bach Sources in America* (1984), were undertaken with the support of its German parent organization. More recently, the chapter's successor, the American Bach Society, sponsored the publication of *A Bach Tribute: Essays in Honor of William H. Scheide.* And from 1989 to 1993 it joined with the Riemenschneider Bach Institute to issue the journal *Bach.*

Now, in initiating its own publication series, the Society seeks to establish a new forum for scholars, teachers, performers, and others interested in Bach and his music. As the title implies, we hope to embrace as wide a variety of perspectives as possible and to publish not only biographical research, source studies, and analytical and interpretive essays but also articles that deal with questions of performance, with social and theological issues, and with the printing and distribution of Bach's music. (The second volume in the series will focus on J. S. Bach and the Breitkopf music publishers in Leipzig.) To assist us in achieving this end, we have assembled an Editorial Board that represents a broadly based view of Bach research and includes several generations of Bach scholars; we plan that a single editor will be responsible for each volume.

The first volume originated as a collection of essays drawn together by Russell Stinson. Its authors address new topics as well as reexamine old questions from a new point of view. David Schulenberg explores the interrelationship of improvisation and composition through a study of Bach's keyboard music. By linking graphological and stylistic evidence, Russell Stinson casts the compositional history of the *Orgelbüchlein* in a new light, while Michael Marissen's consideration of extramusical issues brings a fresh perspective to another of the composer's well-known works. In looking anew at the role of parody in a secular cantata, Stephen Crist elucidates Bach's ingenious working methods when faced with a deadline. And Eric Chafe and James Brokaw use stylistic and critical analysis to illuminate, first, the harmonic and theological dimensions of a New Year's Day cantata and, second, the questions of attribution that surround a little-known keyboard fugue. Two of the authors, Crist and Schulenberg, contribute reviews of a collection of biographical and critical essays by Christoph Wolff and an anthology of keyboard pieces edited by Robert Hill from the manuscripts of Johann Christoph Bach, Johann Sebastian's older brother and teacher.

The inauguration of *Bach Perspectives* comes at an auspicious moment in the history of Bach scholarship. Just as the end of the nineteenth century coincided with the completion of the Bachgesellschaft edition, begun fifty years earlier to commemorate the centenary of Bach's death, so the end of the twentieth century will mark the final stage in the publication of the Neue Bach-Ausgabe (NBA), initiated in 1950. Its implications for Bach research, however, differ markedly from those of its predecessor. In the beginning years of this century, scholars such as Charles Sanford Terry and Albert Schweitzer, following immediately on the heels of Philipp Spitta, sought to paint a detailed and complete picture of a composer still known primarily for his instrumental music. At the century's close, the broad outlines of this picture remain intact. But we now view Bach's career as a composer in a new light as a result of the

diplomatic studies of Alfred Dürr and Georg von Dadelsen, the "new Bach research" of the 1950s that dramatically altered the dating of his compositions
and thereby the context in which he conceived and wrote them. To reassess
Bach's music not only in terms of this new chronology but also in reference to
the society of his day is a process that, as several essays in the present volume
attest, is well under way – and one to which we hope *Bach Perspectives* will make
a significant contribution.

Don O. Franklin, President
The American Bach Society

ABBREVIATIONS

BC — Hans-Joachim Schulze and Christoph Wolff, eds. *Bach Compendium: Analytisch-bibliographisches Repertorium der Werke Johann Sebastian Bachs*. Leipzig: Edition Peters, 1985-.

BDOK — *Bach-Dokumente*. [Edited by the Bach-Archiv, Leipzig, as a supplement to the NBA.] 4 vols. Kassel: Bärenreiter; Leipzig: VEB Deutscher Verlag für Musik, 1963-78.

Vol. 1: Werner Neumann and Hans-Joachim Schulze, eds. *Schriftstücke von der Hand Johann Sebastian Bachs.*

Vol. 2: Werner Neumann and Hans-Joachim Schulze, eds. *Fremdschriftliche und gedruckte Dokumente zur Lebensgeschichte Johann Sebastian Bachs 1685–1750.*

Vol. 3: Hans-Joachim Schulze, ed. *Dokumente zum Nachwirken Johann Sebastian Bachs 1750–1800.*

Vol. 4: Werner Neumann, ed. *Bilddokumente zur Lebensgeschichte Johann Sebastian Bachs.*

BG — [Bachgesellschaft ed.] *Johann Sebastian Bach's Werke*. 47 vols. Leipzig: Breitkopf & Härtel, 1851-99.

BR — Hans T. David and Arthur Mendel, eds. *The Bach Reader: A Life of Johann Sebastian Bach in Letters and Documents*. Rev. ed. New York: W. W. Norton & Co., 1966.

BUXWV — [Buxtehude-Werke-Verzeichnis.] Georg Karstädt. *Thematisch-systematisches Verzeichnis der musikalischen Werke von Dietrich Buxtehude*. Wiesbaden: Breitkopf & Härtel, 1974.

BWV — [Bach-Werke-Verzeichnis.] Wolfgang Schmieder. *Thematisch-systematisches Verzeichnis der musikalischen Werke von Johann Sebastian Bach*. Rev. ed. Wiesbaden: Breitkopf & Härtel, 1990.

BWV ANH. — [Appendix (*Anhang*) to the BWV.]

F. Martin Falck. *Wilhelm Friedemann Bach: Sein Leben und seine Werke.* Studien zur Musikwissenschaft, vol. 1. Leipzig: C. F. Kahnt, 1913. Reprint, Lindau: C. F. Kahnt, 1956.

H. E. Eugene Helm. *Thematic Catalogue of the Works of Carl Philipp Emanuel Bach.* New Haven, Conn.: Yale University Press, 1989.

HWV [Händel-Werke-Verzeichnis.] Bernd Baselt. *Thematisch-systematisches Verzeichnis: Instrumentalmusik, Pasticci und Fragmente.* Händel-Handbuch, vol. 3. Kassel: Bärenreiter, 1986.

KB [Kritischer Bericht (critical report of the NBA).]

MBLPZ Musikbibliothek der Stadt Leipzig.

NBA [Neue Bach-Ausgabe.] *Johann Sebastian Bach: Neue Ausgabe sämtlicher Werke.* Edited by the Johann-Sebastian-Bach-Institut, Göttingen, and the Bach-Archiv, Leipzig. Kassel: Bärenreiter; Leipzig: Deutscher Verlag für Musik, 1954–.

P Partitur. [Music score, abbreviation used by the SBB.]

QV [Quantz-Werkeverzeichnis.] Horst Augsbach. *Johann Joachim Quantz: Thematisches Verzeichnis der musikalischen Werke. Werkgruppe QV2 und QV3.* Studien und Materialien zur Musikgeschichte Dresdens, vol. 5. Dresden: Sächsische Landesbibliothek, 1984.

RV [Ryom-Verzeichnis.] Peter Ryom. *Répertoire des œuvres d'Antonio Vivaldi: Les compositions instrumentales.* Copenhagen: Engstrøm & Sødring, 1986.

SBB Staatsbibliothek zu Berlin–Preussischer Kulturbesitz, Musikabteilung.

ST Stimmen. [Performing parts, abbreviation used by the SBB.]

W. Alfred Wotquenne. *Catalogue thèmatique des œuvres de Charles Philippe Emmanuel Bach (1714–1788).* Leipzig: Breitkopf & Härtel, 1905. Reprint, Wiesbaden: Breitkopf & Härtel, 1972.

Composition and Improvisation in the School of J. S. Bach

David Schulenberg

For almost as long as Bach's music has been studied and enjoyed, his practice and teaching of composition have been a focus of interest nearly as intense. What is offered here is a review of the evidence concerning the subject as well as a consideration of the close relationship in the Bach circle between composition and improvisation and of how this may affect our views of music history during the period. The emphasis here will be on composition and improvisation at the keyboard since this was the primary sphere in which Bach taught these subjects.[1]

The close relationship between composition and improvisation in eighteenth-century music is well known. Yet the details of the improvisation process and the precise nature of its relationship to composition have rarely been considered. Moreover, the apparent paradox of a strong tradition of improvisation within a musical culture that prized rational structure and highly stylized ornament raises historical and aesthetic issues that remain to be explored. Perhaps it is inevitable that Bach studies, even more than most branches of musical scholarship, have tended to focus on documents, in part because Sebastian and Emanuel Bach were themselves avid collectors of scores and careful revisers and editors of their own music. But those who study early chant or non-Western musical traditions understand that what happens to be written down

---

1. Thus C. P. E. Bach wrote to Johann Nicolaus Forkel (letter of 13 January 1775): "Since he himself [Sebastian] had composed the most instructive pieces for the clavier, he brought up his pupils on them" (BDOK 3, no. 803; translation taken from BR, 279). Because of the emphasis here on keyboard music, little reference will be made to what is still the principal study of Bach's compositional process: Robert Lewis Marshall, *The Compositional Process of J. S. Bach: A Study of the Autograph Scores of the Vocal Works*, 2 vols. (Princeton, N.J.: Princeton University Press, 1972).

represents only a small fraction of the musical culture under study. Even in dealing with a composer as strongly oriented to the written note and word as J. S. Bach, we might bear in mind that his musical culture was much more aural than our own. The surviving documents represent only the tip of the iceberg, the visible remains of musical practices and musical thought that are largely hidden to us, although perhaps not entirely unrecoverable.

With respect to keyboard music, many of the documents concerning teaching and practice in the Bach circle relate not to composition as such but to a tradition in which composition and improvisation were two aspects of a single activity. What Bach and other keyboard players of his day actually did in fulfilling their professional obligations involved a great deal of improvisation: the realization of figured-bass accompaniments, the performance of preludes during a church service, and so forth. Written-out solo pieces were employed principally for teaching and study, although Sebastian Bach was noted for his use of written scores in his public recitals, at least "to set his powers of imagination" in motion.[2] Moreover, Sebastian, like other organists, was expected to improvise fugues and chorale fantasies in his auditions for organ posts, and any responsible teacher would have made preparation for such trials an important part of teaching. We might suppose that this, but not composition as such, was part of the "instruction suitable for an organist" that Bach received from his older brother Johann Christoph, according to a report by Emanuel Bach.[3] Emanuel himself and other members of his generation must have received the same from Sebastian.

Although the sources say little if anything specifically about training in improvisation, this skill clearly depended on many of the same concepts and mental disciplines as did composition. Quantz, for example, mentioned the need for flutists to understand "harmony" (*die Harmonie*), presumably meaning figured bass, in order to improvise embellishments in an adagio.[4] Emanuel Bach

2. See the report by T. L. Pitschel in BDOK 2, no. 499; and BR, 290.

3. Letter to Forkel, 13 January 1775. Since Emanuel is evidently answering Forkel's questions about Sebastian's study of composition, the implication is that Emanuel does not believe that Johann Christoph provided instruction in written composition.

4. Johann Joachim Quantz, *Versuch einer Anweisung die Flöte traversiere zu spielen* (Berlin, 1752; reprint, with introduction by Barthold Kuijken, Wiesbaden: Breitkopf & Härtel, 1988); trans. Edward J. Reilly as *An Essay on Playing the Flute* (London: Faber & Faber, 1966), 14.3. According to Burney, Quantz attributed his knowledge of how to perform an adagio and to "compose

refers to his father's pedagogic use of figured-bass realization,[5] and indeed we possess a written-out realization of the bass of an Albinoni sonata by Bach's student Heinrich Nicolaus Gerber.[6] Similar exercises must have led to the scrupulous attention that Emanuel Bach devotes to voice leading in the section of his *Essay* devoted to figured bass.[7] Yet the *Essay* is concerned with the "true manner of keyboard *playing*," and any written exercises given to Emanuel's pupils must have complemented practical ones.

THE SOURCES

The relevant evidence is summarized in the appendix. Obviously, almost any composition and any autograph source by Bach might be considered relevant; the sources listed are those that seem to bear directly on the question of how Bach and his students understood the act of composition or improvisation.[8]

Two aspects of the appendix are noteworthy. First, an important category of material conspicuous by its absence is learned counterpoint. But learned counterpoint occupies a somewhat ambiguous place in the Bach circle. Today we tend to see Bach as a proponent of strict fugue, canon, and other such forms. In this we observe a distinction between him and his contemporaries (such as Handel) that was already being made during his own lifetime.[9] Bach

---

in many parts" to Pisendel (see Charles Burney, *The Present State of Music in Germany* ... [London, 1775]; ed. Percy A. Scholes as *An Eighteenth-Century Musical Tour in Central Europe and the Netherlands* [London: Oxford University Press, 1959], 187).

5. Letter to Forkel, 13 January 1775.

6. Gerber's realization (with Bach's corrections) appears in SBB MUS. MS 455, ed. in Philipp Spitta, *Johann Sebastian Bach*, 2 vols. (Leipzig: Breitkopf & Härtel, 1873-80; reprint, Wiesbaden: Breitkopf & Härtel, 1979), vol. 2, *Musikbeilagen*, pp. 1-11.

7. C. P. E. Bach, *Versuch über die wahre Art das Clavier zu spielen* (Berlin, 1753-62; reprint, Wiesbaden: Breitkopf & Härtel, 1981); trans. William J. Mitchell as *Essay on the True Art of Playing Keyboard Instruments* (New York: W. W. Norton & Co., 1949).

8. The appendix incorporates a number of items included in an earlier overview of the subject in Hans-Joachim Schulze, "Cembaloimprovisation bei Johann Sebastian Bach: Versuch einer Übersicht," *Studien zur Aufführungspraxis und Interpretation von Instrumentalmusik des 18. Jahrhunderts* 10 (1980): 50-57.

9. See, e.g., Marpurg's 1749 distinction between "the works of the invaluable Handel and the learned Bach," emphasizing the latter's appeal to "the practiced ear" (BDOK 2, no. 581).

himself contributed to this impression through his publication of several late works concerned with strict counterpoint. The Art of Fugue was even advertised after Bach's death as a sort of textbook in learned counterpoint, in the form of exemplary compositions.[10]

Yet these publications seem to have been directed less toward students than toward "those already practiced in this study," to quote a phrase that Bach himself used in the title of Book 1 of the Well-Tempered Clavier.[11] Indeed, we possess almost no evidence, in the form of students' notebooks or reports, about Bach's teaching of learned counterpoint. Friedemann and Emanuel Bach must at least have made experimental efforts as composers of learned counterpoint since they contributed a few canonic pieces to writings and anthologies by Marpurg and Kirnberger, and Emanuel Bach's works include a number of essays in strict contrapuntal style.[12] Yet, in his letters and in accounts by Forkel and Charles Burney, C. P. E. Bach has almost nothing good to say about the study of counterpoint. While there appears to have been a resurgence of theoretical interest in strict counterpoint in the decades following Bach's death, in works like Marpurg's *Abhandlung von der Fuge* one can already detect an academic, inorganic approach to the study of fugue. Contrapuntal technique is

10. "Der Kunst der Fuga in 24 Exempeln" (from the notice of 1 June 1751 in the *Leipziger Zeitungen* [BDOK 3, no. 639]).

11. "Derer in diesem studio schon habil" (BDOK 1, no. 152; BR, 85).

12. See the musical examples in Friedrich Wilhelm Marpurg, *Abhandlung von der Fuge*, 2 vols. (Berlin, 1753-54; reprint, Hildesheim: Georg Olms, 1970), vol. 2; and in Johann Philipp Kirnberger, *Die Kunst des reinen Satzes in der Musik*, 3 vols. (Berlin and Königsberg, 1771-79; reprint, Hildesheim: Georg Olms, 1968); vol. 1 and vol. 2, pt. 1, trans. David Beach and Jurgen Thym as *The Art of Strict Musical Composition* [New Haven, Conn.: Yale University Press, 1982]). Marpurg published annotated editions of C. P. E. Bach's fugues H.76 (w.119/1), H.101 (w.119/4), and H.102 (w.119/6); for sources and editions, see E. Eugene Helm, *Thematic Catalogue of the Works of Carl Philipp Emanuel Bach* (New Haven, Conn.: Yale University Press, 1989). The closing fugue of Emanuel's Magnificat H.772 (w.215) was later reworked in his Easter Music of 1784, H.807 (w.243), with many additional "contrapuntal devices" (*viele contrapunktische Künste*), as Emanuel described them in a letter to Princess Anna Amalie (printed in C. H. Bitter, *Carl Philipp Emanuel Bach und Wilhelm Friedemann Bach und deren Brüder*, 2 vols. [Berlin: Wilhelm Müller, 1868; reprint, Kassel: Bärenreiter, 1973], 2:305; newly ed. in Rudolph Angermüller, "Carl Philipp Emanuel Bachiana: Briefe, die bei Ernst Suchalla nicht veröffentlicht wurden," in *Jahrbuch des Staatlichen Instituts für Musikforschung Preussischer Kulturbesitz 1985/86* [Berlin: Merseburger Verlag, 1989], no. 69).

discussed as if it had no relationship to motivic work, tonal planning, and other essential aspects of Bach's own fugues – even though Marpurg purportedly had discussed "matters pertaining to fugue" with Bach himself.[13]

A second point concerns the nature of the evidence regarding improvisation. Recent discussions of medieval music indicate a need for a precise understanding of the concept of improvisation,[14] and the same is doubtless true in eighteenth-century studies as well. It should be self-evident that all improvisation is, to some degree, prepared ahead of time and is controlled by convention and conscious planning. From written documents we may gain some idea of the nature of the conventions governing improvisation in particular traditions as well as of the music that resulted. But all written compositions, including those originating in improvisation, contain a certain amount of rationalization. Thus we cannot assume that improvised pieces attained the pure voice leading and rational architecture found in virtually all written ones from the Bach circle. On the other hand, we should not assume the contrary, that improvised pieces necessarily sounded "improvisatory" in the usual sense of the word. The one work by Bach that we know to have originated in an actual improvisation, the three-part ricercar from the Musical Offering, hardly seems as improvisatory as, say, a toccata by Frescobaldi.

The newspaper account describing Bach's visit to Potsdam in 1747 quoted him as planning to publish a "regular" (*ordentliche*) fugue based on the royal theme. Indeed, in his dedication of the completed Musical Offering to Frederick the Great, Bach apologized for his failure at Berlin to give the king's subject the treatment it deserved.[15] This may have been less an admission of failure than a way of indicating that the published fugue lacked the irregularities that inevitably must have occurred in improvisation. Hence in its printed form the three-part ricercar might be seen in the same light as those engravings of Baroque opera scenes in which heroes rise to heaven or armies attack one another without any visible inconvenience from gravity or balky stage machinery. It presents an idealized version of what actually took place, purged of

13. "Gewisse Materien, welche die Fuge betrafen" (BDOK 3, no. 701; BR, 257).

14. See the "Communications" concerning improvisation in chant and secular monophony by Leo Treitler and Hendrik van der Werf, respectively, in *Journal of the American Musicological Society* 44 (1991): 513–24.

15. See BDOK 2, no. 554; BR, 176; and BDOK 1, no. 173; BR, 179.

the errors in voice leading and the momentary hesitations or changes of direction likely to have occurred in impromptu playing.[16]

To be sure, the relatively uncomplicated sequences used in the first episode of the ricercar (mm. 38–52) might have been easily improvised. Moreover, the unusually long episode that follows the decisive arrival in the dominant minor (m. 109, marking the formal midpoint) is perhaps improvisatory in the usual sense, consisting of a series of rapidly modulating phrases whose material is only loosely connected with that of the rest of the piece. Several ideas are introduced and then quickly abandoned, in particular a little *fuga per diminutionem* (mm. 118–23) and an apparent quotation from the subject of the D-minor fugue in Book 2 of the Well-Tempered Clavier (mm. 128–29). That very fugue, however, is constructed almost as loosely – it contains only one or perhaps two statements of the complete subject after the opening exposition – while the fugue in F major in the same volume contains a central episode that is proportionately even larger than the one in the ricercar.[17] Despite their improvisatory qualities, both the ricercar and the F-major fugue employ a device that seems calculated to produce the impression of a solid "architectural" framework: both conclude only after a transposed recapitulation of the phrase that previously led to the cadence in the dominant (marking the end of the first large section). The ricercar contains several additional and more substantial recurring passages as well.[18] One must doubt that such nearly verbatim restatements or recapitulations could have occurred in an improvisation. Instead, what Bach printed was a piece that captures some of the effect of a discursive improvisation even while satisfying the mid-eighteenth-century demand for a rationally organized symmetrical tonal structure articulated by recurring material.

RHETORIC

What actually would have gone through the mind of an organist called on to improvise a chorale fantasy or a fugue? How would a court composer have

16. One might view in the same light the "cadenza" in the Fifth Brandenburg Concerto, which, as Bach's dedication to Christian Ludwig suggests, apparently records an earlier performance.

17. The episode in mm. 29–52 of the F-major fugue occupies almost precisely a quarter of the total length, the episode in the ricercar only about a sixth.

18. In the F-major fugue, mm. 24–29 are restated in the tonic, with small alterations, in mm. 94–99; mm. 105–9 of the ricercar likewise recur in mm. 180–84. In addition, mm. 31–37 of the ricercar are reused in mm. 129–35, mm. 38–52 in mm. 87–101, and mm. 61–65 in mm. 155–59.

gone about writing a cantata on short notice? These may once have seemed wholly unanswerable questions, but in light of the evidence summarized in the appendix we can at least posit some suggestions.

To judge from literary sources, the basic model for both composition and improvisation was rhetoric. This is clear even from the musical terminology; words such as *thema* and *subjectus* are taken from rhetoric, and the basic idea of playing a fugue on a given theme forms a parallel with the idea of delivering a sermon on a given Bible verse or a disquisition on a given legal question or text. The metaphor proved useful for analysis and criticism, as the writings of Scheibe, Mattheson, and others show, and there is evidence that some musicians really did follow precepts derived from it. Scheibe, for example, wrote in his *Compendium musices* that "the *loci topici* are a great help to those who lack the gift of producing their [musical] thoughts on their own." [19]

Yet beyond providing a convenient list of categories for the musician to consider, such as the time, place, occasion, affect, and other circumstances of a piece or performance, Scheibe provides no concrete examples of how to apply rhetoric to music. Nor is there other contemporary evidence for the application of rhetorical terms in any systematic way to the procedures of instrumental music, as is apparently envisaged in many modern treatments of the subject.[20] Apart from furnishing simple metaphors for musical processes – useful, perhaps, in the instruction of beginners and laypersons – it is difficult to see how rhetoric would have helped a professional performer or composer deal with the purely musical problems at hand. These were of a peculiarly musical character, requiring principles of musical construction for their solution.

VARIATION

One such principle is variation. By this is meant not a series of varied settings of a melody or theme but rather the elaborate realization or composing-out of a figured-bass line, as described, for example, in Friedrich Erhardt Niedt's

19. "Die Loci topici sind insgemein eine gute Hülffe vor Leute, so nicht gleich die Gabe haben ihre Gedancken von sich zu geben" (Johann Adolph Scheibe, *Compendium musices*, ed. in Peter Benary, *Die deutsche Kompositionslehre des 18. Jahrhunderts* [Leipzig: VEB Breitkopf & Härtel, 1960], 3.2.3).

20. See, e.g., Daniel Harrison, "Rhetoric and Fugue: An Analytical Application," *Music Theory Spectrum* 12 (1990): 1–42.

Musicalische Handleitung.[21] The precise connection, if any, between Niedt and the circle around J. S. Bach remains uncertain.[22] But other sources (see sec. 3 of the appendix) make it clear that the principles taught by Niedt were known and used in the Bach circle. Even Scheibe, best known for his criticism of Bach's vocal works, may also be a witness to Bach's teaching. His composition treatise includes a discussion of *variatio* explicitly based on Heinichen's figured-bass treatise,[23] yet the examples illustrating it have a distinctly Bachian flavor. Scheibe's treatise dates from no later than 1736, five years after he had received from Bach a testimonial concerning his "knowledge in *musicis*" and his ability in composition;[24] thus, even if Scheibe was not an actual student of Bach, his writings are likely to reflect familiarity with Bach's teaching.

As for Bach's own studies, Robert Hill has pointed to the considerable number of works on ground basses, among them several variation-suites attributable to Reinken and others, in the Möller Manuscript and the Andreas Bach Book – two large collections assembled by Bach's older brother and teacher Johann Christoph.[25] Reinken was a central figure in the musical life of Ham-

21. Friedrich Erhardt Niedt, *Musicalische Handleitung*, 3 vols. (Hamburg, 1700, 1706, 1717); rev. ed. by Johann Mattheson (Hamburg, 1721; reprint, Buren: Frits Knuf, 1976); trans. Pamela Poulin and Irmgard Taylor as *The Musical Guide* (Oxford: Clarendon Press, 1989).

22. Walter Heimann (*Der Generalbass-Satz und seine Rolle in Bachs Choral-Satz* [Munich: Emil Katzbichler, 1973], 131), identifying the teacher described in the preface to the first volume of Niedt's treatise as Johann Nicolaus Bach of Jena, suggested that Niedt transmitted a Bach family tradition (*Familientradition*). The Niedt-Bach connection is strengthened by Hans-Joachim Schulze (*Studien zur Bach-Überlieferung im 18. Jahrhundert* [Leipzig: Edition Peters, 1984], 126), who shows that the extracts from Niedt in Brussels, Bibliothèque du Conservatoire Royale de Musique, MS AA 27.224, were owned by a student at the Leipzig Thomasschule. Pamela Poulin reports new documentation of Niedt's early career in her preface to *The Musical Guide*, xvii–xix and 25n.

23. Johann David Heinichen, *Der General-Bass in der Composition* (Dresden, 1728), referred to in Scheibe, *Compendium musices*, 3.1.3, and elsewhere.

24. BDOK 1, no. 68; BR, 126.

25. SBB MUS. MS 40644 and MBLPZ III.8.4, respectively. See Robert S. Hill, "Stilanalyse und Überlieferungsproblematik: Das Variationssuiten-Repertoire J. A. Reinkens," in *Dietrich Buxtehude und die europäischer Musik seiner Zeit*, ed. Arnfried Edler and Friedhelm Krummacher (Kassel: Bärenreiter, 1990), 204–14. Variation-suites by Bach, Reinken, and Zachow are published in Robert Hill, ed., *Keyboard Music from the Andreas Bach Book and the Möller Manuscript* (Cambridge, Mass.: Department of Music, Harvard University, 1991).

burg during Bach's student years at nearby Lüneburg; Niedt also appears to have spent time in Hamburg, and his treatise was published there. Hill is properly skeptical of any direct connection between Reinken and Niedt.[26] Nevertheless it seems significant that the pieces in the volume of Niedt's treatise on "variation," while uniformly weak, are close to the north German style – for example, in the inclusion of a chaconne within the Praeludium, a feature also adopted by Buxtehude (e.g., in BUXWV 137).[27]

Whatever the precise relationships between Niedt, Reinken, and Bach, variation technique seems to have been of particular importance to north German composers around 1700, when the young Bach went to Lüneburg. Handel, who arrived in Hamburg shortly after Bach left Lüneburg (in 1703), also seems to have devoted considerable attention to it in his early years. While Handel, like Bach, avoided the thoroughgoing variation-suite in which all movements follow the same harmonic-contrapuntal framework, substantial portions of many of his courantes are based on the preceding allemande. Handel's famous penchant for borrowing might even be seen as a development of the variation technique acquired in his youth since the manner in which the courante quotes from or varies passages of the allemande is often similar to Handel's borrowings from his own works or from works by other composers.[28] Bach is known to have composed only one true variation-suite, the early *Praeludium et partita*, BWV 833, but he also made a keyboard transcription (BWV 965) of one of the chamber sonatas from Reinken's *Hortus musicus*, and here the allemande and the courante form a variation pair.

The purpose and date of this transcription remain in doubt, but Hill has described Reinken's *Hortus musicus* as an important "statement" on the variation-suite, comparable to Niedt's treatise.[29] Bach's transcription is a large and im-

---

26. Hill, "Stilanalyse und Überlieferungsproblematik," 210.

27. Niedt's Praeludium is a multisectional piece built on a bass line related to that used as the basis of the variation-suite that follows. In the printed abstract to a version of this paper read at the 1991 meeting of the American Musicological Society in Chicago, Georg Böhm was mentioned as one of Bach's probable influences in this regard. But, as Hill points out ("Stilanalyse und Überlieferungsproblematik," 211), no firmly attributed suite by Böhm has a variation structure.

28. See, e.g., the free reuse of fragments from the allemande in the courantes of the suites HWV 439 (in G minor) and HWV 451 (in G major).

29. Hill, "Stilanalyse und Überlieferungsproblematik," 205.

portant piece that was copied by both Walther and Kellner, two copyists who were themselves important teachers. Hence besides confirming the importance of Reinken as an example or influence for Bach – a role to which Christoph Wolff has previously drawn attention[30] – BWV 965 might be counted as evidence that Bach himself taught the doctrine of "variation." Although the variation-suite passed out of fashion after the first decade of the century, Bach evidently continued to employ it as a teaching device, for there is a fragmentary example attributed to "Richter" in the *Clavierbüchlein vor Wilhelm Friedemann Bach.*

Several other entries in the *Clavierbüchlein* may also bear a relationship to variation technique. Indeed, the problems surrounding one piece, the little Prelude in A Minor, BWV 931, might be explained by assuming it to have been a realization – by the copyist (Friedemann Bach?) – of a preexisting bass line. Its apparently *unbachisch* stylistic characteristics raise questions about its authorship, and indeed the diffuse upper voices lack the motivic logic found even in Bach's simplest preludes. The bass, however, opens with a paradigmatic progression, and the bass as a whole forms a more cogent line than the upper parts (see ex. 1).

EX. 1. Prelude in A Minor, BWV 931, mm. 1–4

The prelude bears a family likeness to the many pieces by Bach students whose opening themes appear to have been conceived as variations over archetypal bass lines. For example, three of the seven distinct movements in C. P. E. Bach's Magnificat are built over a descending scale in the bass that has been ob-

30. Christoph Wolff, "Johann Adam Reinken und Johann Sebastian Bach: Zum Kontext des Bachschen Frühwerkes," *Bach-Jahrbuch* 71 (1985): 99–117; trans. as "Johann Adam Reinken and Johann Sebastian Bach: On the Context of Bach's Early Works," in *J. S. Bach as Organist: His Instruments, Music, and Performance Practices,* ed. George Stauffer and Ernest May (Bloomington: Indiana University Press, 1986), 57–80; translation reprinted in Christoph Wolff, *Bach: Essays on His Life and Music* (Cambridge, Mass.: Harvard University Press, 1991), 56–71.

served elsewhere in his music.[31] Kirnberger, whose *Kunst des reinen Satzes* was envisioned as a systematic setting out of Bach's pedagogy, illustrated the technique, under the rubric "Von dem verziehrten oder bunten einfachen Contrapunkt" (embellished or florid simple counterpoint), by showing various realizations of a harmonic skeleton derived from Handel's so-called Harmonious Blacksmith air.[32] In an anonymous suite in G major apparently copied by the alleged Bach student Homilius, the opening themes of most of the fourteen movements are built over bass lines selected from just three common types.[33] One of these types, employed in ex. 2, resembles the bass of the Goldberg Variations (see ex. 3*a*), which is, among other things, a more sophisticated demonstration of the same principle of variation.

As Wolff has shown, the bass of the Goldberg Variations is closely related to that of another variation work from the Bach circle, Johann Christoph Bach's *Sarabanda con 12 variazioni* (see ex. 3*b*).[34] Thus it would be hasty to connect the anonymous suite with the Goldberg Variations, even though they are in the

---

31. Suzanne Clercx relates such bass lines to the ostinato technique used in the chaconne ("La Forme du rondo chez Carl Philipp Emanuel Bach," *Revue de musicologie* 16 [1935]: 156–57; see also David Schulenberg, *The Instrumental Music of Carl Philipp Emanuel Bach* [Ann Arbor, Mich.: UMI Research Press, 1984], 34–42). The movements in question in the Magnificat are the chorus no. 1, the aria no. 5, and the duet no. 6; the opening theme of the aria no. 3 includes a prominent sequence (mm. 4–7) built on the same bass line.

32. From the suite HWV 430, published in the *Suites de pièces pour le clavecin* (London, 1720). See Kirnberger, *Die Kunst des reinen Satzes*, 1.11, especially the examples in 1:195, 205–8, etc. (exx. 11.9 and 11.22–26 in the translation). Kirnberger cannot, however, have followed Bach's teaching in all respects; see, e.g., Heimann, *Der Generalbass-Satz*, 16–19.

33. The suite occurs in SBB MUS. MS BACH P 368, listed as a Homilius copy in Paul Kast, *Die Bach-Handschriften der Berliner Staatsbibliothek* (Trossingen: Hohner-Verlag, 1958), 131, despite many inconsistencies in handwriting among the copies in the manuscript assigned to Homilius. The work itself is designated in Kast as *Incerta* 68 and is likely by a Bach student. Homilius is probably not the student in question; indeed, Hans John (*Der Dresdner Kreuzkantor und Bach-Schüler Gottfried August Homilius: Ein Beitrag zur Musikgeschichte Dresdens im 18. Jahrhundert* [Tutzing: Hans Schneider, 1980]) can, despite his title, adduce only slender evidence that Homilius actually studied with Bach (see pp. 12–14). Peter Wollny, however, kindly points out to me that one movement of *Incerta* 68 is a version of the Polonoise H. 340, elsewhere attributed to C. P. E. Bach and identical to Kast's Wq. n. v. 54 (see Helm, *Thematic Catalogue*, 71).

34. Walter Emery and Christoph Wolff, eds., NBA v/2 (*Zweiter Teil der Klavierübung, Vierter Teil der Klavierübung, Vierzehn Kanons BWV 1087*), KB, 110.

EX.2. Anonymous, Suite in G Major, Kast *Incerta* 68:
a, mvt. 4, mm. ob–2a; *b*, mvt. 7, mm. 1–4

EX.3. *a*, Goldberg Variations, BWV 988, aria, mm. 1–8.
b, J. C. Bach (1642–1703), *Sarabanda con 12 variazioni*, sarabanda
(from SBB MUS. MS BACH P 4/2)

same key and appear to be roughly contemporary with one another. Still, the evidence seems clear that among Bach's pupils thematic material was conceived as proceeding from figured-bass realization. *Harmonia* was the mother of *inventio*.[35]

This was probably true even in the contrapuntal genres, where abstract linear subjects had once been the rule (and still tended to be so in works in the *stile antico*). A clear harmonic framework underlies many of Bach's fugue subjects, and even the combination of the subject and its countersubjects is often harmonically conceived (as in the E-minor fugue from Book 2 of the Well-Tempered Clavier). The Goldberg Variations includes a fugue – actually two fugues, if one includes the second part of variation 16 (in overture form) – not to mention the nine canons. Even chorale settings could be understood as products of variation, which could be used to produce works ranging from "simple" four-part settings of a melody to imitative chorale fantasies.[36] The use of the same principle in both homophonic and contrapuntal genres belies the notion that figured bass is based on chords, that it represents "harmony" in some vertical sense, as opposed to "linear" counterpoint.[37] That this is a false dichotomy becomes clear from C. P. E. Bach's detailed treatment of voice leading in the second volume of his *Essay*. Thus it is no contradiction to suppose that Bach and his students conceived of music in the "contrapuntal" genres in much the same terms as other music.

Niedt had already reported that his model teacher, evidently Johann Nicolaus Bach, proceeded from figured bass to the playing of suites and the improvisation of fugues.[38] This may or may not be a reference to improvised

35. Although the term *inventio* has been accorded great significance in some modern writings, it seems often to have been merely an equivalent for *Erfindung*, i.e., the "discovery" of (musical) ideas (see Wulf Arlt, "Zur Handhabung der 'inventio' in der deutschen Musiklehre des frühen achtzehnten Jahrhunderts," in *New Mattheson Studies*, ed. George J. Buelow and Hans Joachim Marx [Cambridge: Cambridge University Press, 1983], 380).

36. See Claus-Jürgen Sachs, "Die 'Anleitung . . . , auff allerhand Arth einen Choral durchzuführen,' als Paradigma der Lehre und der Satzkunst Johann Sebastian Bachs," *Archiv für Musikwissenschaft* 37 (1980): 135–54. I am grateful to Russell Stinson for bringing this article to my attention.

37. As assumed, e.g., in Heimann, *Der Generalbass-Satz*, 40 and 132, evidently following Hans Heinrich Eggebrecht, "Arten des Generalbasses im frühen und mittleren 17. Jahrhundert," *Archiv für Musikwissenschaft* 14 (1957): 74–75.

38. Niedt, *Musicalische Handleitung*, introduction, par. 21.

partimento fugues, such as the four-part example in Niedt's first volume (see ex. 4a).[39] In fact there is little difference between free fugal improvisation and the realization of a figured-bass accompaniment in an a cappella fugue. Both types of exercise seem to have been widely used by teachers during the late seventeenth and early eighteenth centuries, and it would hardly be a surprise if Bach himself employed similar pieces.[40] At any rate, a number of compositions from the Bach circle illustrate techniques similar to those through which a figured-bass line might have been turned into a keyboard piece. Among them are the partimento preludes and fugues BWV 907 and 908 and the so-called sketches for several chorale settings.

While some sources attribute BWV 907 and 908 to J. S. Bach, others contain an alternate attribution to Gottfried Kirchhoff, organist at Halle, and Bach may well have had nothing to do with them.[41] Marpurg mentioned that Kirch-

39. Ibid., chap. 10, labeled "Two-Part Fugue" in *The Musical Guide*, 48, although in fact indicating entries for four distinct voices. Heimann (*Der Generalbass-Satz*, 30n) assumes that Niedt's introduction refers to the realization of partimenti.

40. Among other partimenti one might mention those of Bernardo Pasquini, reproduced in Alexander Silbiger, ed., *London, British Library, Add. ms. 31501 (Bernardo Pasquini, Partial Autograph)*, 17th Century Keyboard Music: Sources Central to the Keyboard Art of the Baroque, vol. 8 (New York: Garland Publishing, 1988). Two modern editions are both inaccurate: Maurice Brookes Haynes, ed., *Bernardo Pasquini: Collected Works for Keyboard*, Corpus of Early Keyboard Music, vol. 5/7 (Rome: American Institute of Musicology, 1968); and Walter Kolneder, ed., *Bernardo Pasquini: Vierzehn Sonaten für bezifferten Bass* (Lottstetten: Albert T. Kunzelmann, 1987). Several examples by Handel and from the Bach circle are reproduced in Alfred Mann, ed., *Georg Friedrich Händel: Aufzeichnungen zur Kompositionslehre aus den Handschriften im Fitzwilliam Museum Cambridge*, Hallische Händel-Ausgabe, Supplement, vol. 1 (Kassel: Bärenreiter, 1978), 46, 48–51; Bach's authorship of the example on p. 47, from SBB MUS. MS BACH P 296, is questioned by Wolfgang Schmieder (*Thematisch-systematisches Verzeichnis der musikalischen Werke von Johann Sebastian Bach*, rev. ed. [Wiesbaden: Breitkopf & Härtel, 1990], xvii), primarily on stylistic grounds. The reference in Schmieder to a set of exercises in keyboard chorale arrangement, corrected by Bach (in MBLPZ, GO. S. 302), is erroneous, according to Hans-Joachim Schulze, ed., *Katalog der Sammlung Manfred Gorke: Bachiana und andere Handschriften und Drucke des 18. und frühen 19. Jahrhunderts* (Leipzig: Musikbibliothek der Stadt Leipzig, 1977), 74. See also Alfred Mann, "Handel's Successor: Notes on John Christopher Smith the Younger," in *Music in Eighteenth-Century England: Essays in Memory of Charles Cudworth*, ed. Christopher Hogwood and Richard Luckett (Cambridge: Cambridge University Press, 1983), 145.

41. See the discussion in Russell Stinson, *The Bach Manuscripts of Johann Peter Kellner and His Circle: A Case Study in Reception History* (Durham, N.C.: Duke University Press, 1989), 127–29.

EX. 4. *a*, Niedt, fugue (*Musicalische Handleitung*, 1.10), mm. 1–8. *b*, Handel, fugal exercise (from Cambridge, Fitzwilliam Museum, MS 30.H.10), mm. 1–7. *c*, Fugue in D Major, BWV 908/2, with realization, articulation, and dynamic indications by Czerny (his fingerings omitted), figures from SBB MUS. MS BACH P 804, mm. 1–10.

hoff had composed a set of partimento fugues, now lost, "to teach his students figured bass together with the manner of the various entries in a fugal composition."[42] This suggests that Kirchhoff's pieces took the same form as Handel's partimento fugues, where entries in the upper parts are merely indicated by letters (see ex. 4b). Handel and Kirchhoff had studied with the same teacher, Zachow; perhaps it is no coincidence that a variation-suite by Zachow follows Bach's (BWV 833) in the Möller Manuscript.

In the fugues of BWV 907 and 908, however, each entry of the subject is written out. Indeed, the opening expositions of both fugues are fully notated through the third entry, as are the episodes (see ex. 4c, where all the unbracketed notes as well as the continuo figures are original). The bass figuration is unusually thorough; thus in m. 7 of ex. 4c the figure "2" dictates a passing tone, included in Czerny's realization. Moreover, both preludes and fugues are in fully idiomatic keyboard style. None could be mistaken for the continuo parts of a chorus in *stile antico*, as is often the case with partimenti. All this suggests that Bach might at least have been responsible for adapting these pieces from works by Kirchhoff. Certainly they go beyond the relatively elementary exercises in Mattheson's *Exemplarische Organisten-Probe*, which contains exercises in figured-bass realization in all keys, as Kirchhoff's collection reportedly did.[43] But Mattheson's pieces do not demand the same level of keyboard skill required by BWV 907 and 908, nor do they include exercises in fugue.

Either Kirchhoff's or Mattheson's works might have suggested to Bach the idea of the Well-Tempered Clavier, although there is no evidence that those publications had reached the Bach circle before 1722, the date of the fair-copy autograph of the first book of Bach's collection.[44] Nevertheless, several Bach fugues seem to resemble the products of an improvised partimento. One is the Fughetta in G Major, BWV 902/2, which was copied along with another simple Bach fugue by Kellner in 1726 or 1727.[45] Here the accompaniments to

42. "Dass er seinen Schülern zugleich den Generalbass und die Art der verschiedenen Eintritte eines Fugensatzes beybrächte" (Marpurg, *Abhandlung von der Fuge*, 1:150). Marpurg's reference to Kirchhoff is noted by Schulze, *Studien*, 124–25.

43. Johann Mattheson's *Exemplarische Organisten-Probe* (Hamburg, 1719) was later incorporated into his *Grosse General-Bass-Schule* (Hamburg, 1731).

44. The earliest surviving copies of BWV 907 and 908 cannot be earlier than the mid-1720s (see Stinson, *Bach Manuscripts*, 127–28).

45. In SBB MUS. MS BACH P 804/5; the dating is from Stinson, *Bach Manuscripts*, 23. The other

the subject consist largely of chords in two, sometimes three, voices, such as might arise in a realization of BWV 907/2 or 908/2 (compare exx. 4*c* and 5). The G-major fughetta was later included in the second book of the Well-Tempered Clavier (see BWV 884/2), but only after revisions that seem to have been prompted, in part, by the perfunctory nature of the original counterpoint. Presumably Bach did not wish anything that looked unduly improvisatory to appear in one of his "official" compendia. Nevertheless, the earlier version may represent the sort of counterpoint that one heard often in improvised fugues, in the Bach household and elsewhere. Bach himself could reportedly tell immediately whether a particular fugue subject was suitable for use in

---

work in this fascicle of P 804 is BWV 953, also preserved in the *Clavierbüchlein vor Wilhelm Friedemann Bach*.

EX.6. *a*, "Vom Himmel hoch, da komm ich her," BWV 738a, opening.
b, Suite in A Major, BWV 806a, prelude, mm. 1–2

stretto or some other learned technique.[46] But the report refers to Bach listening to a fugue by someone else, and even his own improvisations are likely to have employed, at least occasionally, the simple and quite free counterpoint of BWV 902/2.

Similar considerations apply to the so-called chorale sketches, which are preserved in copies by Johann Tobias Krebs, who studied with Bach at Weimar (see ex. 6*a*). Together with their later versions, these suggest the manner in which a simple four-part chorale setting could be turned into a keyboard prelude or even a fantasy.[47] Yet the Beethovenian idea of a "sketch" seems inappropriate here, for even in their "unfinished" forms the pieces were evidently copied out by a student and put to practical use. While Bach did occasionally

46. See, e.g., C. P. E. Bach's letter of around the end of 1774 to Forkel (BDOK 3, no. 802; BR, 277).

47. See BWV 722a, 729a, 732a, and 738a, all *unica* from SBB MUS. MS BACH P 802. These are edited, together with the later versions BWV 722, 729, etc., in Hans Klotz, ed., NBA IV/3 (*Die einzeln überlieferten Orgelchoräle*).

jot down ideas and even work them out in a manner that could be described as "sketching," these chorale settings – like the early versions of the French Suites (which lack most of their ornaments) or the early forms of some of the preludes from the Well-Tempered Clavier – are better regarded as incompletely notated compositions, meant to be fully realized in performance, than as unfinished works in the nineteenth-century sense.[48] Although we cannot be sure how Krebs might have used them, in conjunction with their "finished" versions – either studied in score or heard in performances by Bach – they could have served as models for both improvisation and composition.

In fact the "sketches" are conceptually identical to a partimento fugue with partially written-out upper parts, the only difference being that the "subject" is a chorale melody, employed as a cantus firmus in the soprano, rather than as a theme wandering from one voice to another. This indictes the close relationship between the improvisation of fugues and chorales. Bach even treated certain fugue subjects, including those of the Chromatic Fugue, BWV 903/2, and the Musical Offering, somewhat like cantus firmi; these subjects consist primarily of long notes that are combined with livelier figuration. The expositions of a fugue, of course, often alternate with bridges or episodes; this appears to have been especially true of improvised fugues, if BWV 907 and 908, or the three-part ricercar and other Bach works, accurately reflect improvisatory practices. But ritornellos or interludes could equally well be inserted into a simple chorale setting. Indeed, the phrases of the chorale melodies in the "sketches" are already articulated by short passages of free figuration (as was apparently customary).

48. Marshall (*Compositional Process*, 1:31–32) discusses "sketches," but these are limited for the most part to "memory aids" and "tentative marginal sketches for ... opening themes." Several of Bach's early keyboard works employ a sketch-like type of notation that includes figured bass. But in the partita BWV 833 and the capriccio BWV 922 this occurs in movements intended to imitate genres scored for voice and continuo. Similarly, the figures in the sonata BWV 967 and the echo movement of the doubtful suite BWV 821 may have been intended to reflect the orchestral scoring imitated in these pieces. Thus, while these works may call for improvisational realization comparable to that employed in playing the chorale "sketches," none of these pieces provides evidence that Bach actually wrote preliminary sketches that employed figured bass.

VARIATION AND FORMULA

One of these flourishes (in BWV 738a) recurs almost note for note at the opening of the First English Suite, probably a Weimar work (see ex. 6b).[49] Moreover, practically the same figure occurs in an anonymous chorale "sketch" from P 802; the latter resembles the "sketches" attributed to Bach but is possibly the work of the copyist Krebs (see ex. 7).[50] Although the exactness of the paral-

EX. 7. J. T. Krebs (?), "Jesu, der du meine Seele," Kast *Incerta* 29
(from SBB MUS. MS BACH P 802), *Stollen*

lels between these examples may be unusual, the implication is that Bach and his students possessed a vocabulary of flourishes and other ornamental gestures that could be inserted at appropriate points into pieces of various genres. Some formulas, such as the virtuoso alternating-hand figures seen in exx. 6 and 7, might have been favorite personal inventions. Others would have corresponded to conventional cadential and sequential patterns or to established opening and closing gestures. Indeed, in genres such as the prelude there must have been a fairly well-established protocol regarding the proper use of such formulas. Many preludes in Book 1 of the Well-Tempered Clavier, for example, begin with a variation on a simple cadential progression – often over a pedal point, as in ex. 8.

It is easy to multiply these examples of opening formulas. Another occurs at the opening of the C-major prelude BWV 924, the first prelude in the *Clavier-*

49. The early version, BWV 806a, exists in a copy by Walther in SBB MUS. MS BACH P 803, a manuscript closely related to the source containing the chorale "sketches."

50. I am grateful to Russell Stinson for bringing this and several other Krebs copies to my attention and for supplying a facsimile.

EX. 8. *a*, Prelude in C Major, BWV 846a/1, mm. 1–4.
   b, Prelude in G Major, BWV 860/1, mm. 1–2

EX. 9. Prelude in C Major, mm. 1–2: *a*, BWV 924; *b*, BWV 924a

büchlein vor Wilhelm Friedemann Bach, which also contains another prelude in the same key, BWV 924a. The latter is often referred to as an alternate version of BWV 924, but it is better described as a second realization of the same basic plan (see ex. 9). The plans of both are summarized in table 1 (upper portion): both pieces open with the same initiating gesture, proceeding to a simple

21

Table 1. Formal Plans

Version	Number of Measures in Each Section						Total
BWV 924	6		11		1		18
BWV 924a	7		3		4		14
Formal device	sequence(s)		pedal point		close		
Key or cadence	C		V		I		
BWV 846a	4	5	7	3	4	1	24
Clavierbüchlein vor Wilhelm Friede-mann Bach (post correc-turam)	4	7	8	3	4	1	27
Final version	4	7	8	4	8	4	35
Formal device			sequences		pedal point	close	
Key or cadence	C	→	G→	C→	C:V→	I	
Measure number (final version)	1	4	12	20	24	32	

EX.10. W. F. Bach, Fantasy in C Major, F.14, mm.1–2

Presto

modulating sequence that leads eventually to a dominant pedal. The final cadence soon follows, preceded by a simple cadenza in BWV 924a. A similar plan recurs, on a somewhat larger scale, in the various versions of the prelude in the same key that opens the first book of the Well-Tempered Clavier (see table 1, lower portion).

Much the same initiating gesture – that is, the ascending triad in the bass – recurs in one of Friedemann's fantasies (F.14), also in C major (see ex.10). Another common initiating gesture, the cadential formula over a pedal point, recurs in a fantasy recently identified as a work of Emanuel Bach, H.348

EX.11. C. P. E. Bach, Fantasy in E♭ Major, H.348, opening

(ex.11).[51] In both cases the bass gesture is dressed up in new figuration, but this too can be found elsewhere. The figuration of F.14 recurs in Friedemann's Fantasy in E Minor, F.21 (see ex.12*a*), while that of H.348 seems to come from a much better-known source, the Chromatic Fantasy (ex.12*b*).

The use of formula is not confined to pieces in the expressly improvisatory genres, such as preludes and fantasies, although it is naturally most common there and in passages such as cadenzas that were meant to sound like improvisations (even if they did not actually originate as such). Thus George Stauffer has pointed to the similarity of certain figuration in the Chromatic Fantasy to that in the great harpsichord solo ("cadenza") in the first movement of the Fifth Brandenburg Concerto.[52] Another passage in this solo, the sequence of

51. On the authorship of H.348, previously ascribed to Nichelmann, see Douglas A. Lee, "C. P. E. Bach and the Free Fantasia for Keyboard: Deutsche Staatsbibliothek Mus. Ms. Nichelmann 1N," in *C. P. E. Bach Studies*, ed. Stephen L. Clark (Oxford: Clarendon Press, 1988), 177–84.

52. George B. Stauffer, "'This fantasia ... never had its like': On the Enigma and Chronology of Bach's Chromatic Fantasia and Fugue in D Minor, BWV 903," in *Bach Studies*, ed. Don O. Franklin (Cambridge: Cambridge University Press, 1989), 176.

EX.12. *a*, W. F. Bach, Fantasy in E Minor, F.21, mm.54–55.
b, J. S. Bach, Chromatic Fantasy in D Minor, BWV 903/1, mm.3–4

descending diminished chords in mm.199–201 – whose dazzling effect remains undiminished by nineteenth-century abuse of the same harmonic progression – recurs in somewhat different form in the hand-crossing gigue of the First Partita (BWV 825/7, mm.34–39). Here the formula consists not of the figuration as such but of the underlying harmonic progression. Although the latter is unusual in earlier music, it is quite simple, and we might imagine Bach astonishing first-time listeners – among them the margrave of Brandenburg at Berlin or Volumier and other notables at Dresden – with what was, in fact, a relatively cheap trick from his arsenal. It was evidently a favorite, for it is already present in the early version of the "cadenza," where Bach jumps to it in the third measure (BWV 1050a/1, mm.157–58).

The passage suggests that (like the analogous "capriccios" inserted into Bach's models) the entire "cadenza" was the product of a series of improvised interpolations.[53] Sebastian probably expected players to insert improvised solos into other concertos; there is a *Cadenza al arbitrio* in the third movement (just before the last ritornello) of what appears to be an early version of the D-minor harpsichord concerto BWV 1052a.[54] Since BWV 1052a is independent of

53. The likely models for the Brandenburg "cadenza" are the two long optional solos in Vivaldi's concerto RV 208 (see Luigi Ferdinando Tagliavini, "Bach's Organ Transcription of Vivaldi's 'Grosso Mogul' Concerto," in *Bach as Organist*, 240–55).

54. The indication occurs in the string parts of the sole source, SBB MUS. MS BACH ST 350; the keyboard part at this point has the direction *ad libitum*. The occasional corrections in ST

the organ versions in Cantatas 146 and 188, it might reproduce an early state of Bach's own performing material – which would thus have resembled Handel's organ concertos in requiring the improvisation of certain solo passages.

Extended solos such as those found in BWV 1050 and 1052 can be constructed relatively easily through the more or less formulaic composing-out of routine sequences. Even counterpoint could be reduced to formula. In a sense, this is what happens in the permutational designs that Bach must have learned from works such as the fugues in Reinken's *Hortus musicus*. Certainly Bach was aware of various ready-made canons and strettos that could be inserted into contrapuntal pieces whose subjects incorporated appropriate motives. One such is the little canon known as the *Trias harmonica*,[55] which bears a close relationship to the strettos in Contrapunctus 5 of the Art of Fugue. Naturally Bach avoided a too obvious reliance on contrapuntal formulas in his written fugues. But ready-made strettos bearing some relation to the opening motive of a fugue subject – such as occurs in the central harpsichord solo in the last movement of the Fifth Brandenburg Concerto (mm. 163-77) – might well have impressed a jury hearing an organist's audition.

The use of formula by Bach and his students is hardly surprising in the light of what we know of Baroque style in general. Following the model of Printz and earlier writers, Niedt set out various melodic embellishments that might be applied to a bass line and evidently assumed a similar approach in the invention of melodic material in the upper voices.[56] George Buelow has pointed to a discussion of *moduli* in Mattheson's *Vollkommener Capellmeister* and has shown how Handel repeatedly employed certain archetypal melodic patterns in his opening themes.[57] Among the papers of C. P. E. Bach and the Bach stu-

---

350 provide little evidence that the arrangement is the work of the copyist, C. P. E. Bach, confirming the doubts expressed in Helm, *Thematic Catalogue*, 105, about Emanuel's authorship of BWV 1052a (which is listed in Helm as the "doubtful" work H. 484). For an argument to the contrary, see Andreas Glöckner, "Neuerkenntnisse zu Johann Sebastian Bachs Aufführungskalender zwischen 1729 und 1735," *Bach-Jahrbuch* 67 (1981): 43-75. I am grateful to Joshua Rifkin for making available his copy of ST 350.

55. BWV 1072, given in Marpurg's *Abhandlung von der Fuge*, vol. 2, *Tabula* 37.

56. Compare the examples in the first volume of Niedt's *Musicalische Handleitung* with those in Wolfgang Caspar Printz, *Phrynis Mytilenaeus oder Satyrischer Componist* (Quedlinburg, 1676-77).

57. George Buelow, "Mattheson's Concept of 'Moduli' as a Clue to Handel's Compositional

dent and associate Johann Gottfried Müthel are collections of fragments and cadenzas that appear to represent exercises or exemplary "ideas" for use in improvisation and composition. No doubt individual players also invented their own formulas, and indeed the "discovery of ideas" was evidently something that Sebastian looked for in his composition students.[58] But, once discovered, many ideas might have served as modular devices that could be inserted into almost any improvisation or composition.

One by-product of the reliance on formula, especially in little preludes and the like, may be the questions of attribution that they frequently raise. Indeed, it is striking how many of the pieces under discussion here are of uncertain authorship. The copy of BWV 924a is in the hand of Wilhelm Friedemann, who might have been its composer. But the idea of a composer in such a piece may be something of an anachronism. Many such pieces may, to some degree, be the products of collaboration between student and teacher.[59] Even when this is not the case, such pieces may belong to a network of related works using recurring formulas that were regarded as common property. Indeed, when we consider how many of these pieces are probably merely the visible survivals of an improvising tradition, we are faced with a situation not unlike the traditions of early chant or, for that matter, oral poetry.

It is possible that some of these pieces, especially the simpler preludes, might be described in terms derived from the study of oral literature, as Leo Treitler

---

Practice," *Göttinger Händel-Beiträge* 3 (1989): 272–78. The reference is to Johann Mattheson, *Der vollkommene Capellmeister* (Hamburg, 1739), 122–23.

58. "Was die Erfindung der Gedancken betrifft, so forderte er gleich anfangs die Fähigkeit dazu" (C. P. E. Bach, letter to Forkel, 13 January 1775). C. P. E. Bach's collection of "ideas" is represented by the *Miscellanea musica*, H.867 (W.121), a manuscript collection of unpublished sketches and other fragments; for Müthel, see the so-called *Technische Übungen* in SBB MUS. MS 15,762/1.2, discussed in Peter Reidemeister, "Johann Gottfried Müthels 'Technische Übungen,' oder Von der Mehrdeutigkeit der Quellen," *Basler Jahrbuch für historische Musikpraxis* 13 (1989): 55–98. Müthel includes extracts not only from the Chromatic Fantasy (as noted by Reidemeister) but also from Emanuel's fantasy-like sonata H.46 (W.65/16); copies by Müthel survive of both works. No doubt other pieces are quoted or echoed in both collections.

59. Evidence of such collaborations in the Bach circle can be found in Bach's having participated in the copying of parts for BWV 1025 and 1038, both probably student works, and in references to a joint composition by him and Emanuel (on the apparently lost trio sonata H.566, see Helm, *Thematic Catalogue*, 123). Likewise, the symphony H.667 appears to be a collaboration between Emanuel and Prince Lobkowitz.

has done for chant and Lawrence Gushee for jazz.[60] Yet, even if the works in question could be shown to display the characteristics of an oral repertory,[61] a study along the lines of "Homer, Gregory, and Sebastian" might not be terribly enlightening.[62] For one thing, it is difficult to apply the details of the Parry-Lord theory of oral-formulaic composition to music, especially in the absence of authentic eighteenth-century improvisers. Individual melodic ideas might be matched with the formulas of oral poetry, and what are called *themes* in the study of oral literature perhaps correspond with the formal protocols mentioned earlier. But there appears to be nothing in Bach's musical structures to correspond to the strict poetic meter and foreordained narratives of epic and other types of traditional verse, whose exacting formal requirements have no precise parallel in eighteenth-century music.[63]

Hence the analogies to oral poetry are at best imprecise. Perhaps the formulas bear a closer relationship to what Robert Gjerdingen has described as *schemata* in eighteenth-century music.[64] These schemata appear to be, in

60. See Leo Treitler, "Homer and Gregory: The Transmission of Epic Poetry and Plainchant," *Musical Quarterly* 60 (1974): 333–72; and the contributions by Lawrence Gushee and Treitler to the panel discussion "Transmission and Form in Oral Traditions," published in *International Musicological Society: Report of the Twelfth Congress, Berkeley, 1977*, ed. Daniel Heartz and Bonnie Wade (Kassel: Bärenreiter, 1981), 151–69, 202–11.

61. The classic account of the oral-formulaic theory of ancient Greek epic is A. B. Lord, *The Singer of Tales* (Cambridge, Mass.: Harvard University Press, 1960). For one set of criteria for an "oral" literature, see Ruth Finnegan, *Oral Poetry: Its Nature, Significance and Social Context* (Cambridge: Cambridge University Press, 1977), 16–24.

62. See Gregory Eugene Smith, "Homer, Gregory, and Bill Evans? The Theory of Formulaic Composition in the Context of Jazz Piano Improvisation" (Ph.D. diss., Harvard University, 1983), esp. 142–58 and 207–15.

63. See, e.g., the discussion of epic economy or "thrift" in Milman Parry, "Studies in the Epic Technique of Oral Verse-Making: I. Homer and Homeric Style," in *The Making of Homeric Verse: The Collected Papers of Milman Parry*, ed. Adam Parry (Oxford: Oxford University Press, 1987), 278–79; see also Adam Parry's introduction, pp. xxviii, xxxi. The role of economy in Homer has been questioned in recent years (see, e.g., David M. Shive, *Naming Achilles* [Oxford: Oxford University Press, 1987], esp. 123–39). Its use (and the degree of "orality") in Homeric epic remains controversial, with possible implications for studies of oral-formulaic composition in Western music.

64. Robert O. Gjerdingen, *A Classic Turn of Phrase: The Psychology of Convention* (Philadelphia: University of Pennsylvania Press, 1988).

essence, certain types of pattern that a listener extrapolates from their recurrences in various pieces. While not every formula is a schema, schemata provide the basis of many formulas. They represent, for example, the elements common to the initiating gestures of the Chromatic Fantasy and certain preludes from the Well-Tempered Clavier.[65]

MUSICAL DESIGN

While variation, formula, and schema may account for much in the surface of the music and even (to some degree) at deeper levels of structure, they cannot adequately explain the design or shape of the whole. In the real world one does not find whole sonatas and other such pieces composed on preexisting bass lines. Yet this is indeed the case with several presumably pedagogic works listed in the appendix.[66] Moreover, in his *Essay*, C. P. E. Bach presents the rule of the octave and other bass lines as the foundation for the improvisation of fantasies.[67] It is conceivable that the most elaborate of these bass lines, which Emanuel presents as the generating principle for the model free fantasy H.160 (W.117/14), is actually an analytical construct, produced after the fact. Yet, where we would employ the symbols of functional harmony to describe modulations or tonal plans, Emanuel seems routinely to have used figured-bass notation.[68]

From this and other evidence, two principles can be inferred about how form or design was conceived at the large level. First, the rounded modulating designs that characterize mature eighteenth-century style were understood in terms of cadences in a series of different keys; second, large designs were expansions of smaller ones. These ideas are familiar to us from the writings of

65. Schemata also seem close to the phenomenon referred to by van der Werf, in his writings on medieval song, as the "frame of reference" or "underlying structure" (see his "Communication," 520).

66. In particular BWV 1021 and 1038 and H.150, 156, and 157. These works are discussed in David Schulenberg, "Composition as Variation: Inquiries into the Compositional Procedures of the Bach Circle of Composers," *Current Musicology* 33 (1982): 57–87.

67. See the last two chapters of the *Essay* (pp. 426ff. in the Mitchell translation).

68. Much of the *Miscellanea musica* consists of figured bass lines delineating a great variety of harmonic progressions and modulations. For further examples of C. P. E. Bach's contrapuntal conception of harmonic progression, see Richard Kramer, "The New Modulation of the 1770s: C. P. E. Bach in Theory, Criticism, and Practice," *Journal of the American Musicological Society* 38 (1985): 552n.

Koch and other theorists of the later eighteenth century, and there is good reason to think that Bach and his students held similar ideas.[69]

Thus the bass lines underlying works like Richter's variation-suite, the fantasy H.160, or the Goldberg Variations define not only the immediate successions of harmonies but the larger modulating design. That such designs were understood as flexible, expandable skeletons is already clear from Bach's early variation-suite BWV 833. There, after the double bar, the allemande makes a passing move through the supertonic G minor (m.14); in the courante this becomes a formal cadence (mm.24–25).

More substantial types of expansion occurred in Bach's revisions of many later works, notably the preludes from the first book of the Well-Tempered Clavier and several chorale settings. In addition, a few chorale fantasies of doubtful authorship (see sec.7 of the appendix) apparently originated as student exercises, produced through the insertion of ritornellos into Bach's own chorale preludes. One such arrangement, BWV ANH.73, is preserved in two copies; one of these is attributed to Emanuel Bach by the copyist, Anonymous 303. The style of the added ritornellos bears out the contention that Emanuel is indeed the composer.[70] It seems obvious why Emanuel would not have acknowledged such an exercise in the posthumously published catalog of his works known as the *Nachlassverzeichnis*,[71] despite the skillfulness of the adaptation.

69. See, e.g., Marpurg's *Principes du clavecin* (Berlin, 1756; reprint, Geneva: Minkoff Reprint, 1974), 44–50, containing analytic material not in the German edition, *Anleitung zum Clavier-spielen* (Berlin, 1755; facsimile of the *zweyte, verbesserte Auflage* [Berlin, 1765], Hildesheim: Georg Olms, 1970). On Heinrich Christoph Koch and concerto form, see Jane R. Stevens, "An Eighteenth-Century Description of Concerto First-Movement Form," *Journal of the American Musicological Society* 24 (1971): 85–95.

70. For a legible facsimile from MBLPZ MS R 25, see Heinz-Harald Löhlein, ed., NBA IV/1 (*Orgelbüchlein, Sechs Choräle von verschiedener Art [Schübler Choräle], Orgelpartiten*), KB, 122–24. Löhlein regards the work as "probably" by C. P. E. Bach (p.82); I am grateful to Russell Stinson for bringing it to my attention. Another example of the same process, also perhaps carried out by a Bach student, can be observed in BWV 691a, based on a work copied in both the second *Clavierbüchlein* for Anna Magdalena Bach (SBB MUS. MS BACH P 225) and the *Clavierbüchlein vor Wilhelm Friedemann Bach*. For further discussion, see Ulrich Leisinger and Peter Wollny, "'Altes Zeug von mir': Carl Philipp Emanuel Bachs kompositorisches Schaffen vor 1740," *Bach-Jahrbuch* 79 (1993): 127–204.

71. *Verzeichniss des musikalischen Nachlasses des verstorbenen Capellmeisters* (Hamburg, 1790); ed. Heinrich Miesner as "Philipp Emanuel Bachs musikalischer Nachlass," *Bach-Jahrbuch* 35 (1938):

A comparable procedure was carried out to form the outer movements of the Triple Concerto, BWV 1044 – whether or not it was Sebastian himself who was responsible for the arrangement.[72] Sebastian certainly carried out a similar process in at least two chorale preludes from the *Orgelbüchlein*, BWV 631 and 641, in the latter instance producing the piece once regarded as his "deathbed chorale."[73] But, while expansion of this sort might have originated in impromptu playing at the keyboard, reports of the wholesale improvisation of chorale fantasies must be taken with a grain of salt. Any organist would have prepared himself for auditions by practicing variations and fantasies on the chorale melodies most likely to be selected by juries. Bach's obituary reports that he "performed extempore the chorale *An Wasserflüssen Babylon*" in Reinken's presence at a Hamburg concert in 1720, provoking a much-quoted compliment from the aged Reinken.[74] But it would be no surprise if this improvisation had incorporated – perhaps as a climactic conclusion – the double-pedal fantasy BWV 653b composed at Weimar.[75]

That Sebastian Bach actually taught along the lines suggested here might be inferred from several students' copies of preludes and fugues from the Well-

---

103-36, 36 (1939): 81-112, and 37 (1940-48): 161-81; facsimile ed. Rachel W. Wade as *The Catalog of Carl Philipp Emanuel Bach's Estate* (New York: Garland, 1981).

72. The most recent (1989) discussion of BWV 1044 (in Dietrich Kilian, ed., NBA VII/3 [*Konzerte für Violine, für zwei Violinen, für Cembalo, Flöte und Violine*], KB, 47-48) does not entirely lay to rest the doubts raised by the lateness of the sources, the absence of an autograph, and questions of style and keyboard range. The outer movements of BWV 1044 are based on the prelude and fugue BWV 894; the slow movement is based on that of the organ sonata BWV 527 (or its prototype), with the addition of varied reprises. The ritornello theme of the last movement is a reduction of the fugue subject used in the solo passages.

73. BWV 668 is based not directly on BWV 641 but apparently on a somewhat simpler prototype. On the origins of BWV 668, see Christoph Wolff, "Johann Sebastian Bachs 'Sterbechoral': Kritische Fragen zu einem Mythos," in *Studies in Baroque Music in Honor of Arthur Mendel*, ed. Robert L. Marshall (Hackensack, N.J.: Joseph Boonin; Kassel: Bärenreiter, 1974), 283-97; trans. as "The Deathbed Chorale: Exposing a Myth," in Wolff, *Bach: Essays on His Life and Music*, 282-94.

74. BDOK 3, no. 666; BR, 219. The obituary was written in part by C. P. E. Bach, according to his 1774 letter to Forkel (BDOK 3, no. 801; BR, 276) – which does not mean that it is precisely accurate concerning events at which C. P. E. Bach could not have been present.

75. Russell Stinson kindly points out to me that Reinken's enormous fantasy on the same chorale melody ends, like Bach's, with a descending scale.

Tempered Clavier. The significance of these copies has been noted by Alfred Dürr, who identified Bach as probably having added the analytical figures and other markings in one of the copies (see ex.13).[76] Each figure marks the inter-

EX.13. Fugue in C Minor, BWV 847/2
(from SBB MUS. MS BACH P 401), mm.18b-20

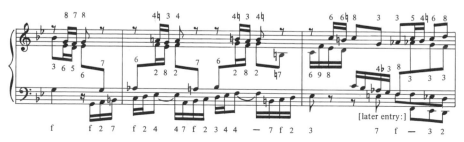

val between a tone in the musical surface and a local tonic (*finalis*) designated in each phrase by the letter *f*. This is, among other things, a way of setting out the tonal plan of the piece in relation to the bass – thus in effect a simple reductive analysis.[77] As such it might have provided the germ for Kirnberger's more sophisticated analyses, including those of two movements from the Well-Tempered Clavier.[78]

76. Alfred Dürr, "Ein Dokument aus dem Unterricht Bachs?" *Musiktheorie* 1 (1986): 163–70. Errors have been pointed out, however, that must cast Bach's connection with these annotations in some doubt (see Joel Lester, *Compositional Theory in the Eighteenth Century* [Cambridge, Mass.: Harvard University Press, 1992], 82–87; as well as the "Anmerkungen" by Heinrich Deppert, *Musiktheorie* 2 [1987]: 107–8). The failure of the annotator to recognize a copying mistake in BWV 851/1 is particularly telling; other analytical "errors" cited by Lester and Deppert possibly reflect only their twentieth-century understanding of modulation.

77. Reductive analyses of a somewhat different type are also found in Scheibe's *Compendium musices*, in the discussion of *Variatio* (3.1.5).

78. In *Die wahren Grundsätze zum Gebrauch der Harmonie* ... (Berlin, 1773; reprint, Hildesheim: Georg Olms, 1970). The treatise was actually written by Kirnberger's student Schulz, according to David Williams Beach, "The Harmonic Theories of Johann Philipp Kirnberger: Their Origins and Influences" (Ph.D. diss., Yale University, 1974), 11; but see Lester, *Compositional Theory*, 240, n.5. A *Zugabe* to vol.1 of *Die Kunst des reinen Satzes* includes a similar analysis of what is apparently one of Kirnberger's own fugues (no.35 in the thematic catalog in Ruth Engelhardt, "Untersuchungen über Einflüsse Johann Sebastian Bachs auf das theoretische und praktische Wirken seines Schülers Johann Philipp Kirnberger" [Ph.D. diss., Univer-

Yet the analysis seems strangely superficial. It reveals nothing about motivic work or large form; even the entries of the subject are not marked. Perhaps this is because the analytical notations were intended merely to identify the vertical intervals. But even in fugue there is little evidence that Bach or his students engaged in the type of precompositional planning that we tend to assume must have taken place.[79] Planning the series of entrances ahead of time would have been necessary only in the relatively small number of fugues that follow unconventional modulatory designs or complicated contrapuntal schemes.

Still, ex. 13 does contain evidence of Bach's conscious concern with formal design. In m. 20, the last three notes of the bass have been doubled at the octave below; the lower notes correspond with a revised reading in the autograph. In the same measure, the soprano enters with the subject in the tonic – the first such entry since the opening exposition. Moving the bass to the deeper register lends the passage greater weight and perhaps strengthens the sense of tonic return at this point, exactly two-thirds of the way through the piece.

This is hardly the only Bach work to rely on the principle of the double return, familiar to us from its use in Classical sonata form. The principle is especially prominent in the preludes from Book 2 of the Well-Tempered Clavier, many of which are in fact sonata movements. Indeed, when Friedemann, Emanuel, and Bach's later students began to compose, they appear to have adopted as models the regular, clearly articulated formal designs found in sonata and concerto movements by Telemann, the Graun brothers, and other German contemporaries admired by J. S. Bach himself, according to Emanuel Bach's testimony.[80] The remarkably close stylistic and formal parallelisms between the flute sonatas BWV 1031 and 1020 appear to reflect this, regardless of which member or members of the Bach circle actually composed them and of whether they were modeled specifically on Quantz's sonata QV 2:18.[81] Forkel,

---

sity of Erlangen, 1974] = BWV ANH. 94). The piece is misplaced in the reprint to just after the preface (*Vorrede*) to vol. 1. A note in the Beach-Thym translation of *Die Kunst des reinen Satzes* (p. 234) points out other eighteenth-century examples of reductive analysis.

79. A recent study of this very work makes just that assumption (see Ulrich Siegele, "The Four Conceptual Stages of the Fugue in C Minor, WTC I," in *Bach Studies*, 197–224).

80. Letter to Forkel, 13 January 1775.

81. As Jeanne Swack argues in "Quantz and the Sonata in E-flat Major for Flute and Cembalo, BWV 1031," read at the 1991 meeting of the American Musicological Society (forthcoming in *Early Music*). The vexed issue of the authorship of BWV 1031 is also discussed in Robert L. Mar-

evidently repeating a comment that Emanuel Bach had also made to Burney, mentioned that Bach's sons had had to invent their own styles since they could not match their father on his own terms.[82] Yet their styles depended to a considerable degree on the individualistic elaboration of fairly simple designs, as Charles Rosen recognized in designating their generation as "mannerist." [83]

The result was a significant change in the relationship between invention and design, for large form became far more conventionalized than it had been with J. S. Bach. While originality or "invention" was evidently prized, it seems often to have involved only the most superficial level of the music, structurally speaking: the addition of chromaticism to a diatonic skeleton or the substitution of unexpected embellishments or arpeggiations for expected ones. Although Friedemann and Emanuel became famous for their improvisations and their improvisatory free fantasies, they appear to have written down few such pieces until relatively late in life. Perhaps this was because such music did not seem to satisfy the demanding requirements for written composition as established at Leipzig in the 1720s and 1730s.

THE FREE FANTASY

Sebastian himself was responsible for at least one exception. George Stauffer brought attention to this in the title of his article on the Chromatic Fantasy, quoting Forkel's remark that "this fantasia is unique, and never had its like." [84]

---

shall, "J. S. Bach's Compositions for Solo Flute: A Reconsideration of Their Authenticity and Chronology," *Journal of the American Musicological Society* 32 (1979): 465–66; reprinted, with additions, in Robert L. Marshall, *The Music of Johann Sebastian Bach: The Sources, the Style, the Significance* (New York: Schirmer Books, 1989), 201–25. I am grateful to Professor Swack for allowing me to see an advance copy of her paper, and to both authors for kindly sharing their thoughts with me on this and related matters.

82. Johann Nicolaus Forkel, *Ueber Johann Sebastian Bachs Leben, Kunst und Kunstwerke* (Leipzig, 1802; reprint, Frankfurt a.M.: H. L. Grahl, 1950), 44; BR, 333. Compare Burney, *Musical Tour,* 217: "he [C. P. E. Bach] has ever disdained imitation," i.e., of his father (this passage is in the section that was replaced by Emanuel's autobiography in the German edition).

83. Charles Rosen, *The Classical Style: Haydn, Mozart, Beethoven* (New York: W. W. Norton & Co., 1972), 47.

84. Stauffer, "This fantasia … ," quoting Forkel, *Bachs Leben,* 55–56 (BR, 342). Forkel seems to have actively sought out other such works from Bach's sons. He took some trouble to obtain two such works by W. F. Bach (see George B. Stauffer, ed., *The Forkel–Hoffmeister & Kühnel Correspondence: A Document of the Early 19th-Century Bach Revival* [New York: C. F. Peters,

The apparent singularity of the Chromatic Fantasy has led to a romantic view of it and probably encouraged the romanticizing accretions to its text that are already evident in the versions stemming from Forkel; these reached a climax in the notorious edition by Hans von Bülow.[85] The same view remains evident in twentieth-century efforts to resuscitate Spitta's interpretation of the work as a quasi-programmatic composition.[86]

Yet it might be better to say merely that the fantasy was the only one of its like ever written down. For it is hard to believe that such a piece could have emerged out of thin air, as an isolated and indeed anomalous *unicum* in Bach's output. Not only does it open with a formulaic harmonic progression; the entire first section is an enormous expansion of what was referred to above as the protocol of a simple prelude, and a striking progression in one of the arpeggio sections recurs in the little-known Prelude in B Minor, BWV 923.[87] Even the idea of an embellished instrumental recitative has a likely precedent in the second movement of the "Grosso Mogul" Concerto, RV 208, one of the Vivaldi works that Bach transcribed for organ (as BWV 594), and perhaps in other works as well.[88] The chromatic harmony and the modulating plan are exceptional, of course. Yet even the bizarre half-step dislocation, from A to Ab at

---

1990], letter 28 [4 April 1803]). C. P. E. Bach's letter of 7 October 1774 to Forkel was evidently written in reply to a request for fantasies or fantasy-like pieces (see no.191 in Ernst Suchalla, ed., *Briefe von Carl Philipp Emanuel Bach an Johann Gottlob Immanuel Breitkopf und Johann Nikolaus Forkel* [Tutzing: Hans Schneider, 1985]).

85. Forkel's edition was published in 1802 (Leipzig: Hoffmeister & Kühnel) and influenced later ones by Griepenkerl (Leipzig: C. F. Peters, 1819) and Naumann (in BG 36:71ff.). Bülow's edition (Berlin: Bote & Bock, 1859–65) is still available in reprints.

86. See Wolfgang Wiemer, "Carl Philipp Emanuel Bachs Fantasie in c-Moll – ein Lamento auf den Tod des Vaters?" *Bach-Jahrbuch* 74 (1988): 166.

87. Compare BWV 903/1, mm.35–36, with the progression developed sequentially in BWV 923, mm.24–25, 27–28, 31–32, etc. BWV 923 is preserved at (among other places) the end of SBB MUS. MS BACH P 401, a copy of the first book of the Well-Tempered Clavier in the hand identified as Anonymous 5 – possibly Johann Schneider, who was praised by Mizler in 1747 for his (improvised?) organ preludes (BDOK 3, no.565; BR, 233n). On the identity of Anonymous 5, see the discussion by Marianne Helms in Alfred Dürr, ed., NBA v/7 (*Die sechs Englischen Suiten*), KB, 183–95.

88. I am grateful to Penny Zokaie for pointing out to me the presence of *Recitativo* movements (so designated) in Bonporti's *Inventioni*, op.10 (1712), and Telemann's *Essercizii musici* (1739–40), although the latter was published too late to have influenced the Chromatic Fantasy.

the beginning of the recitative section, has a precedent of a sort in the central modulating episode in the fugue of the early *Ouverture* in G Minor, BWV 822, which makes an astonishing move to G♭.[89] From such examples one gathers that the principles of tonal design explained by C. P. E. Bach in the last chapter of his 1762 treatise had been guiding his father since the first years of the eighteenth century.

Understanding the Chromatic Fantasy as one exemplar of a continuous tradition helps demystify it, making it seem less of a historical anomaly.[90] On the other hand, although it seems more improvisatory than most Bach works, even the Chromatic Fantasy shows signs of having been rationalized or idealized. Two of the cadenza-like passages in the opening section underwent revision,[91] and one wonders whether the chords in the recitative were originally written out, as they are in all surviving sources, or were notated in figured bass (like the chorale "sketches"), as in the recitative passages of works by W. F. Bach (fantasy F. 21) and C. P. E. Bach (Prussian Sonata no. 1, H. 24 [w. 48/1]). Here, as elsewhere, Bach must have preferred not to leave a piece in sketchy or ungrammatical form.

The tradition represented by the Chromatic Fantasy hardly ended with its being written down. Attempts have long been made to connect it with the free fantasies of Bach's sons.[92] To the intermediary examples by Johann Ludwig Krebs, which have been placed in the 1740s,[93] one might now add the much

---

89. See BWV 822, mvt. 1, mm. 68–76. On the attribution and original form of BWV 822, see Hartwig Eichberg and Thomas Kohlhase, eds., NBA v/10 (*Einzeln überlieferte Klavierwerke II und Kompositionen für Lauteninstrumente*), KB, 77–85; further discussion can be found in David Schulenberg, *The Keyboard Music of J. S. Bach* (New York: Schirmer Books, 1992), 33.

90. The same argument suggests that apparent references to BWV 903/1 in later works – such as the "Reminiszenz" that Wiemer ("Bachs Fantasie in c-Moll," 168–69) finds in the Largo section of C. P. E. Bach's C-minor fantasy H. 75/3 (w. 63/6/3) – are fortuitous.

91. See the alternate readings for mm. 17 and 21–24, respectively, in the early version BWV 903a (given in BG 36:125) and in the copy by J. T. Krebs in P 803 (see BG 36:xliii).

92. As early as 1955 Heinrich Besseler argued for the influence of J. S. Bach's improvised fantasias on the style of his sons Emanuel and Friedemann (see "Bach als Wegbereiter," *Archiv für Musikwissenschaft* 12 [1955]: 1–39; reprinted in *Johann Sebastian Bach*, ed. Walter Blankenburg [Darmstadt: Wissenschaftliche Buchgesellschaft, 1970], 196–246).

93. See Peter Schleuning, *Die Freie Fantasie: Ein Beitrag zur Erforschung der klassischen Klaviermusik* (Göppingen: Alfred Kümmerle, 1973), 109.

more important fantasy H.348, which Douglas Lee convincingly dates "before 1749."[94] As Lee notes, this work already shows many features of Emanuel Bach's later fantasies, such as the use of an opening *arpeggiando* passage that is later recapitulated. Interspersed with this "quasi-ritornello section," as Lee calls it, are modulatory passages in a style resembling accompanied recitative. In addition, its tonal plan, which includes a central move to a key removed by one half step from the tonic, has parallels not only in Emanuel's later works but in the Chromatic Fantasy.

These parallels, however, probably point not to the direct modeling of one composition on another but to their emergence out of a common tradition. By the 1740s the traditions governing improvisation might have dictated the use of distant, experimental modulations as well as the free reuse of opening material as a sort of ritornello, although in practice the restatements were probably never as exact as in the written examples. References to recitative may have been another conventional element, although this is unlikely to have had any specific expressive significance, such as the *Traueraffekt* that has been claimed for it.[95] Actual recitative has a broad range of expressive effects, and thus there is no reason to associate its imitation in instrumental music with any particular affect, although it presumably does indicate a heightened expressive intent. It is true that the poet Gerstenberg added two texts to C. P. E. Bach's C-minor fantasy H.75/3; both texts are related in some way to death.[96] But while representing moments of great pathos – Hamlet's soliloquy and the death of Socrates, respectively – neither text can be described precisely as a "lament," and, in his letters to Gerstenberg and others, C. P. E. Bach hardly encourages such hermeneutic interpretations.

One attraction of recitative style may simply have been that it made possible the use of Heinichen's "theatrical" liberties of harmony, not to mention irregularities of tempo and meter impossible in a more "composed" piece.[97] This,

94. Lee, "C. P. E. Bach and the Free Fantasia," 180.

95. Schleuning, *Die Freie Fantasie*, 136.

96. On these texts, see E. Eugene Helm, "The 'Hamlet' Fantasy and the Literary Element in C. P. E. Bach's Music," *Musical Quarterly* 58 (1972): 281–82.

97. Heinichen's *General-Bass in der Composition* allows various licenses in the "theatrical" treatment of dissonances (*theatralische Resolutiones der Dissonantien*) (see George Buelow, "Heinichen's Treatment of Dissonance," *Journal of Music Theory* 6 [1962]: 216–73).

however, presented a danger if the score was to fall into the wrong hands. As Emanuel wrote – with an explicit reference to Gerstenberg – "how many are there who love free fantasias, and can also understand and play them well?"[98] The likelihood of being misunderstood was evidently one of the reasons for C. P. E. Bach's reluctance, noted by Lee, to publish his fantasies.[99]

That the unwritten free fantasy was, however, already flourishing by the 1740s is evident from a number of sonatas by Emanuel Bach from that decade that incorporate apparent borrowings from the improvised genre. For example, a formula used in H.348 to prolong the dominant of G minor recurs – in the same key – in the sonata H.47 (W.65/17), whose first movement opens with an unbarred passage in the style of a fantasy that serves as the opening theme (see ex.14).[100] The sonata dates from 1747 and may in fact have been composed before the fantasy was written down. Yet the point of the passage is clear: to incorporate fantasy style into a sonata, just as Emanuel had previously incorporated recitative into his First Prussian Sonata of 1740. The idea might have been suggested not only by the Chromatic Fantasy but also by instances in Sebastian's cantatas where recitative interrupts choruses or arias.[101] Such effects would have had little meaning if the interruption were not immediately recognized as representing the incursion of a free or improvisatory genre into the formal architecture of a sonata movement or an aria.

But even if fantasies, along with preludes, fugues, and chorales, were commonly improvised in the Bach household, Sebastian's apparent use of written exercises and Emanuel Bach's testimony that his father generally composed away from the keyboard imply a certain suspicion of improvisation. To judge from his own late publications, Sebastian wished to be remembered as a rational, even scientific, composer of learned contrapuntal works. Emanuel, too, was reluctant to write down and publish his improvisations, but eventually did so, as he wrote to Breitkopf, so that after his death people might know what

98. Letter to Forkel, 10 February 1775; no.191 in Suchalla, ed., *Briefe*.

99. Lee, "C. P. E. Bach and the Free Fantasia," 183.

100. The passage in question is not visible in the facsimile from H.348 given in Lee, "C. P. E. Bach and the Free Fantasia," 180. H.47 is best consulted in the facsimile edition by Darrell Berg, *The Collected Works for Solo Keyboard by Carl Philipp Emanuel Bach, 1714–1788*, 6 vols. (New York: Garland Publishing, 1985), 3:291ff.

101. See, e.g., the tenor aria "Die schäumenden Wellen" in Cantata 81.

EX.14. C. P. E. Bach: *a*, Fantasy in E♭ Major, H.348, from first section;
b, Sonata in G Minor, H.47 (W.65/17), mvt.1, from m.1

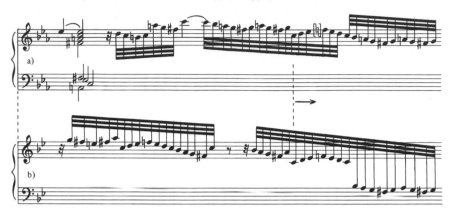

a *Fantast* he had been.[102] The change in musical aesthetics that had occurred during the intervening thirty years is clear.

There is, however, a constant factor, one that seems to have been a special characteristic of music in the Bach circle: that embellishments, cadenzas, even entire pieces that might have originated in disciplined but still improvisatory flights of fancy could – indeed, must – be fixed and brought to perfection by writing them down as precisely as possible. To be sure, writing down a free fan-

102. Letter of 15 October 1782; no.123 in Suchalla, ed., *Briefe*.

tasy, even if only as part of a sonata, was an admission that music did not always follow the rules and patterns of eighteenth-century style, even as formulated and taught in the Bach household. Bach's habit (shared by his son Emanuel) of revising, indeed editing, his keyboard music led to an image – encouraged by Forkel, among others – of Bach as the model composer of an unblemished corpus of masterpieces. This view tended to emphasize the archaic contrapuntal aspects of the keyboard works over their "galant" elements while suppressing the early, more improvisatory pieces – discounted as youthful indiscretions by Forkel – and the early versions of familiar works such as the Well-Tempered Clavier. But the messy reality of surviving early versions belies this view, as does the likelihood that improvisations not preserved would have presented a somewhat different picture of Bach. In short, we cannot consider the history of music in the school of J. S. Bach solely from the surviving scores; they are at best a pale reflection of music as studied in the Bach circle.

AUTHOR'S NOTE

Joel Lester's *Compositional Theory in the Eighteenth Century* (Cambridge, Mass.: Harvard University Press, 1992) appeared too late for me to incorporate substantial references to it in the body of this essay. I am grateful to the editor for permitting me to add the following:

Lester's most important suggestion regarding the Bach circle is that C. P. E. Bach, Kirnberger, and others incorporated significant elements of Rameau's harmonic theories into their thought. In particular, Lester suggests that Nichelmann and Kirnberger could have had a "common source for their fundamental-bass ideas" (p. 255). Elsewhere he cites the claim by Christoph Gottlob Schröter to have studied Rameau's *Traité de l'harmonie* (1722) with Johann Nicolaus Bach of Jena (pp. 124–25) and argues that C. P. E. Bach "orders his chapters [on thoroughbass] according to [Rameau's] theory" (p. 58).

C. P. E. Bach's reported remark that he and his father were "anti-Ramellian" (see Lester, p. 232) implies that both were nevertheless acquainted with some aspect of Rameau's thought. But, as Lester shows, it is difficult to determine how familiar Rameau's theories were even to writers like Marpurg who acknowledged his influence. J. S. Bach himself used the term *Fundamental-Noten* for the underlying bass in works like the Goldberg Variations, but this has little to do with Rameau apart from the use of the word "fundamental."

The ordering of C. P. E. Bach's chapters on figured bass only incidentally resembles Rameau's. Proceeding from purely consonant to increasingly dissonant chords, they treat each progression through a strictly contrapuntal type of analysis reflecting an orientation toward harmony and improvisation very different from that of Rameau, whose figured-bass method (bk. 4 of the *Traité*) is close in its surprisingly pragmatic approach to earlier French treatises. Rameau, for example, offers advice on fingering, while Emanuel makes few concessions to the convenience of the player even when contrapuntal considerations lead to progressions that lie awkwardly under the hands. Far from "reflecting the gradual disappearance of extempore thoroughbass realizations" (Lester, p. 52), the attention to correct voice leading evidently demanded even in improvised accompaniments suggests the degree to which Bach trained his pupils to be guided by rigorous musical thinking, not by speculative theory or by considerations of performance technique.

APPENDIX
Sources

Full bibliographic information is found in the notes.

1. WRITINGS BY BACH STUDENTS AND ASSOCIATES

Niedt, *Musicalische Handleitung* (1700–1717/21; manuscript extracts copied ? by a Bach student)

Scheibe, *Compendium musices* (MS, ca. 1736)

Marpurg, *Abhandlung von der Fuge* (1753–54), etc.

C. P. E. Bach, *Versuch* (1753–62); letters to Forkel

Kirnberger, *Kunst des reinen Satzes* (1771–79), etc.

2. ANALYTICAL ANNOTATIONS IN WORKS BY BACH

SBB P 401 (Anonymous 5). Well-Tempered Clavier, Book 1: preludes in D minor, B minor; fugue in C minor

SBB P 1075 (Penzel). Well-Tempered Clavier, Book 1: preludes in C major, C minor, D major, E♭ minor, E minor

Kirnberger, *Die wahren Grundsätze* (1773). Well-Tempered Clavier, Book 1: prelude in A minor; fugue in B minor

3. MUSICAL WORKS TRANSMITTED IN THE BACH CIRCLE EXEMPLIFYING "VARIATION"

Variation-suites (including BWV 833) in the Andreas Bach Book and the Möller Manuscript

Reinken, sonatas from *Hortus musicus* (1684), arranged as BWV 965–66

Concerto transcriptions, BWV 592–96, 972–87 (esp. BWV 975, mvt. 3)

Agrémens and *doubles* in English Suites, BWV 806a, 806–11

Alternate movements and *doubles* in suites BWV 818–19

Richter, allemande and courante (*Clavierbüchlein* for W. F. Bach)

Polonoise BWV ANH.117 (two versions in *Clavierbüchlein* for Anna Magdalena Bach)

Alternate versions (BWV 855a/855) of Well-Tempered Clavier, Book 1, prelude in E minor

Goldberg Variations BWV 988

Violin sonata BWV 1021

Triple concerto BWV 1044

C. P. E. Bach, varied reprises in many pieces; *Veränderungen … für Scholaren*, H.164; sonata H.150 "zweymahl durchaus verändert" (H.156–57)

4. REALIZED FIGURED BASSES

Of Albinoni, op. 6, no. 6 (by H. N. Gerber, corrected by J. S. Bach)

Of the trio sonata from the Musical Offering, BWV 1079/3 (by Kirnberger; in BDOK 3, no. 855)

5. "SKETCHES," PARTIMENTI, AND RELATED PIECES

Keyboard chorales in SBB P 802 (BWV 722a, 729a, 732a, 738a; Kast *Incerta* 26, 29)

Fantasy BWV 944/1; preludes BWV 923, 846a/1, 872a/1

Preludes and fugues BWV 907–8

Mattheson, *Exemplarische Organisten-Probe* (1719)

Short fugues in SBB P 296

Müthel, *Technische Übungen*

C. P. E. Bach, *Miscellanea musica*, H.867

6. PRESERVED IMPROVISATIONS (?)

"Cadenzas" in BWV 894, 1050, 1052, etc.

Well-Tempered Clavier, Book 2: prelude in B♭ major, fugue in G major (revision of BWV 902/2)

Ricercar a 3 from the Musical Offering, BWV 1079/1

Fantasies: BWV 903/1; H.348, 75/3, 160, etc.; F.14–23

7. STUDENT EXERCISES (?) ILLUSTRATING PARTICULAR COMPOSITIONAL TECHNIQUES

Preludes, BWV 924a, 931 (in *Clavierbüchlein* for W. F. Bach)

Pieces in *Clavierbüchlein* for Anna Magdalena Bach

Suite, Kast *Incerta* 68

Trio sonata BWV 1038 (same bass as violin sonata BWV 1021; arranged and expanded as BWV 1022)

Flute sonatas BWV 1020, 1031

Keyboard chorales BWV 691a, ANH. 73 (? by C. P. E. Bach)

The Compositional History of Bach's *Orgelbüchlein* Reconsidered

Russell Stinson

J ohann Sebastian Bach's *Orgelbüchlein*, a collection of forty-six organ chorales, has enjoyed more than a modicum of popularity since its composition. No other organ chorales – by Bach or anyone else – have been
so frequently performed or written about, and none have been studied
from a wider range of perspectives: philology, style criticism, biography, hym-
nology, and organology, to name but some. Musicologists have pursued these
disciplines to address various questions about the *Orgelbüchlein*, not least of
which is its compositional history. Despite the great and diverse interest in this
topic, however, that history has not been resolved to the extent of discouraging further research.

In exploring the vast literature on the *Orgelbüchlein*, it is easy to understand
why its compositional history is still unclear, for the autograph manuscript has
yet to be scrutinized in such a way as to date its contents properly or to determine the sequence in which the contents originated, and the issue of musical
style has been dealt with for the most part only in general terms. I am not suggesting that a systematic graphological analysis of the autograph, coupled with
detailed stylistic observations about the music, can reveal precisely when and
in what order Bach composed the *Orgelbüchlein*. But I do hope to demonstrate
that this approach can considerably sharpen the existing picture.

The autograph (SBB MUS. MS BACH P 283) reveals that Bach originally

I would like to thank the staff of the Musikabteilung of the former Deutsche Staatsbibliothek,
Berlin (now Staatsbibliothek zu Berlin–Preussischer Kulturbesitz), for kindly allowing me ac-
cess to the autograph of the *Orgelbüchlein* for the preparation of this study. Funding for my
research in Berlin was provided by the New York State/United University Professions Joint
Labor-Management Committees and the Humanities Division of the State University of New
York at Stony Brook.

planned to include no fewer than 164 chorales – that is the number of chorale titles he entered – arranged according to the liturgical year. For reasons we will never know, only about a fourth of the titles were ever set; consequently, most of the pages of the manuscript contain only chorale titles and blank staves. The first thirty-six works in this source are *de tempore* (i.e., intended for a particular season or festival of the church year); the remaining ten are *omne tempore* (i.e., appropriate at any time during the church year and dealing with, e.g., such everyday themes as "Christian life and conduct" and "death and dying").

It used to be believed that the collection originated either late in Bach's Weimar period (1708–17) or during his years in Cöthen (1717–23). The fact that Bach lists his position on the title page of the autograph as Kapellmeister at Cöthen was evidence enough for Wilhelm Rust, a nineteenth-century editor of the *Orgelbüchlein*, that all the pieces were composed in Cöthen, even though producing organ music was not among Bach's duties there.[1] The nineteenth-century Bach biographer Philipp Spitta, on the other hand, maintained that the actual composition took place while Bach was court organist in Weimar and that only the title page was penned in Cöthen.[2] For reasons unstated, Spitta assigned the works to the late rather than the early Weimar period.[3]

About thirty years ago, Georg von Dadelsen also argued for a Weimar dating, but, unlike Spitta, on the basis of strong philological evidence.[4] He observed, for instance, that the only other Bach holographs bearing the watermark found in the autograph of the *Orgelbüchlein* are two Weimar cantata

1. Wilhelm Rust, ed., BG 25/2:v. Regarding the (once popular) notion that the *Orgelbüchlein* was written for Bach's oldest son, Wilhelm Friedemann (b.1710), see Heinz-Harald Löhlein, ed., NBA IV/1 (*Orgelbüchlein, Sechs Choräle von verschiedener Art [Schübler Choräle], Orgelpartiten*), KB, 107.

2. Philipp Spitta, *Johann Sebastian Bach*, 2 vols. (Leipzig: Breitkopf & Härtel, 1873–80; reprint, Wiesbaden: Breitkopf & Härtel, 1979), 1:588, 818–21.

3. According to Charles Sanford Terry ("The 'Orgelbüchlein': Another Bach Problem," *Musical Times* 58 [1917]: 109), the *Orgelbüchlein* was authored late in 1717, during Bach's "incarceration" in Weimar.

4. Georg von Dadelsen, *Beiträge zur Chronologie der Werke Johann Sebastian Bachs* (Trossingen: Hohner-Verlag, 1958), 80, and "Zur Entstehung des Bachschen Orgelbüchleins," in *Festschrift Friedrich Blume*, ed. Anna Amalie Abert and Wilhelm Pfannkuch (Kassel: Bärenreiter, 1963), 74–79.

scores from 1714,[5] and he pointed out the existence of numerous manuscript copies of *Orgelbüchlein* chorales by Bach's Weimar colleague J. G. Walther and Weimar pupil J. T. Krebs, presumably prepared during Bach's Weimar period.[6]

Dadelsen contended, furthermore, that several of the pieces could not have been entered into the autograph any later than 1714. In these works Bach cancels sharps with flats instead of natural signs, a habit, judging from cantata autographs, that he relinquished progressively during 1714.[7] Dadelsen noted, too, that in several instances Bach draws half notes and whole notes with the same peculiar symbols most characteristic of cantata autographs from his Mühlhausen period (1707–8). In these sources half notes with ascending stems are often drawn with two distinct strokes, one each for the note head and stem; the notes appear to recline since the stem frequently veers to the right, suggesting the shape of a spoon or ladle. The half notes with descending stems, often drawn with two strokes, sometimes contain note heads that have been likened to the shape of a bird's head. The whole notes are usually in a reclining position as well and often consist of a slanting semicircle, connected at the top by a diagonal line. (I will refer to such half notes and whole notes as "Mühlhausen" symbols.) Finally, in several entries Bach draws tiny, almost decorative

5. It now appears that the watermark of the autograph of the *Orgelbüchlein* is not identical to, but is rather a variant of, that found in the two cantata autographs (see Wisso Weiss and Yoshitake Kobayashi, *Katalog der Wasserzeichen in Bachs Originalhandschriften* [= NBA IX/1], *Textband*, 89–90). Further philological evidence of a Weimar dating is that Bach used the same rastra to draw staves in the autograph of the *Orgelbüchlein* as he used for various Weimar cantata autographs (see Christoph Wolff, "Die Rastrierungen in den Originalhandschriften Joh. Seb. Bachs und ihre Bedeutung für die diplomatische Quellenkritik," in *Festschrift für Friedrich Smend* [Berlin: Merseburger Verlag, 1963], 80–92).

6. Other scholars have claimed that Bach used as liturgical models Weimar hymnals published in 1708 and 1713, which would yield further evidence that the *Orgelbüchlein* dates from Bach's Weimar years. Recent research indicates, however, that Bach probably devised his own liturgical scheme, based on his acquaintance with various hymnals and his general knowledge of hymnody (see Robin A. Leaver, "Bach and Hymnody: The Evidence of the *Orgelbüchlein*," *Early Music* 13 [1985]: 231). (All the liturgical designations used in the present study are taken from Leaver.)

7. For data on this trend, see Alfred Dürr, ed., NBA I/35 (*Festmusiken für die Fürstenhäuser von Weimar, Weissenfels und Köthen*), KB, 40–41. According to NBA IV/1, KB, 95, it may have been Bach's study of Italian music that caused him to change symbols.

symbols for accidentals and note values smaller than a half note. This type of script, Dadelsen asserted, is found in the Mühlhausen autographs as well as cantata autographs from 1714.

Dadelsen observed that in other entries Bach uses natural signs instead of flats, half notes and whole notes of a more conventional shape, and generally the same sort of symbols encountered in cantata autographs from 1715-16. With regard to the three different types of C clefs employed in the manuscript, Dadelsen pointed out that two of them are common among the Weimar and pre-Weimar autographs but that the "hook" form used in two of the entries (BWV 613 and the fragment BWV ANH.200) is documented only for Bach's Leipzig tenure (1723-50).[8] These discrepancies led Dadelsen to posit three different chronological layers within the autograph: an early, pre-1715 group of chorales; a later (post-1714) Weimar group; and a much later Leipzig group dating from ca.1740 at the earliest. (Dadelsen also demonstrated that the pieces could not have been inscribed in the sequence in which they appear in the autograph and that the autograph contains composing scores as well as fair copies.)

Using Dadelsen's findings as a point of departure, Heinz-Harald Löhlein has recently postulated that the vast majority of the works originated in Weimar during one of three annual cycles (1713-14, 1714-15, 1715-16), each corresponding to the church year.[9] Despite Dadelsen's belief that a precise chronology is impossible, Löhlein has proposed specific years for most of these pieces. He was able to add to the Leipzig entries the revised versions of two chorales (BWV 620 and 631), which Bach notated in the autograph directly on top of the original versions (BWV 620a and 631a). The original versions are also found in a manuscript copy prepared between 1727 and 1730 by C. G. Meissner,

8. Rust took the different C-clef symbols as proof that the compilation spanned the entire Cöthen period (BG 25/2:vii–viii).

9. Heinz-Harald Löhlein, ed., *Johann Sebastian Bach: Orgelbüchlein*, Faksimile-Reihe Bachscher Werke und Schriftstücke, vol.17 (Leipzig: VEB Deutscher Verlag für Musik, 1981); and NBA IV/1, KB, 90–95. The composition dates for *Orgelbüchlein* chorales given in various recent publications are based largely on Löhlein's findings (see, e.g., Christoph Wolff et al., *The New Grove Bach Family* [New York: W. W. Norton & Co., 1983], 201-2; Alfred Dürr, *Johann Sebastian Bach: Seine Handschrift – Abbild seines Schaffens* [Wiesbaden: Breitkopf & Härtel, 1984], commentary to "Blatt 5"; and Yoshitake Kobayashi, *Die Notenschrift Johann Sebastian Bachs: Dokumentation ihrer Entwicklung* [= NBA IX/2], 38, 207).

who from 1723 to 1729 worked for Bach as a copyist.[10] Assuming that Meissner copied directly from the autograph, Bach could not have prepared the revised versions (BWV 620 and 631) before 1727. It was Meissner's copy, presumably, that led Löhlein to date the revised versions "not before 1730." In accordance with Dadelsen, Löhlein dates the other Leipzig entries around 1740.

Significantly, Löhlein is the only scholar thus far who has detected patterns in how the *Orgelbüchlein* evolved stylistically. He maintains that some of the earliest works are nothing more than "diminished cantional settings" (*variierte Kantionalsätze*) while later on the lower three voices exhibit greater thematic content and a heightened sense of motivic unity; in the latest entries, Löhlein contends, four-part writing is sometimes abandoned in favor of thicker textures, and the cantus firmus may appear in voices other than the soprano.[11]

More recently, Christoph Wolff has suggested that the origins of the collection may be earlier still.[12] Citing sources unknown to Dadelsen (but known to Löhlein), Wolff argues that Bach's handwriting during his first seven years in Weimar (1708–15) was extremely stable and that graphological evidence alone is insufficient to assign works to specific years. A biographical factor that Wolff finds to be chronologically suggestive is Bach's appointment on 2 March 1714 as Weimar Konzertmeister. Prior to this date, Bach was court organist only; beginning on it, he was Konzertmeister as well. His new post entailed composing church cantatas at the rate of one per month, effectively reducing the time available to him for writing organ music. Wolff is skeptical that Bach was in the process of composing the *Orgelbüchlein* chorales (and, by way of implication, that he had time to compose them?) while he was engaged in the monthly production of church cantatas, and he therefore suggests that the chorales originated before Bach became Konzertmeister, perhaps at the very

10. See NBA IV/1, KB, 50–51, 66–67, 228.

11. Löhlein, facsimile ed., 11–12.

12. Christoph Wolff, "Zur Problematik der Chronologie und der Stilentwicklung des Bachschen Frühwerkes, inbesondere zur musikalischen Vorgeschichte des Orgelbüchleins," in *Bericht über die Wissenschaftliche Konferenz zum V. Internationalen Bachfest der DDR in Verbindung mit dem 60. Bachfest der Neuen Bachgesellschaft*, ed. Winfried Hoffmann and Armin Schneiderheinze (Leipzig: VEB Deutscher Verlag für Musik, 1988), 449–55; trans. as "Chronology and Style in the Early Works: A Background for the Orgel-Büchlein," in Christoph Wolff, *Bach: Essays on His Life and Music* (Cambridge, Mass.: Harvard University Press, 1991), 297–305.

beginning of the Weimar period, when the new court organist would have had an immediate need for a large chorale repertory. Wolff sees no reason why the earliest entries could not be as early as 1708–10, even though there are no autographs from these years dated by Bach himself that could be used to support this dating (the earliest music manuscript from Weimar dated by Bach himself is from 1713, which poses a fundamental problem in assigning autographs to the early Weimar period). The graphological layers, which Wolff fears cannot be dated precisely, suggest to him that the compilation unfolded over a period of a few years, with the major share of the work (i.e., all the pieces save the Leipzig entries) completed before 1714.

We would do well at this juncture to examine portions of the autograph that reflect different chronological layers. Plate 1 contains what is obviously an early entry, the Christmas chorale BWV 605. Bach cancels sharps nine times in this piece, using flats in eight instances (only in m. 13 is a natural used). Other signs of an early date are the small script and the Mühlhausen half notes in the upper staff of mm. 1 and 5. Observe also that the symbol for the soprano clef resembles the numeral "3."[13] Knowing what we do about Bach's working methods as a composer of church cantatas (and using common sense), it is a foregone conclusion that he composed the work in close proximity to the Christmas season, in either December or early January.[14]

Plate 2, obviously a late entry, contains the Passiontide chorale BWV 623. Here sharps are canceled by naturals exclusively, the Mühlhausen half notes have been replaced by oval note heads, the symbols in general are considerably larger, and a different, "ornate" form of the soprano clef is used. Bach probably composed the work and entered it into the autograph around Passiontide (the last two weeks in Lent).

Appendix 1 gives graphological data on all the works entered by Bach into the autograph during the Weimar period. To alleviate any potential confusion about this information, the following explanatory remarks are necessary. Beginning with the "BWV" column, BWV 620a/620 and BWV 631a/631 are entries

13. Plate 1 is representative of Bach's clef usage and stave layout throughout the autograph in that there are two staves, the upper notated exclusively in soprano clef, the lower in bass clef. Only in BWV 633 is a pedal line allotted its own staff, and only in BWV 624 is the bottom staff notated in a clef other than bass (it is notated in both bass and soprano clef).

14. This accords with remarks about the *de tempore* chorales in Dadelsen, "Zur Entstehung," 76; and NBA IV/1, KB, 91.

PL.1. Autograph MS of "Der Tag, der ist so freudenreich," BWV 605
(Staatsbibliothek zu Berlin–Preussischer Kulturbesitz,
Musikabteilung, MUS. MS BACH P 283, fol. 6r)

in which two versions of the same piece are notated literally one on top of the
other; the original entries are designated as BWV 620a and 631a. The abbreviation NA (not applicable) is used in the second column for any work where
sharps are not canceled[15] and in the third and fifth columns for works that
lack half notes and whole notes or common-time signatures, respectively. The
singular (*flat, natural*) is employed in the second column for works in which
only one sharp is canceled. The word *mostly* is used in the second and fourth

15. Although in BWV 625 a sharp is canceled in one instance, it is impossible to determine
whether the cancellation symbol is a flat or a natural. I have therefore chosen to use "NA" for
this entry as well. My findings on the method of sharp cancellation differ substantially from
those given by Löhlein in NBA IV/1, KB, 95, which are erroneous as well as incomplete.

PL. 2. Autograph MS of "Wir danken dir, Herr Jesu Christ, dass du für uns gestorben bist," BWV 623 (Staatsbibliothek zu Berlin–Preussischer Kulturbesitz, Musikabteilung, MUS. MS BACH P 283, fol. 16v)

columns for entries that contain a mixture of flats and naturals or a mixture of "3" and ornate symbols, respectively, but in which one symbol is employed more frequently than the other. Turning to the third column, the only Mühlhausen half note or whole note in BWV 607 is a half note on D in m. 2 that Bach changed to a quarter note. The C-clef symbols in BWV 624 (see the fourth column) require a further word of explanation since this is the only entry where C clefs are utilized for the lower as well as the upper staff. Here Bach employs the ornate symbol for his soprano clefs in the upper staff while alternating between the bass clef and the "3" form of the soprano clef in the lower staff (the pedal line is notated in tablature). In those entries where different common-time symbols are present (see the fifth column), the symbol for the top staff is listed first and then, following a "+" sign, the symbol for the bottom staff.

BWV 627 consists of three sections or "verses," each of which has its own pair of symbols. Upright symbols with a decorative vertical (or slightly curved) line at the crest are referred to as *upright with flourish*.

The final column is devoted to entry types. Three different types are given, based on the type and number of revisions: a *composing score* is an entry that apparently contains numerous compositional revisions of a formative nature and, consequently, appears to be an original draft; a *revision copy* is an entry in which Bach was apparently copying from an existing source but simultaneously making a few compositional revisions more "grammatical" than formative in nature; a *fair copy* is an entry evidently free of compositional revisions.[16] The entries encountered in the autograph represent a veritable continuum, and their categorization into only three types is to some degree arbitrary. The types listed are by no means absolute and are somewhat conjectural.[17]

Wolff's point about the uniformity of Bach's script in 1708–15 is well taken, as there is undeniably a certain sameness of appearance among the autographs from these years.[18] Yet the few chronological indicators that do exist offer general guidelines that should not be ignored. With this in mind, let us begin our reconsideration of the *Orgelbüchlein*'s compositional history by establish-

16. My use of these three entry types is based on Robert Lewis Marshall, *The Compositional Process of J. S. Bach: A Study of the Autograph Scores of the Vocal Works*, 2 vols. (Princeton, N.J.: Princeton University Press, 1972), 1:3–36. By comparing app. 1 with app. 2, the reader will see that my conclusions regarding entry types are rather different from Löhlein's. A discussion of how I arrived at these conclusions lies outside the scope of this essay, but my forthcoming monograph on the *Orgelbüchlein*, to be published by Schirmer Books (New York), will contain much commentary on the issue of entry types as well as on compositional process in general. Its central chapters will survey the *Orgelbüchlein* chorales not according to the order in which they appear in the autograph – the tack taken in every existing piece-by-piece description of the collection – but rather according to the (approximate) order of their composition, as proposed in app. 3.

17. I have chosen basically not to rely on the ink types present in the autograph as a means of corroborating graphological evidence, for, owing to certain restoration measures, many pages have a faded appearance, rendering it impossible to determine the ink's original color (see NBA IV/1, KB, 20). Only in the case of the Leipzig entries, for which Bach used a black ink distinct from all the other ink types in the manuscript, will this issue assume any importance.

18. There are no Weimar autographs that can be dated with certainty to 1708, but the autograph score and parts to Cantata 71, *Gott ist mein König*, performed by Bach in Mühlhausen in February 1708, give a clear picture of his script early in that year.

ing criteria for a relatively early dating, proceeding in the order of the columns in app. 1. First of all, as discussed earlier, it is fairly certain that all the works in which sharps are canceled by flats, either wholly or partially, were entered (and thus composed) before 1715. (It is not at all clear, though, that the group in which naturals are used exclusively dates from after 1714 since Bach occasionally employed naturals to cancel sharps prior to 1715.)[19] The presence of Mühlhausen half-note and whole-note symbols would seem to indicate a date of before 1714; the latest datable source in which Bach draws such symbols is the autograph score of Cantata 199, *Mein Herze schwimmt im Blut*, evidently dating from the summer of 1713.[20] In every work where flats are used, either wholly or partially, the "3" form of the soprano clef is also employed, either wholly or partially. (With respect to the works using naturals exclusively, the correlation is not so direct: in eight works the "3" form is used, in two works the "3" form is used in tandem with the ornate form, and in three works the ornate form is used exclusively.) Moreover, with only one exception (BWV 610), all the entries that make use of Mühlhausen symbols employ the "3" form exclusively. It would seem, then, that the "3" form itself is indicative of a relatively early date.[21]

19. For example, he uses a mixture of naturals and flats in what is evidently his earliest surviving autograph, that of the two organ chorales on "Wie schön leuchtet der Morgenstern," BWV 739 and 764 (see Russell Stinson, "Bach's Earliest Autograph," *Musical Quarterly* 71 [1985]: 235–63). There is even one instance of a pre-1714 autograph, that of the parts to Cantata 18, *Gleichwie der Regen und Schnee vom Himmel fällt*, in which naturals are used exclusively. According to Yoshitake Kobayashi ("Diplomatische Überlegungen zur Chronologie der Weimarer Vokalwerke" [paper delivered at the Bach-Kolloquium, Rostock, 1990], these parts date from 1713. For further data on this source, see Werner Neumann, ed., NBA I/7 (*Kantaten zu den Sonntagen Septuagesimae und Sexagesimae*), KB, 102–6; and BC I/1:201.

20. See Kobayashi, "Diplomatische Überlegungen." For further information on this source, see Klaus Hofmann and Ernest May, eds., NBA I/20 (*Kantaten zum 11. und 12. Sonntag nach Trinitatis*), KB, 13–22; and BC I/2:519.

21. Regarding the distribution of C-clef symbols among contemporaneous holographs, the two pre-Weimar keyboard autographs in staff notation use the ornate form, whereas the Weimar keyboard autographs adopt the "3" (see Dadelsen, *Beiträge*, 73–80). In the two Mühlhausen cantata autographs the voices are assigned the ornate form and the instruments the "3," while in the Weimar cantatas the "3" is employed almost exclusively for both voices and instruments. (According to Dadelsen [*Beiträge*, 78], the ornate form does not appear at all in the Weimar cantata autographs. In actuality, however, it is found not only in the autograph score

To these three criteria may be added a fourth: relatively thin common-time signatures that slant to the left (such as those in pl. 1). The symbols used for common-time signatures in the autograph of the *Orgelbüchlein* have never before been mentioned as potential chronological clues. Yet all the entries that use the thin, slanting symbols are notated with the "3" form of the soprano clef exclusively, and most of these entries that cancel sharps or contain half notes or whole notes also employ flats and Mühlhausen symbols. There is no pattern among common-time signatures in Bach's Weimar and pre-Weimar autographs that unambiguously supports the notion that the slanting symbols are suggestive of an early date – Bach uses such symbols in his very earliest autographs as well as in Weimar autographs from after 1714. But the overwhelming majority of common-time signatures in the pre-Weimar autographs are slanting symbols (of varying widths) as opposed to upright symbols. Furthermore, in his earliest keyboard autographs Bach uses the thin, slanting symbols exclusively.[22]

Finally, there is the size of the script. For most of the entries only one page was allotted; only where a relatively long cantus firmus was to be set did Bach allow for more room. (He did this, obviously, not only out of a sense of parsimony but also to avoid page turns.) In order not to exceed the allotted space, Bach was often forced to utilize small symbols. Thus the small, quasi-decorative script is not so viable a chronological criterion as it would be had Bach not imposed these severe space restrictions on himself. It is also important to realize, though, that he does not adopt the small script for all the one-page entries (see, e.g., pl. 2). It is used frequently toward the beginning of the volume but rarely so near the end. Moreover, all the entries with the small script, except for BWV 612, employ the "3" form of the soprano clef exclusively, and most of these entries that cancel sharps, contain half notes or whole notes, and are in common time also employ flats, Mühlhausen symbols, and thin,

---

of Cantata 199 but also in the soprano and alto parts to Cantata 12, *Weinen, Klagen, Sorgen, Zagen.* For further information on the latter, see Reinmar Emans, ed., NBA I/11, pt. 2 [*Kantaten zum Sonntag Jubilate*], KB, 16–17; and BC I/1:284.) Because of these inconsistencies, the clef patterns among the pre-Cöthen autographs cannot be invoked as evidence of the *Orgelbüchlein*'s compositional history; rather, the patterns within the autograph of the *Orgelbüchlein* must stand as a separate entity.

22. See the autographs of the two chorales on "Wie schön leuchtet," BWV 739 and 764, and the Prelude and Fugue in G Minor, BWV 535a.

slanting time signatures. There is also the fact that in no autograph that can be dated after 1714 does Bach employ this type of script. We may therefore view the small script as a further chronological signpost, giving us five graphological criteria – which are viable regardless of entry type – for an early dating.

Having established some chronological guidelines, it seems appropriate now to list those works that completely satisfy all applicable criteria for an early dating: BWV 601, 603, 606, 622, and 635. To these can be added entries that, while failing to meet all the criteria, contain a sufficiently large number of flats and/or Mühlhausen symbols to warrant an early dating: BWV 605, 608, 630, and 637. For reasons to be given below, the following entries also appear to be among the earliest: BWV 604, 609, 621, 632, 636, and 638.

Since Löhlein relied on all our criteria except common-time signatures, it is not surprising that most of these works are also among the entries he takes to be the earliest (see app. 2).[23] The exceptions are BWV 632, 635, and 636, all of which employ thin, slanting common-time signatures. The only Advent chorale in this group is BWV 601 ("Herr Christ, der einge Gottessohn"), which Löhlein believes to be the very first entry. That the earliest entry would be an Advent chorale is entirely expected since the Advent chorales occupy the opening pages of the manuscript. Löhlein asserts that BWV 601 was entered before the two works that precede it in the autograph (both Advent chorales) because they lack Mühlhausen symbols. One major problem with this criterion is that the number of half notes or whole notes in *Orgelbüchlein* chorales varies, depending on the time signature. The works in duple meter, which are mostly in common (or cut) time, use relatively few of these values; those in triple meter, notated with one exception in $\frac{3}{2}$ time, contain an abundance. But with respect to the work that stands at the very beginning of the manuscript, BWV 599, we are lucky to have a piece in common time that contains a large number (fourteen) of these values. The entry on the next two pages, BWV 600, is in $\frac{3}{2}$ time and contains several times this many. Three of the six values in BWV 601 are Mühlhausen symbols, suggesting that it is earlier than the other two chorales.

Precisely when BWV 601 was entered is less clear than its status as one of the

---

23. Appendix 2 is based on a table supplied by Löhlein in NBA IV/1, KB, 93, that is erroneous in designating as *omne tempore* the Pentecost chorales BWV 632–34. But judging from NBA IV/1, KB, 92, Löhlein is aware of the correct liturgical association of these settings, and I have modified his table accordingly.

earliest entries. Löhlein has pointed out that in the Weimar hymnals of 1708 and 1713 the chorale "Herr Christ, der einge Gottessohn" is designated for either the third or the fourth Sunday in Advent, while the cantus firmi of the other three Advent chorales in the *Orgelbüchlein* (BWV 599, 600, 602) are assigned to the first Sunday of the season. Why Bach would have devoted the first entry to a chorale not for the first Sunday of the church year but for the third or fourth is a question whose answer, Löhlein hypothesizes, lies in Bach's trip to Halle in late 1713. We do not know exactly when the trip began, but Bach could not have left Weimar before 27 November, when he stood as godfather to J. G. Trebs, son of the Weimar organ builder Heinrich Nikolaus.[24] During his visit to Halle, Bach successfully auditioned for the post of organist at the city's Liebfrauenkirche. He attended a meeting at the church on 13 December and returned to Weimar, it seems, shortly thereafter. The first Sunday service for which he could have played on returning to Weimar was either the third or the fourth Sunday in Advent (17 or 24 December).

I agree with Löhlein's view that there is nothing in the script of BWV 601 at odds with a dating of December 1713. It is difficult to reconcile this dating, however, with what appears to have been the state of the organ at the court church at this time, for the instrument seems to have been out of commission from soon after Pentecost 1713 until at least Easter 1714.[25] This information, which Löhlein expressly chooses to ignore, casts doubts not only on his dating of the BWV 601 entry but on his chronology as a whole.[26] A further problem with Löhlein's chronology involves BWV 628-29, 632, and 635-36; it

24. See BDOK 2, nos. 61–65; and BR, 65–68.

25. See Hans-Joachim Schulze, *Studien zur Bach-Überlieferung im 18. Jahrhundert* (Leipzig: Edition Peters, 1984), 170; and Peter Williams, *The Organ Music of J. S. Bach*, 3 vols. (Cambridge: Cambridge University Press, 1980–84), 2:8. The organ, originally built by Ludwig Compenius, was repaired and partially rebuilt in 1707-8 and 1713-14 by J. Conrad Weishaupt and H. N. Trebs, respectively.

26. I do, of course, allow for the possibility that Bach could have composed certain *Orgelbüch-lein* chorales during this period, despite the status of the court church organ. He could have had the organ of the Weimar town church (where his colleague J. G. Walther was organist) in mind, or he could originally have conceived of them as "abstract" music. But it is hard to imagine a musician as pragmatic as Bach launching such an ambitious collection – and entering as many as fifteen works into the autograph – without having a serviceable instrument of his own at hand.

is highly questionable that these entries could have originated as late as 1715 since they all meet at least one of our criteria for an early (i.e., pre-1715 or pre-1714) date.[27]

Löhlein identified the entry of BWV 601 as a fair copy, but he had no way of knowing that the piece exists in a different and clearly earlier version in the recently discovered Neumeister Collection.[28] So there is a good reason why the BWV 601 entry is not a composing score: the work had already been composed, albeit in a slightly different version. It is impossible to date the early version with any measure of precision since the Neumeister Collection was compiled well after Bach's death, probably during the 1790s. Arguably the most important discrepancies between the two versions have to do with the repetition of entire halves of the piece, whose cantus firmus, like so many chorale melodies, is in bar form (AAB). In its original form only the *Stollen* is repeated; in the *Orgelbüchlein* version both the *Stollen* and the *Abgesang* are repeated (the latter unnecessarily so, of course), resulting in an AABB design.

On examining what was apparently the next entry, a composing score of the Christmas chorale BWV 603 ("Puer natus in Bethlehem"), we see that Bach takes the repetition idea a step further by indicating that the entire piece is to be repeated. It is highly unusual for him to repeat passages in organ chorales (or vocal chorales) where the chorale text does not dictate a repetition, although he does just this in six *Orgelbüchlein* settings.[29] Because these two entries may have originated within very close chronological proximity – they were conceivably entered just a week or two apart – the addition of an unnecessary repeat in the

27. See app. 1. As with the vast majority of the settings, Löhlein does not discuss any of these entries individually. In most instances one is left to surmise from Löhlein's generalizations why he assigns a given entry to a particular year.

28. See Christoph Wolff, ed., *The Neumeister Collection of Chorale Preludes from the Bach Circle* (New Haven, Conn.: Yale University Press, 1986), 9. For a detailed discussion of the discrepancies between the versions of BWV 601, see Russell Stinson, "Some Thoughts on Bach's Neumeister Chorales," *Journal of Musicology* 11 (1993): 455–77.

29. BWV 601 and 603, already cited; BWV 612, where the last three phrases of the cantus firmus are repeated; BWV 632, where the last two phrases of the cantus firmus are repeated; and BWV 633 and 634, where the *Abgesang* is repeated. A further Bach organ chorale whose *Abgesang* is restated unnecessarily is the miscellaneous setting of "Wer nur den lieben Gott lässt walten," BWV 690.

Advent chorale may well have influenced Bach's use of one in the Christmas chorale.

Bach's next step, evidently, was to enter five other Christmas chorales: BWV 604, 605, 606, 608, and 609. That BWV 605 ("Der Tag, der ist so freuden-reich") employs a natural in one instance to cancel a sharp seems inconsequen-tial because in the other eight instances where sharps are canceled, flats are used. In addition to their common liturgical designation, BWV 605 and BWV 606 ("Vom Himmel hoch, da komm ich her") are immediately adjacent in the autograph and are virtually identical from a graphological standpoint. They also share a close stylistic affinity. Like most of the *Orgelbüchlein* chorales, they use four-part texture and exemplify the chorale type known as the *melody chorale*, wherein the cantus firmus is stated once in its entirety in the soprano, with little if any embellishment.[30] But there are few chorales from the collec-tion whose bass lines are so clearly intended as accompaniment to the cantus firmus. With their regular eighth-note motion, these lines are reminiscent of "walking basses" from contemporaneous chamber music, and they cadence with the soprano in every instance.[31] These works represent the first of several side-by-side entries that may be referred to as *pairs* since they form a two-

---

30. See Ernest May, "The Types, Uses, and Historical Position of Bach's Organ Chorales," in *J. S. Bach as Organist: His Instruments, Music, and Performance Practices*, ed. George Stauffer and Ernest May (Bloomington: Indiana University Press, 1986), 92.

31. Lest there be any doubt, a "walking bass" is characterized by the predominance of one rhythmic value, usually the value half as large as that of the main pulse (e.g., an eighth note in common time or a quarter note in $\frac{3}{2}$ time); the use of stepwise motion; and the avoidance of pitch repetition. The manner in which the bass line of BWV 605 cadences with the soprano is a feature that Peter Williams (*Organ Music*, 2:28) has found suggestive of an early date. According to Williams's program notes to Peter Hurford's recording of the complete Bach organ works on the Decca label (D228D 4, K228K 44 [1982]), "The setting is ... naive ... and must be one of the earliest chorales of the *Orgelbüchlein*." According to Ernst Arfken ("Zur Entstehungsgeschichte des Orgelbüchleins," *Bach-Jahrbuch* 52 [1966]: 52), BWV 605 and 606, along with BWV 609 and 638, are the only common-time works in the *Orgelbüchlein* containing bass lines of this type – a view to which I completely subscribe. Arfken's study, based largely on Dadelsen's findings, is most helpful in its stylistic groupings according to bass lines. But his chronology is badly flawed, as it essentially divides the pieces into two groups, almost solely on the basis of soprano-clef symbols (the entries with the "3" form are assigned to 1713-14, those with the ornate symbol to 1714-15).

entry unit on liturgical, graphological, and stylistic grounds. It would follow that they were not only entered in direct succession but composed at about the same time as well.[32]

On the next page of the autograph is the Christmas chorale BWV 607, which, like BWV 599 and 600, appears to be a later entry since among its many half notes and whole notes is nary a Mühlhausen symbol. BWV 607 was obviously entered later than BWV 606 because its final measures were squeezed onto space at the bottom of the preceding page left unused in the notation of BWV 606. The double canon BWV 608 ("In dulci jubilo") seems unquestionably early, though, despite its use of naturals; only in BWV 630 is there such a proliferation of Mühlhausen symbols.

For the remaining two chorales (BWV 604 and 609), we must rely equally on handwriting and musical style. They are the only common-time works of the seven entries thus far proposed as early that adopt upright as well as slanting symbols. Still, BWV 604 ("Gelobet seist du, Jesu Christ") otherwise meets all the criteria. BWV 609 ("Lobt Gott, ihr Christen, allzugleich") otherwise meets all the criteria except Mühlhausen symbols. Yet it contains only three half notes and no whole notes, so the fact that no Mühlhausen symbols are used is hardly compelling evidence against an early date. In terms of musical style, BWV 609 clearly belongs with BWV 605 and 606. It features a walking bass that cadences in four out of five instances with the soprano. Despite some genuine motivic content, the bass line of BWV 604 is even more subservient to the soprano at phrase endings – they cadence together without fail. Further, this work is related stylistically to BWV 605 in its alto and tenor figuration. Frequently, one of the two voices is given a ♩♪♪ motive, which usually consists of repeated notes or notes a step apart, while the other simultaneously states a ♪ ♪♪ motive in mostly stepwise motion.[33] In effect, the two voices "function

---

32. It will be assumed here that all the *Orgelbüchlein* chorales, regardless of entry type, were composed at about the time they were entered into the autograph, unless there is evidence to the contrary (such as the existence of an earlier version).

33. This figuration, found regularly in organ music by Bach's predecessors (Böhm, Buxtehude, Lübeck, and Pachelbel) and contemporaries (J. G. Walther), is most typical of Bach's earliest organ chorales, such as the miscellaneous setting of "Valet will ich dir geben," BWV 735a; variation 7 of the partita on "Christ, der du bist der helle Tag," BWV 766; variation 4 of the partita on "Ach, was soll ich Sünder machen," BWV 770; and the Neumeister Chorales.

rhythmically as a single voice."[34] No other *Orgelbüchlein* chorales so extensively utilize this figuration.

The next unquestionably early entries are the back-to-back Passiontide chorales BWV 621 and 622, found several pages later but entered perhaps only a few months after the Christmas chorales. They represent different chorale genres – BWV 621 ("Da Jesus an dem Kreuze stund") is a melody chorale, while BWV 622 ("O Mensch, bewein dein Sünde gross") is a "short ornamental chorale" – but they are clearly a liturgical-graphological unit.[35] Their graphological similarity is greatly enhanced in being surrounded on either side by entries in a substantially different script. That BWV 621 fails to meet the criterion of Mühlhausen symbols is not strong evidence against an early date since it contains only four half notes and no whole notes. In addition to its graphological affinity with BWV 622, it uses figuration very similar to that of the early Christmas chorale BWV 606.[36] And the syncopated stepwise figure from which the bass line is derived recalls m.3 of the tenor part of BWV 601, presumably the earliest entry of all.

It would appear that, perhaps only a week or so later, Bach next entered the Easter chorale BWV 630 ("Heut triumphieret Gottes Sohn"). Despite the larger ("medium") script, there can be no doubt that this is one of the earliest entries.[37] Bach had generously reserved two pages for this chorale, so he could afford to use symbols larger than those in any of the other entries designated so far as early. Otherwise, all the criteria for an early date are met. This is particularly true with respect to the abundant Mühlhausen symbols. Like BWV 601, this work had already been composed in a slightly different version (BWV 630a) by the time Bach entered it into the autograph.[38] The early version exists only in a copy by J. G. Walther, presumably made during Bach's Weimar

34. See Robert Clark and John David Peterson, eds., *Johann Sebastian Bach: Orgelbüchlein* (St. Louis: Concordia, 1984), 40.

35. The short ornamental chorale differs from the melody chorale only in that the chorale tune is heavily ornamented (see May, "Bach's Organ Chorales," 93-94).

36. See Williams, *Organ Music*, 2:30, 58.

37. This is also the conclusion in Kobayashi, *Notenschrift*, 38.

38. Neither BWV 630a nor BWV 638a, another early version to be cited shortly, is listed in the BWV; both numbers are used in NBA IV/1.

period,[39] but because the precise date of this source is unknown, it cannot furnish a *terminus post quem* for the entry of BWV 630.

Löhlein proposes that during the same Easter season Bach entered the Easter chorales BWV 625–27. While there are indications that these entries are certainly not among the latest – flats are used to cancel sharps, and there are Mühlhausen symbols as well – they do not appear to be as early as BWV 630. Positioned side by side in the autograph, they constitute a further liturgical-graphological unit (some minor graphological discrepancies notwithstanding) and were apparently entered one after the other. What most separates them from the BWV 630 entry are their half-note and whole-note symbols. Whereas BWV 625 and 626 contain few of these values, in BWV 627 they are numerous, just as in BWV 630; BWV 627 contains only two Mühlhausen symbols, while in BWV 630 they are ubiquitous. In addition, of the ten entries designated thus far as early, the seven works in common time employ the thin, slanting symbol; BWV 625 and 627 use upright symbols exclusively. A further difference between BWV 630 and BWV 625–27, which at first glance might not appear significant, involves pedal cues (i.e., the abbreviations *p.* or *ped.* used to denote pedal lines). The three previously discussed early entries that have pedal cues use the *ped.* formulation exclusively; in BWV 625–27 *p.* is used.

Bach's next course of action, evidently, was to notate the Pentecost chorale BWV 632 and the *omne tempore* Catechism chorales BWV 635–38. Only BWV 635 ("Dies sind die heilgen zehn Gebot") satisfies all the criteria for an early dating. To judge from app. 1, BWV 637 ("Durch Adams Fall ist ganz verderbt") shows few signs of an early date, but it contains only one half note and no whole notes, and it uses flats six out of seven times. BWV 637 and BWV 638 ("Es ist das Heil uns kommen her"), a side-by-side pair surrounded on either side by numerous blank pages, obviously constitute a further graphological-liturgical unit. The BWV 638 entry, too, has only one half note and no whole notes, and it uses naturals exclusively in no fewer than eight instances. Still, its medium-sized script is identical to that of BWV 637, and in both works Bach furnishes fermatas for the pedal line wherever he did so for the soprano, something about which he was usually not so consistent. The two works are very close liturgically in that they are Catechism chorales of "confession, penitence,

39. See NBA IV/1, KB, 119.

and justification."[40] They are also both melody chorales whose pedal lines cadence without fail at the same time as the soprano. (The pedal lines themselves, though, are rather different; BWV 637 has a motivic pedal, whereas BWV 638 has a walking bass.) Finally, it has been suggested that the two pieces form a unique "antecedent-consequent" pair in which BWV 638 serves as an "exuberant, assertive answer to the problems of Adam's fall."[41] All the above suggests that they were entered in direct succession.

The entry of BWV 638 appears to be a fair copy of a work already composed in a somewhat different version (BWV 638a). The early version survives in copies by Walther and J. T. Krebs, presumably prepared during Bach's Weimar tenure.[42] But, as was true of BWV 630a/630, because we do not know the precise year(s) in which these copies were made, they cannot supply a *terminus post quem* for the entry of BWV 638.

This leaves BWV 632 and 636. Except for its medium-sized script, BWV 632 ("Herr Jesu Christ, dich zu uns wend") satisfies all the criteria for an early date. It is physically separated from BWV 635 – which, it will be recalled, meets all the criteria – only by the obviously late entries BWV 634 and 633. A more telling link between BWV 632 and 635, however, is their stylistic orientation, for they are the only two melody chorales in the collection, save the Leipzig entry BWV 613, whose bass lines allude almost continuously to the cantus firmus. In BWV 632 the bass imitates the soprano in quasi-canonic fashion for the first three phrases, while the bass of BWV 635 appropriates the opening phrase as an ostinato of sorts. We may conclude that the two works were composed at around the same time and entered into the autograph in direct succession.

BWV 636 ("Vater unser im Himmelreich") is related both graphologically and stylistically to BWV 637 and 638. Like these two entries, it consists of only one half note and no whole notes, so the fact that its lone half note is not a Mühlhausen symbol cannot be marshaled as evidence against an early date. Only once is a sharp canceled; therefore, its use of a natural does not constitute compelling evidence against an early date either. In its first three phrases the bass cadences simultaneously with the soprano, as in BWV 637 and 638.

40. See Leaver, "Bach and Hymnody," 233–34.

41. See Williams, program notes.

42. See NBA IV/1, KB, 119.

Having identified the entries that seem to be the earliest, let us continue with those that are evidently the latest from the Weimar period: BWV 611, 615, 620a, 623, 624, and 633–34. These entries share a number of graphological features: the exclusive use of naturals to cancel sharps; the complete absence of Mühlhausen symbols; a preference for the ornate form of the soprano clef; common-time signatures consisting of either the upright symbol without the flourish or the thick, slanting symbol; medium or large script size; and the use of the *ped.* formulation for pedal cues.

As a stylistic entity, they are far removed from the relatively simple melody chorales of the early group. In the Christmas chorale BWV 611 ("Christum wir sollen loben schon"), for example, the chorale tune is stated by the alto alone, making it the only work in which the cantus firmus is assigned exclusively to a voice other than the soprano. What is more, only in the two short ornamental chorales BWV 614 and 622 is the cantus firmus subjected to such chromatic elaboration. Witness also the relatively independent pedal part, which cadences with the alto cantus firmus only in the first phrase; the unusually wide spacing between voices, as in BWV 611; and the thickening of texture toward the end from four to five voices by means of a double pedal (the only use of this technique in the collection).[43]

The New Year chorale BWV 615 ("In dir ist Freude") constitutes the only work in the collection that can properly be called a chorale fantasy. A virtuoso showpiece, the cantus firmus is stated in its entirety by the soprano, but with frequent repetitions and flashy interludes. The chorale tune often appears in the tenor as well. Other salient features include exceedingly free voice leading, sometimes encompassing as many as six parts, and unusually wide spacing between voices, as in BWV 611. The pedal is assigned a wide range of material, including portions of the cantus firmus, alternate-feet eighths, and a quasi-ostinato figure (♪♩♩♪♩♩♩♩♩♩|♩). Sui generis in so many ways, this work is more akin to Bach's large organ chorales from the presumably later "Great Eighteen

---

43. According to Clark and Peterson (*Orgelbüchlein*, 57), the simultaneous appearance of pitches four octaves apart – a particularly striking example of the wide spacing – may have been inspired by the concluding phrase of the chorale's first stanza, "and reaches to all the ends of the world" (*und an aller Welt Ende reicht*). According to Williams (*Organ Music*, 2:38), the added voice may be intended for the left hand. But since Bach brackets this voice only with the bass line, and not the tenor, it seems beyond doubt that it was meant to be pedaled. This is also the conclusion in NBA IV/1 and Clark and Peterson, eds., *Orgelbüchlein*.

Chorales" and the unquestionably later third part of the *Clavierübung* (1739) than to any other settings in the *Orgelbüchlein*.[44]

In the Passiontide chorale BWV 620a ("Christus, der uns selig macht") four-voice texture is strictly maintained. The work departs from the early entries in setting its cantus firmus as a canon at the fifteenth between the soprano and the bass. Frequently, there is also canonic interplay between the inner voices, whose chromaticism is redolent of BWV 611.

The immediately adjacent entries BWV 623 ("Wir danken dir, Herr Jesu Christ, dass du für uns gestorben bist") and BWV 624 ("Hilf Gott, dass mir's gelinge") appear to have been entered at around the same time as BWV 620a: all three are Passiontide chorales; they agree graphologically in every respect, save the size of the script; and they share stylistic features. The two common-time works, BWV 620a and 624, are the only ones in the *Orgelbüchlein* that adopt the thick, slanting symbol. BWV 623 is the only triple-meter work in the collection in $\frac{3}{4}$ rather than $\frac{3}{2}$ time, a further clue that it is among the latest entries. In his triple-meter organ chorales that clearly predate the *Orgelbüchlein* (such as the Neumeister Chorales) Bach uses $\frac{3}{2}$ almost exclusively; in his triple-meter organ chorales that definitely or presumably postdate the *Orgelbüchlein* (such as the chorales from *Clavierübung* III and the "Great Eighteen," respectively) $\frac{3}{4}$ is the rule. Like BWV 620a, BWV 624 is a four-part canon, although it sets the chorale tune as a canon at the fifth and (in the fifth and sixth phrases) at the fourth between the soprano and the alto; its pedal part is completely independent of the soprano at cadences. BWV 623 is a melody chorale in four voices whose bass cadences with the soprano only in the third phrase.

The inclination toward canonic writing is seen once again in the Pentecost chorales BWV 633–34 ("Liebster Jesu, wir sind hier"), which, as mentioned above, represent different versions of the same piece. Bach first penned the composing score BWV 634 and then on the next page the fair copy BWV 633.[45] As in BWV 624, the chorale tune is set as a canon at the fifth between the upper two parts. Five voices are maintained from beginning to end, imparting to the

---

44. On the relative chronology of the *Orgelbüchlein* and the "Great Eighteen," see Wolff, "Zur Problematik," 451.

45. The BWV considers BWV 634 a "variant" of BWV 633, implying (correctly) that the latter represents the final, definitive version. This presumably explains why BWV 633, the second of the two settings to be entered into the autograph, is the first to be listed in the BWV.

pungent harmonic writing an unusually rich sonority; the bass cadences with the soprano in two of the four phrases.

There are some obvious generalizations to be made about the musical style of these late entries: (1) they exhibit a predilection for canon, especially at the fifth between the upper two voices; (2) they often opt for textures thicker than four parts; (3) they tend to place the cantus firmus in voices other than the soprano (largely a by-product of the canonic writing); (4) the bass lines, compared to those in the early entries, are rather independent of the cantus firmus at phrase endings.

An awareness of the stylistic gulf between the early and the late entries is of considerable import in dealing with those that remain to be discussed. The graphological evidence suggests that these entries, which will be referred to as *middle* entries, are situated chronologically between the early and the late. Two of these works, the immediately adjacent Passiontide chorales BWV 618 and 619, may have originated very shortly before the late entries. A further liturgical-graphological-stylistic pair, their musical style betrays a relatively late date, and they differ graphologically from the late entries only in their use of "3" soprano-clef symbols. Both set their cantus firmi as canons at the fifth (in BWV 619, actually the twelfth). In BWV 618 ("O Lamm Gottes, unschuldig") the canon is between the tenor and the alto and is prefaced by a measure-long introduction; in BWV 619 ("Christe, du Lamm Gottes"), which is scored for five voices, the canon is between the tenor and the soprano and is preceded by three measures of introductory material. In only two other *Orgelbüchlein* chorales does Bach begin with material other than the initial note of the cantus firmus. In one, the early entry BWV 637, the prefatory material consists merely of two sixteenths; the other (the middle entry BWV 617) will be discussed shortly.

BWV 618 and 619 are preceded immediately by two other side-by-side entries, the Purification chorales BWV 616 and 617. A liturgical-graphological pair, their exclusive use of naturals and their lack of Mühlhausen symbols suggest a relatively late date. While BWV 616 ("Mit Fried und Freud ich fahr dahin") is a strict melody chorale, BWV 617 ("Herr Gott, nun schleuss den Himmel auf") displays such progressive features as a half-measure introduction and, more important, regular interludes between phrases (only in the late entry BWV 615 are interludes incorporated to this extent). Moreover, the texture of BWV 617 is almost identical to that of the late entry BWV 624. In both works the upper two voices form slow-moving chords; the tenor voice, played by the left hand obviously (even though not prescribed in BWV 617) on a different manual, consists only of perpetual-motion sixteenths that often rise above the alto and even the soprano; and the pedal line is composed largely of syncopated eighth notes. (No other *Orgelbüchlein* chorales approach this type of texture, although the middle entry BWV 607 uses similar hand crossings.) There is, then, sufficient graphological and stylistic evidence to place BWV 616 and 617 alongside BWV 618 and 619 as late "middle" entries.

A further unifying factor between these four works and the seven "late" entries is the influence of French organ music, specifically that of Nicholas de Grigny. The late entries BWV 624 and 633–34 and the middle entry BWV 619 are the only pieces in the collection that openly betray Gallic style.[46] The style is most manifest in BWV 619 and 633–34, owing both to their imitative five-voice texture and to their manner of voice distribution: Bach prescribes that the right hand is to play the two upper parts on one manual and the left hand the two middle parts on a different manual, while the pedal is assigned the lowest part – along the lines of a de Grigny organ fugue.[47] While BWV 624 is scored for only four parts, it seems to be similarly inspired. Here, through the use of a heading and a bracket for the upper two voices, Bach indicates that the right hand plays the upper two canonic parts on a manual other than that employed for the lone left-hand voice.[48]

The rest of the middle entries have more in common with the early ones. They are for the most part strict melody chorales, but, in contrast to the early entries, their pedal lines are almost exclusively motivic (there is only one walk-

46. The sixteenth-note figuration in BWV 599 is usually cited as an attempt by Bach to simulate the *style brisé* of the French harpsichord school, but this is questionable since the figuration is common in organ music by Bach's German predecessors (see, e.g., the opening of Buxtehude's E-minor chaconne BUXWV 160 and mm. 7–9 of Pachelbel's E-minor toccata).

47. The voice distribution is indicated in BWV 619 and 634 by the heading *à 2 Clav.* and by the use of brackets for the paired voices. For a discussion of French influence in BWV 633–34, see Victoria Horn, "French Influence in Bach's Organ Works," in *Bach as Organist*, 263–64.

48. A logical inference to be drawn from the French influence is that all these eleven works were entered sometime after Bach had prepared his copy of de Grigny's *Livre d'Orgue* (which is one of the presumably early Weimar sources in Bach's hand that cannot be precisely dated). To judge from the abundance of Mühlhausen symbols in that manuscript, this is clearly the case. On Bach's de Grigny copy, see NBA IV/1, KB, 87; and Kobayashi, *Notenschrift*, 38.

ing bass out of the twenty-three pieces in the middle compilation phase, compared to four out of fifteen in the early phase). The Advent chorale BWV 599 ("Nun komm, der Heiden Heiland") is a melody chorale whose bass always cadences with the soprano, while the Advent chorale BWV 600 ("Gott, durch deine Güte") stylistically parallels the early Christmas chorale BWV 608: both BWV 600 and 608 set their chorale tunes as a canon at the octave between soprano and tenor (and in that order); the chorale tunes themselves open with essentially the same melodic contour; the canonic voices are a measure apart; and they use the same time signature and note values.

The Christmas chorale BWV 607 ("Vom Himmel kam der Engel Schar") is stylistically reminiscent of the early Christmas chorales BWV 605 and 606; it contains a true walking bass that cadences invariably with the soprano. The remaining Advent/Christmas chorales BWV 602 ("Lob sei dem allmächtigen Gott"), BWV 610 ("Jesu, meine Freude"), and BWV 612 ("Wir Christenleut") feature bass lines that are somewhat independent of the soprano. In BWV 610 Bach utilizes a pedal motive that is also employed in the late entry BWV 611, but he notates it differently. The notation in BWV 610 is ♪⌐ ♫♫, in BWV 611 ♪. ♫♫.

The short ornamental New Year chorale BWV 614 ("Das alte Jahr vergangen ist") contains numerous flats, suggesting a very early date, but also uses ornate soprano-clef symbols. Several pages later are the five side-by-side Easter chorales BWV 625 ("Christ lag in Todesbanden"), BWV 626 ("Jesus Christus, unser Heiland, der den Tod überwand"), BWV 627 ("Christ ist erstanden"), BWV 628 ("Erstanden ist der heilge Christ"), and BWV 629 ("Erschienen ist der herrliche Tag"). The graphological and stylistic similarities between these works are sufficiently strong to suggest that they were entered during the same Easter season. Signs of a relatively early origin are the flats and Mühlhausen symbols as well as the adoption of the melody-chorale genre in the first four.[49] The bass lines of BWV 625, 626, and 628 usually cadence with the soprano. BWV 627, with its three "verses," may be viewed as a set of three melody chorales, with relatively independent pedal parts. Somewhat monotonously, Bach has the soprano state the cantus firmus in each verse, even though it seems only natural that the register might be varied from verse to verse (as

49. These graphological similarities were presumably among the factors that led Löhlein to include the first three in his first annual cycle.

happens in, say, "O Lamm Gottes, unschuldig" from the "Great Eighteen").[50] The contrast between this rigidity and the free treatment of cantus firmi in the late entries is remarkable. BWV 629 sets its chorale tune as a canon at the fifteenth between the soprano and the bass, in the manner of BWV 600 and 608.

Several pages later and surrounded by blank pages on either side is the Pentecost chorale BWV 631a ("Komm, Gott Schöpfer, Heiliger Geist"). Its pedal sounds for the most part only on the third eighth note of the beat, preceded by two eighth rests (surely a symbolic reference to the *third* member of the Holy Trinity). At the cadences, it sounds invariably on the downbeat and simultaneously with the soprano.

The remaining works are *omne tempore*. There is first of all the unique BWV 639 ("Ich ruf zu dir, Herr Jesu Christ"), a three-voice setting that may well be some sort of transcription.[51] Isolated both conceptually and geographically – it too is separated on either side by blank pages, as are all the remaining chorales – it, like BWV 601, is also contained in the Neumeister Collection. Unlike BWV 601, though, the differences in this case between the Neumeister manuscript and the autograph are so trifling that it seems ill advised to speak of different "versions."

BWV 640 ("In dich hab ich gehoffet, Herr") is much in the style of the early entry BWV 630. Although their pedal lines are motivically constructed, they never fail to cadence with the soprano, and these are the only works in the collection to end with a pedal flourish.[52] BWV 641 ("Wenn wir in höchsten Nöten sein") is the third and final ornamental setting. Löhlein sees as evidence against a late date the relatively high percentage of eighths and sixteenths with descending stems drawn on the right, instead of the left, of the note head.[53] The

---

50. See Löhlein, facsimile ed., 12.

51. See Williams, *Organ Music*, 2:91; and Klaus Peter Richter, *Orgelchoral und Ensemblesatz bei J. S. Bach* (Tutzing: Hans Schneider, 1982), 181–200.

52. Dadelsen takes BWV 640 to be a late entry, presumably because of its large script. He draws the same conclusion about BWV 644, one assumes, for the same reason. Curiously, at least in terms of the script size (and for reasons unstated), he believes BWV 642 to be among the early entries (see *Beiträge*, 80; and "Zur Entstehung," 76).

53. NBA IV/1, KB, 95. This method of drawing stems is characteristic of Bach's Mühlhausen cantata autographs. On the whole, it is rarely encountered in the autograph of the *Orgelbüchlein*, but in BWV 641 and the early ornamental setting BWV 622, two of the most hastily penned entries, it is common.

last three chorales in the autograph – BWV 642 ("Wer nur den lieben Gott lässt walten"), BWV 643 ("Alle Menschen müssen sterben"), and BWV 644 ("Ach wie nichtig, ach wie flüchtig") – feature fairly independent bass lines.

Identifying these compilation phases is a far easier task than dating them. We can feel most confident about the late entries, for their script is the same found in (securely dated) cantata autographs from 1715-16. It is conceivable, though, that some of them could have been entered as late as 1717, almost all of which Bach spent in Weimar,[54] despite the absence of autographs that can be assigned with certainty to this year. The late "middle" entries probably originated during 1715 or 1716. As Purfication (2 February) or Passiontide chorales, they would presumably not have been composed during 1714 since the Weimar court organ seems to have been unplayable at least through Easter of that year, and their script seems much too late for 1713. Nor does it seem that these chorales could have been entered as late as 1717. They clearly appear to predate the "late" entries, which probably did not originate any later than 1717;[55] if the New Year chorale BWV 615 and the Passiontide chorales BWV 620a, 623, and 624 represent Bach's script in early 1717, then, because of their designation as either Purification or Passiontide chorales (i.e., chorales intended for the early calendar year), BWV 616-19 could not be any later than 1716.

The considerable stylistic disparities between these eleven entries and the others imply a fairly large chronological interval. Although we have no way of knowing precisely, I would propose that the interval was at least a year long and that it was taken up to some extent by the organ renovation project of 1713-14. At all events, it is only reasonable to assume that the organ repairs interrupted Bach's work on the collection for about a year. The *de tempore* chorales of the early and early "middle" entries would seem to indicate that these works encompass at least two annual cycles. Because six of the early "middle" entries

54. According to Wolff et al. (*New Grove Bach Family*, 71), Bach moved to Cöthen probably on 3 or 4 December.

55. There is no graphological evidence that the late entries could not have originated as late as 1718, merely the (important) fact that Bach was not responsible for writing organ music in Cöthen. However, the first datable autograph from the Cöthen period, from early 1719, is sufficiently different (from a graphological standpoint) from the cantata autographs of 1715-16 that 1718 is surely the latest year in which these entries could have been made (see Dadelsen, *Beiträge*, 81-85; and Kobayashi, *Notenschrift*, 18-19).

use Mühlhausen symbols – a practice that Bach appears to have relinquished by 1714 – the latter of these cycles presumably could not have ended any later than 1713 (and, considering the organ repairs, no later than the spring of 1713). We can do little more than propose a dating of 1708–12 for the early entries and 1709–13 for the early "middle" entries.

Bach returned to the autograph of the *Orgelbüchlein* during his years in Leipzig, but exactly when (and for what reasons) cannot be ascertained. He entered the New Year chorale BWV 613, began an entry of the Passiontide chorale BWV ANH.200, and substantially revised two existing entries to form the Passiontide chorale BWV 620 and the Pentecost chorale BWV 631. What most distinguishes these portions of the autograph from all the others is their black ink.[56] Dadelsen was convinced that the new entries were from late in Bach's life, ca.1740 at the earliest, but his only specific evidence of such a late date was the form of the C clef. In his recent monograph on Bach's script, which represents the most detailed and comprehensive study of this topic to date, Kobayashi is far more cautious, offering for the new entries as well as the revisions only a dating of after 1724.[57] To judge from Meissner's copy of BWV 620a and 631a, this dating may be narrowed, but only by a couple of years. As mentioned earlier, this source, dating from 1727–30 and presumably copied from the autograph, suggests that Bach could not have penned the revised versions before 1727. Since the same ink was used for both the new entries and the revisions, it stands to reason that all the Leipzig entries were made at around the same time, possibly during the winter and spring (New Year–Pentecost) of the same year.[58] But we may offer no more precise a dating than "after 1726."

56. Only by viewing the autograph firsthand can one appreciate just how distinct this black ink is from the various shades of brown used for all the other entries (in Löhlein's facsimile edition the black ink is rendered mostly as a dark shade of brown).

57. Kobayashi, *Notenschrift*, 207.

58. The same black ink also appears to some degree in the entry of BWV 619, which occupies the recto side of the folio that contains BWV 620a/620. Bach used the black ink to notate brackets in mm.8, 9, 10, and 13 that clarify how the voices are to be distributed between the two hands; to complete one such bracket in m.5; and to draw a diagonal line between the first and the second bass notes in m.5, thereby clarifying the voice leading. All these symbols can be interpreted as performance instructions, indicating that Bach returned to this chorale in Leipzig to perform or teach it.

The only complete and entirely new setting in this group, the New Year chorale BWV 613 ("Helft mir Gotts Güte preisen"), is a melody chorale.[59] Bach had allowed only one page for this entry, and by this point the page was immediately preceded and followed by the entries of BWV 612 and 614. Obviously, he was somewhat restricted in his choice of chorale types here; he could not have chosen the chorale fantasy or any other genre that would have occupied two or more pages. The melody chorale, though, was not his only option; a short ornamental chorale, chorale canon, or chorale fughetta (a fugue usually on the first phrase of the chorale tune) on this cantus firmus would also have fit on a single page. In choosing this simple yet effective design, Bach returned to the genre most representative of the collection, suggesting that his choice was not incidental but rather was made out of concern for the *Orgelbüchlein* as a unified whole.

Appendix 3 summarizes the conclusions set forth here regarding the compositional history of the *Orgelbüchlein*. If nothing else, these findings substantiate Löhlein's conclusions, cited earlier, on the stylistic evolution of the collection. But it is also hoped that a compelling case has been made for the existence of specific stages within that evolution, stages during which Bach appears to have focused on particular chorale types or compositional practices. This diversity of genres and techniques is closely tied to the main didactic goal of the *Orgelbüchlein*, which, as its composer declares on the title page, is to instruct the beginning organist in how to set a chorale "in all kinds of ways."

59. To judge from the two surviving measures of the Passiontide chorale BWV ANH.200, Bach originally conceived of this work as a melody chorale, too, but in revising it added ornamentation to the cantus firmus (see Marshall, *The Compositional Process*, vol. 2, no. 166).

APPENDIX ONE
The Graphological Makeup of the Autograph of the *Orgelbüchlein*

BWV No.	Method of Sharp Cancellation	"Mühlhausen" Half Notes or Whole Notes?	Soprano-Clef Symbols	Common-Time Signature Symbols	Size of Script	Proposed Entry Type
599	NA	no	3	slanting	small	composing score
600	NA	no	3	NA	small	composing score
601	NA	yes	3	slanting	small	fair copy
602	NA	no	3	upright	small	composing score
603	NA	yes	3	NA	small	composing score
604	NA	yes	3	upright + slanting	small	composing score
605	mostly flats	yes	3	slanting	small	composing score
606	flats	yes	3	slanting	small	revision copy
607	NA	yes	3	NA	small	composing score
608	naturals	yes	3	NA	small	composing score
609	flats	no	3	upright + slanting	small	composing score
610	NA	yes	mostly 3	upright	small	fair copy
611	natural	no	ornate	upright	medium	revision copy
612	NA	no	3	upright	small	composing score
613	[Leipzig entry]					fair copy
614	flats	no	mostly ornate	upright	small	revision copy
615	naturals	no	mostly 3	NA	medium	revision copy
616	naturals	no	3	upright with flourish + upright	medium	fair copy

BWV No.	Method of Sharp Cancellation	"Mühl-hausen" Half Notes or Whole Notes?	Soprano-Clef Symbols	Common-Time Signature Symbols	Size of Script	Proposed Entry Type
617	naturals	no	3	upright with flourish + upright	medium	revision copy
618	NA	no	3	upright	medium	revision copy
619	NA	no	3	NA	large	revision copy
620a	naturals	no	ornate	slanting (thick)	medium	fair copy
620	[Leipzig entry]					revision copy
621	NA	no	3	slanting	small	revision copy
622	NA	yes	3	slanting	small	composing score
623	naturals	no	ornate	NA	large	revision copy
624	naturals	no	ornate/3	slanting (thick)	medium	revision copy
ANH. 200	[Leipzig entry]					composing score
625	NA	yes	3	upright with flourish + upright	small	revision copy
626	mostly naturals	no	3	upright with flourish + upright	medium	revision copy
627	NA	yes	3	upright with flourish + upright; upright; upright	small	composing score
628	mostly naturals	no	3	NA	small	composing score

BWV No.	Method of Sharp Cancellation	"Mühlhausen" Half Notes or Whole Notes?	Soprano-Clef Symbols	Common-Time Signature Symbols	Size of Script	Proposed Entry Type
629	NA	yes	3	NA	small	composing score
630	NA	yes	3	NA	medium	revision copy
631a	flat	no	3	upright	medium	composing score
631	[Leipzig entry]					revision copy
632	NA	yes	3	slanting	medium	fair copy
634	NA	no	mostly 3	upright	medium	composing score
633	NA	no	ornate	upright	medium	fair copy
635	NA	yes	3	slanting	small	composing score
636	natural	no	3	slanting	medium	fair copy
637	mostly flats	no	3	upright + slanting	medium	composing score
638	naturals	no	3	slanting	medium	fair copy
639	NA	no	3	upright with flourish + upright	medium-large	fair copy
640	natural	NA	3	upright	medium-large	revision copy
641	NA	no	3	upright with flourish + upright	medium-large	composing score
642	naturals	no	3	upright	medium	revision copy
643	natural	yes	3	upright	medium	composing score
644	NA	NA	3	upright	medium-large	fair copy

APPENDIX TWO
Heinz-Harald Löhlein's Chronology of the *Orgelbüchlein*

	Composing Scores	Fair Copies
First annual cycle:		
3d or 4th Sunday in Advent 1713		BWV 601
Christmas 1713	BWV 603, 608, 609	BWV 604-6, 610
New Year 1714		BWV 614
Passiontide 1714	BWV 622	BWV 621
Easter 1714	BWV 627	BWV 625, 626, 630
Pentecost 1714	BWV 631a	
Omne tempore 1714	BWV 637, 641, 643	BWV 638-40, 642, 644
Second annual cycle:		
Advent 1714	BWV 599, 600, 602	
Christmas 1714	BWV 607, 612	
Purification (2 February) 1715		BWV 616, 617
Passiontide 1715		BWV 618, 619, 620a
Easter 1715	BWV 628, 629	
Pentecost 1715	BWV 634	BWV 632, 633
Omne tempore 1715	BWV 635	BWV 636
Third annual cycle:		
Christmas 1715		BWV 611
New Year 1716		BWV 615
Passiontide 1716		BWV 623, 624
Leipzig entries		
New Year (ca. 1740)		BWV 613
Passiontide (ca. 1740)	BWV ANH. 200 (fragment)	
(Further Leipzig entries, made after 1729: BWV 620 and 631)		

APPENDIX THREE
Bach's *Orgelbüchlein:* A Proposed Compositional History

BWV *No.*	*Title*	*Liturgical Season or Festival*	*Compilation Phase*	*Proposed Date*
601	"Herr Christ, der einge Gottessohn"	Advent	Early	1708–12
603	"Puer natus in Bethlehem"	Christmas	Early	1708–12
604	"Gelobet seist du, Jesu Christ"	Christmas	Early	1708–12
605	"Der Tag, der ist so freudenreich"	Christmas	Early	1708–12
606	"Vom Himmel hoch, da komm ich her"	Christmas	Early	1708–12
608	"In dulci jubilo"	Christmas	Early	1708–12
609	"Lobt Gott, ihr Christen, allzugleich"	Christmas	Early	1708–12
621	"Da Jesus an dem Kreuze stund"	Passiontide	Early	1708–12
622	"O Mensch, bewein dein Sünde gross"	Passiontide	Early	1708–12
630	"Heut triumphieret Gottes Sohn"	Easter	Early	1708–12
632	"Herr Jesu Christ, dich zu uns wend"	Pentecost	Early	1708–12
635	"Dies sind die heilgen zehn Gebot"		Early	1708–12
636	"Vater unser im Himmelreich"		Early	1708–12
637	"Durch Adams Fall ist ganz verderbt"		Early	1708–12
638	"Es ist das Heil uns kommen her"		Early	1708–12

BWV *No.*	*Title*	*Liturgical Season or Festival*	*Compilation Phase*	*Proposed Date*
599	"Nun komm, der Heiden Heiland"	Advent	Middle (early)	1709–13
600	"Gott, durch deine Güte"	Advent	Middle (early)	1709–13
602	"Lob sei dem allmächtigen Gott"	Advent	Middle (early)	1709–13
607	"Vom Himmel kam der Engel Schar"	Christmas	Middle (early)	1709–13
610	"Jesu, meine Freude"	Christmas	Middle (early)	1709–13
612	"Wir Christenleut"	Christmas	Middle (early)	1709–13
614	"Das alte Jahr vergangen ist"	New Year	Middle (early)	1709–13
625	"Christ lag in Todesbanden"	Easter	Middle (early)	1709–13
626	"Jesus Christus, unser Heiland, der den Tod überwand"	Easter	Middle (early)	1709–13
627	"Christ ist erstanden"	Easter	Middle (early)	1709–13
628	"Erstanden ist der heilge Christ"	Easter	Middle (early)	1709–13
629	"Erschienen ist der herrliche Tag"	Easter	Middle (early)	1709–13
631a	"Komm, Gott Schöpfer, Heiliger Geist"	Pentecost	Middle (early)	1709–13
639	"Ich ruf zu dir, Herr Jesu Christ"		Middle (early)	1709–13
640	"In dich hab ich gehoffet, Herr"		Middle (early)	1709–13
641	"Wenn wir in höchsten Nöten sein"		Middle (early)	1709–13

BWV No.	Title	Liturgical Season or Festival	Compilation Phase	Proposed Date
642	"Wer nur den lieben Gott lässt walten"		Middle (early)	1709–13
643	"Alle Menschen müssen sterben"		Middle (early)	1709–13
644	"Ach wie nichtig, ach wie flüchtig"		Middle (early)	1709–13
616	"Mit Fried und Freud ich fahr dahin"	Purification (2 February)	Middle (late)	1715–16
617	"Herr Gott, nun schleuss den Himmel auf"	Purification	Middle (late)	1715–16
618	"O Lamm Gottes, unschuldig"	Passiontide	Middle (late)	1715–16
619	"Christe, du Lamm Gottes"	Passiontide	Middle (late)	1715–16
611	"Christum wir sollen loben schon"	Christmas	Late	1715–17
615	"In dir ist Freude"	New Year	Late	1715–17
620a	"Christus, der uns selig macht"	Passiontide	Late	1715–17
623	"Wir danken dir, Herr Jesu Christ, dass du für uns gestorben bist"	Passiontide	Late	1715–17
624	"Hilf Gott, dass mir's gelinge"	Passiontide	Late	1715–17
633	"Liebster Jesu, wir sind hier"	Pentecost	Late	1715–17
634	"Liebster Jesu, wir sind hier"	Pentecost	Late	1715–17
613	"Helft mir Gotts Güte preisen"	New Year	Leipzig	after 1726

BWV No.	Title	Liturgical Season or Festival	Compilation Phase	Proposed Date
620	"Christus, der uns selig macht"	Passiontide	Leipzig	after 1726
631	"Komm, Gott Schöpfer, Heiliger Geist"	Pentecost	Leipzig	after 1726
ANH. 200 (fragment)	"O Traurigkeit, o Herzeleid"	Passiontide	Leipzig	after 1726

Concerto Styles and Signification in Bach's First Brandenburg Concerto

Michael Marissen

The unquestionably vital role that "Vivaldi fever" played in the dramatic change around 1713 in J. S. Bach's compositional style is referred to regularly in recent general studies of Bach's life and works.[1] At the same time, though, investigations into this phenomenon are all too often plagued by serious analytical problems. In specialized studies on the reception of Vivaldi in Bach's concertos, for example, the usual tack has been to construct formal models for Vivaldi, against which to compare the content of Bach's music.[2] Although this approach reveals the relative richness and com-

---

1. Hans-Joachim Schulze has shown by means of detailed archival research that Bach's first encounter with the new concerto style of Vivaldi's *L'Estro Armonico* collection probably took place in 1713, after Prince Johann Ernst of Weimar had forwarded to Weimar a large quantity of music purchased during his travels in the Netherlands, including, presumably, Vivaldi's *L'Estro Armonico*, published in Amsterdam a year or two earlier (see "J. S. Bach's Concerto-Arrangements for Organ – Studies or Commissioned Works?" *Organ Yearbook* 3 [1972]: 4–13, "Johann Sebastian Bachs Konzertbearbeitungen nach Vivaldi und anderen – Studien- oder Auftragswerke?" *Deutsches Jahrbuch der Musikwissenschaft* 18 [1978]: 80–100, and *Studien zur Bach-Überlieferung im 18. Jahrhundert* [Leipzig: Edition Peters, 1984], 146–73). For an interesting discussion of Vivaldi's influence on Bach's compositional thinking, see Christoph Wolff, "Vivaldi's Compositional Art, Bach, and the Process of 'Musical Thinking,'" in *Bach: Essays on His Life and Music* (Cambridge, Mass.: Harvard University Press, 1991), 72–83.

2. See, e.g., Pippa Drummond, *The German Concerto: Five Eighteenth-Century Studies* (Oxford: Oxford University Press, 1980); and Martin Geck, "Gattungstraditionen und Altersschichten in den Brandenburgischen Konzerten," *Die Musikforschung* 23 (1970): 139–52. For a more sophisticated approach to formal issues, see Laurence Dreyfus, "J. S. Bach's Concerto Ritornellos and the Question of Invention," *Musical Quarterly* 71 (1985): 327–58.

plexity of Bach's concertos, it has the unfortunate methodological consequence of considering Bach's concertos to be Vivaldian only when Bach's content is manifestly molded into Vivaldi's form.

Bach's concertos for an ensemble without a consistently detached soloistic subgroup represent an especially intriguing field for this sort of inquiry since their surface stylistic features frequently tend to obscure the application of Vivaldi's ritornello procedures. For example, in the First, Third, and Sixth Brandenburg Concertos textural and thematic contrasts are attenuated, which has led scholars to place these works outside Bach's reception of Vivaldi. In addition, the critical report in the standard scholarly edition of the concertos implies misleadingly that early versions of these pieces predate the known arrival of Vivaldi's concertos in Germany,[3] thus providing an objective, text-critical basis for a pre-Vivaldian view of the concertos.[4] I propose to show, however, in an interpretation of relationships between structure and scoring in the First Brandenburg Concerto, that this apparently old-fashioned ensemble work of Bach is better understood as a sophisticated response to formal possibilities presented by Vivaldi's new concerto style and, furthermore, that Bach's procedures have interesting social implications.[5]

For the purposes of the present discussion only a brief review of Vivaldian concerto style will be necessary. In the concertos of Vivaldi the alternation between the tutti (entire ensemble) and the concertino (subgroup) involves contrasts in texture as well as in the type of music performed by the two groups. The tutti plays "ritornello" thematic material, and the concertino plays "episode" material. The ritornellos are expository in character, and normally they are tonally closed (i.e., they begin and end in the same key). Considered in terms of a continuum from expository to episodic, the episodes tend to be less

3. Heinrich Besseler, ed., NBA VII/2 (*Sechs Brandenburgische Konzerte*), KB.

4. This argument is advanced most forcefully by Geck, "Gattungstraditionen und Altersschichten."

5. Vivaldi's formal influence on the First Brandenburg Concerto is discussed in Hans-Günter Klein, *Der Einfluss der Vivaldischen Konzertform im Instrumentalwerk Johann Sebastian Bachs* (Strasbourg: Heitz, 1970), 52–56; and Peter Ansehl, "Genesis, Wesen, Weiterwirken: Miszellen zur Vivaldischen Ritornellform," *Informazioni e Studi Vivaldiani* 6 (1985): 74–85 (the excerpts concerning Bach are reprinted in Ansehl's "Zum Problem der Ritornellstrukturen in den Brandenburgischen Konzerten von Johann Sebastian Bach," *Cöthener Bach-Hefte* 4 [1986]: 96–100).

expository in character. They are often virtuosic, and normally they begin in one key and end in another. A Vivaldian concerto movement consists mainly of free episode material with occasional returns of part or all of the ritornello. In fact, Vivaldi's specific contributions to the development of the Venetian Baroque concerto were to make opening tuttis tonally closed and to intensify the stabilizing function of the tuttis by employing literal or transposed quotations from all the now easily separable segments in the opening tutti. By contrast, in the concertos of Vivaldi's predecessors often only the head of the first – tonally "open" – tutti would return in the course of a movement, while the continuations – also tonally open, save the final one – might employ different thematic material in each instance.[6] The rationality of Vivaldi's formal innovations probably goes a long way in helping explain why Vivaldi's concertos evidently appealed to Bach so much more than the concertos of Vivaldi's predecessors.

In his concerto-style works Bach shows a predilection for a Vivaldian ritornello type containing three clearly differentiated segments, a type that falls within the category of what modern German-speaking students of Vivaldi's music have labeled the *Fortspinnungstypus* (spinning-forth type). In the Vivaldian ritornello favored by Bach the first segment grounds the tonality with primarily tonic and dominant harmonies, ending on either the tonic or the dominant (more typically the dominant). The second segment follows with sequential thematic material whose harmonic rhythm is marked mostly by root movement by fifths. And the third segment, whether involving further sequencing or other procedures, brings the ritornello to a satisfying close by way of a cadential gesture in the tonic.[7] Writers in various languages still refer to the three segments of this particular variety of *Fortspinnung*-type ritornello with the German terms *Vordersatz*, *Fortspinnung*, and *Epilog*.[8] I will

6. On the Baroque concerto and Vivaldi's specific formal contributions to the genre, see Michael Talbot, "The Concerto Allegro in the Early Eighteenth Century," *Music and Letters* 52 (1971): 8–18, 159–72.

7. For an example of a Vivaldi ritornello clearly structured along these lines, see the opening ritornello of the third movement of his E-major violin concerto, op. 3, no. 12 (RV 265; cf. Bach's arrangement of this piece for keyboard solo, BWV 976), where the points of division occur at mm. 7 and 17.

8. These terms are derived from similar ones employed in Wilhelm Fischer, "Zur Entwicklungsgeschichte des Wiener klassischen Stils," *Studien zur Musikwissenschaft* 3 (1915): 24–84.

use *Fortspinnung-type* here to describe this specific type of Vivaldian ritornello.[9]

The opening movement of the First Brandenburg Concerto certainly has none of the obvious external features of the new Vivaldian concerto form. The Vivaldi concertos that Bach transcribed for keyboard in the early 1710s were scored for violin (or violins) and string ensemble, and they featured relatively clear textural and thematic contrasts between the ritornellos and the episodes. Bach's concerto, on the other hand, is scored for several choirs of instruments (two horns, three oboes with bassoon, and string ensemble), and its continually changing subgroups do not necessarily coincide with contrasts in thematic material. On the face of it, the scoring and the style appear to have more in common with German ensemble music of earlier decades than with the Vivaldian string concertos that had become modish in Saxony by the time Bach sent his dedication score of the Brandenburg Concertos to the margrave of Brandenburg (in 1721).[10]

On formulating these categories primarily in terms of harmonic properties rather than thematic ones, see Dreyfus, "Bach's Concerto Ritornellos."

9. At times Bach scholars also use the term *Fortspinnung-type ritornello* for ritornellos with other sorts of spinning forth than sequencing (e.g., sixteenth-note figures repeated at the same pitch level) as well as for ritornellos without initial segments having the properties described above under the term *Vordersatz*. See, e.g., the discussions of the arias "Jagen ist die Lust der Götter" and "Schafe können sicher weiden" from *Was mir behagt, ist nur die muntre Jagd!* BWV 208, and "Er segnet, die den Herrn fürchten" from *Der Herr denket an uns*, BWV 196, in Miriam K. Whaples, "Bach's Earliest Arias," *Bach: The Journal of the Riemenschneider Bach Institute* 20, no.1 (Spring 1989): 35, 39, 45. See also Alfred Dürr, *Studien über die frühen Kantaten Johann Sebastian Bachs: Verbesserte und erweiterte Fassung der im Jahr 1951 erschienenen Dissertation* (Wiesbaden: Breitkopf & Härtel, 1977), 123–24, 172.

10. Geck ("Gattungstraditionen und Altersschichten," 145) associates the opening movement of the First Brandenburg Concerto stylistically and chronologically with the instrumental preludes to German sacred vocal works of the late seventeenth and early eighteenth centuries, especially those of Friedrich Wilhelm Zachow (1663-1712), who scores several of his cantatas with horns, oboes, and strings. But Vivaldian concertos scored with similar combinations of wind instruments were cultivated decades later by composers at the Dresden court during Bach's lifetime (see Rudolf Eller, "Vivaldi and Bach," in *Vivaldi Veneziano Europeo*, ed. Francesco Degrada, Studi di Musica Veneta Quaderni Vivaldiana, vol.1 [Florence: Olschki, 1980], 55-66). That is, Geck's concern with the dating of the First Brandenburg Concerto and his comparison with Zachow will initially appear compelling more on the questions of contrapuntal styles than on the scorings.

But consider how Bach organizes the opening thirteen measures. He structures mm.1–6 with *Vordersatz* (hereafter "V"), *Fortspinnung* ("Fa"), and *Epilog* ("Ea") segments (closing, however, on the dominant); mm.1–3 emphasize the tonic and dominant triads, mm.3–4 feature sequential material, and mm.4–6 approach a clearly defined cadence. A second and third *Fortspinnung* segment (hereafter "Fb 1" and "Fb 2") follow: in mm.6–10 the oboe and string families proceed, separately in mm.6–7 and then together in mm.8–10, with sequential material loosely derived from the *Vordersatz* segment. The design concludes with a second and third *Epilog* (hereafter "Eb 1" and "Eb 2"): mm.10–13 twice lead to a cadence on the tonic (first deceptive, then authentic). Since various permutations of segments from this tonally closed block of material are used during the course of the movement (in most cases more than once),[11] mm.1–13 and the returns would correctly be viewed as modeled, thematically and tonally, on the new Vivaldian *Fortspinnung*-type ritornello procedure.

Texturally, however, mm.1–13 do not correspond at all to the Vivaldian ritornello procedure. Bach engineers a reduction in the scoring toward the middle of the ritornello (from full ensemble with horns, to oboe and string families together, to oboe and string families alternating). He also designs a buildup of the scoring toward the close (from oboe and string families alternating, to oboe and string families together, to full ensemble with horns). Furthermore, m.13 does not mark the entrance of a soloist or soloists with entirely new thematic material but initiates alternating full-ensemble and subgroup textures with thematic material obviously derived from mm.1–6 of the ritornello. Measures 13–15 emphasize the tonic and dominant triads, mm.16–17 proceed sequentially, and mm.17–18 approach a close on the dominant. In other words, Bach structures this block too with *Vordersatz*, *Fortspinnung*, and *Epilog* segmentation. Since this syntactically ritornello-like block of material (hereafter "episode i") does recur (see mm.58–63), it could be thought of as a second (though, in this case, tonally open) ritornello.

Owing to the exact tonal and thematic correspondence to Fb 1 in mm.6–8, mm.18–19a will initially be experienced as a return of a segment from the "first ritornello." This is the case even though the textural contrast occurs in the "wrong direction" (the episode of mm.13–18 closes in full-ensemble texture with horns, and m.18 commences with only the string group). In mm.19b–

11. See mm.21–24 (Fa–Ea), 27–33 (V–Fb2–Eb1), 43–48 (V–Fb2–Eb1′), 52 (part of V), 57 (part of V), and 72–85 (entire ritornello).

21 Bach alters and extends the sequence of mm. 6–8, however, and closes on F major. Thus, although the segments of episode material in mm. 13–21 modulate from the tonic to the dominant and touch on both the supertonic and the submediant, the episode closes back at the tonic. Bach breaks this potential tonal monotony in m. 21 with a subdominant ritornello featuring the initial Fa and Ea segments (see mm. 3–6), performed by the tutti minus the horns.

The run of mm. 1–24, then, appears to be strikingly at odds with the stylistic premises of the Vivaldian string concerto. The one palpable trace of this concerto style lies in the subsequent literal quotation of thematic material with internal *Vordersatz-Fortspinnung-Epilog* segmentation. The textural and thematic contrasts conform rather less closely to Vivaldian expectations.

"Properly" contrasting and modulating episodes arrive in mm. 24–27 (hereafter "episode ii") and mm. 33–36 (hereafter "episode iii"), both featuring alternating quasi-Corellian textures (i.e., two treble lines and continuo: from horns and continuo, to the first two oboes and continuo, to violins and continuo).[12] A more extended episode at mm. 36–43 (hereafter "episode iv") is scored for the full ensemble, thereby allowing Bach to turn Vivaldi's textural contrast on its head: the ritornello of mm. 43–48 has a thinner texture and sonority than the previous (blasting) episode for horns, oboes, and strings.

The complexity of the formal and contrapuntal relationships encountered in mm. 1–24 is nowhere relieved in the rest of the movement. For one thing, Bach has each of the subsequent episodes come back as well (episode ii, mm. 48–52 and 53–57; episode iii, mm. 63–65; and episode iv, mm. 65–72). What is more, all the episodes are ultimately derived from the thematic material of the opening ritornello. Episode i, as mentioned earlier, opens with thematic material from the beginning of the ritornello (cf. mm. 13–18 and 1–6) and continues with the-

---

12. Arcangelo Corelli's concertos represent a different Italian concerto tradition from the Venetian. Corelli's concertos rarely feature thematic contrasts between tutti and solo; they concentrate rather on textural contrasts of the same thematic material, typically between the tutti and a subgroup of two violins and continuo. There is no evidence that Corelli's concertos were known outside his native Rome before they were published in 1714. For example, Vivaldi's incorporation of Corellian features in some concertos in *L'Estro Armonico* stems not from an independent study of Corelli but from the influence of Giuseppi Valentini's op. 7 concertos published in 1710 in Bologna (see Michael Talbot, "Vivaldi and Rome: Observations and Hypotheses," *Journal of the Royal Musical Association* 113 [1988]: 28). That Bach had direct knowledge of Corelli's trio-sonata style is attested to by his B-minor organ fugue BWV 579, which is based on the fourth sonata from Corelli's op. 3.

matic and tonal material based on the Fb 1 ritornello segment in mm. 6–8; the continuo of episode ii adopts the falling sequence of ascending tetrachords in the continuo line of Fb 1 but adds new counterpoint in the treble; episode iii takes from episode ii the treble line and the ascending tetrachords of the continuo but inverts and extends them; episode iv adopts the descending version of the tetrachord but presents it in augmentation (see horn 1, mm. 36–37a) above a continuo line adapted from the treble counterpoint of episode iii. From this outline, it should be clear that each of the latter three episodes is based on some novel feature of the episode that precedes it and that, consequently, the episodes gradually distance themselves thematically from the ritornello.

Throughout the movement these five blocks of related material (the ritornello and the ritornello-derived episodes i–iv) are juxtaposed to each other. Since all this material returns, *everything* in the movement is, strictly speaking, "ritornello." A composer's proceeding in this unusual and limiting manner could easily yield an uninteresting concerto movement. Yet there is nothing dull or inevitable about the form of Bach's concerto, for the ordering of the blocks of material is unpredictable. This is not to say that Bach's compositional procedure is haphazard, for he may have planned out his various returning segments in this seemingly arbitrary way specifically to contravene the regularity of his Vivaldian models, works in which segments of the same ritornello more predictably punctuate ever-changing episode material.

The opening movement of Bach's First Brandenburg Concerto, then, can be viewed as a rigorous, complex, and sophisticated manifestation of the formal possibilities presented by Vivaldi's mercurial, simple, and flamboyant new concerto style. Bach's methods of shaping the tonal and thematic material in this movement are no doubt indebted to his encounter in the early 1710s with Vivaldi's *L'Estro Armonico* concertos. Yet at the same time his carefully worked out "architectural" approach to the whole, with its involved contrapuntal procedures and step-by-step moving away from the ritornello in its episodes, is essentially foreign to Vivaldi's more "spontaneous" style. In fact, Bach reintroduces the very kind of complexity that the Italian concerto style had presumably been admired for avoiding.

According to the interpretation offered here, Bach both expands and contracts a Vivaldian model. While this model assumes a two-way contrast between an expository *Fortspinnung*-type ritornello for the ensemble and episodic material for the soloists, Bach creates a structure with a *five*-way contrast between a *Fortspinnung*-type ritornello, a *Fortspinnung*-type episode, and, finally, three only somewhat less expository episodes, two of which (episodes i and iv) are scored for full ensemble. And, while Vivaldi assumes a contrast between a continually returning ensemble ritornello and mostly new episodes, all of Bach's material returns throughout the movement, and all of it is related thematically. Bach appears interested not merely in the binary opposition of ritornello and episode but also in the notion of episodic distance from the ritornello. He does not merely fill a Vivaldian formal model with complex or more "developed" content: he develops the model itself – and in a way that, unlike Vivaldi's, does not readily lend itself to mass production.[13] In this singular

13. An alternative explanation would be that Bach adopted the *Vordersatz-Fortspinnung-Epilog* syntax found occasionally in the opening tuttis of some pre-Vivaldian concertos but, in contrast to the procedures of those pieces – where initial tuttis are not tonally closed and subsequent tuttis often do not quote the opening *Fortspinnung* and *Epilog* segments, providing new material instead – decided to make his opening tutti tonally closed and have all his material, including the episodes, come back in literal quotations later in the movement. Accordingly, Bach's procedure for his literally quoted, tonally closed ritornellos would not actually be Vivaldian but rather the logical by-product of a fusion of ideas taken from the pre-Vivaldian concerto for strings and the block-like permutation fugue for keyboard (or voices). A fundamental problem with this explanation, though, is that the *Vordersatz-Fortspinnung-Epilog* syntax (leaving aside whether it is tonally closed or whether its specific thematic material is quoted subsequently in the movement, in the "Vivaldian" manner) does not appear in any of Bach's works that can be securely dated to before about 1713. There is in fact no nonmusical evidence to support the prevalent view that this movement from the First Brandenburg Concerto was conceived at an early (pre-Vivaldian) point in Bach's career (the dating suggested by Geck). Following Johannes Krey ("Zur Entstehungsgeschichte des ersten Brandenburgischen Konzerts," in *Festschrift Heinrich Besseler zum sechzigsten Geburtstag*, ed. Institut für Musikwissenschaft der Karl-Marx-Universität [Leipzig: VEB Deutscher Verlag für Musik, 1961], 337–42), many Bach scholars maintain that an earlier version of the First Brandenburg Concerto probably served as a sinfonia for the cantata *Was mir behagt, ist nur die muntre Jagd!* BWV 208, a work that, according to Alfred Dürr (NBA I/35 [*Festmusiken für die Fürstenhäuser von Weimar, Weissenfels und Köthen*], KB, 39–43), was in existence by early 1713 and that, according to Yoshitake Kobayashi ("Diplomatische Überlegungen zur Chronologie der Weimarer Vokalwerke" [paper delivered at the Bach-Kolloquium, Rostock, 1990]), might have originated as early as 1712 (Krey mistakenly believed that Bach composed the cantata in 1716). But it turns out that Krey's arguments in support of his cantata-sinfonia hypothesis are riddled with factual errors; on this issue, which involves too many details for inclusion here, see my "On Linking Bach's F-Major Sinfonia and His Hunt Cantata," *Bach: The Journal of the Riemenschneider Bach Insti-*

concerto movement Bach appears antithetically to "complete" his predecessor by retaining some of the original terms but assigning them different meanings. By this procedure Bach realized the inherent formal potential of the new concerto style much more fully than Vivaldi's equally enthusiastic but more literal German imitators.[14]

* * *

Having explored Bach's unique approach to Vivaldian concerto procedure in the opening movement, we now have a meaningful context in which to consider questions of signification in his unusual treatment of early eighteenth-century instruments.

The participation of two *Corni di caccia* (hunting horns) in a concerto grosso must have seemed unusual to early eighteenth-century audiences since in the 1710s and 1720s the hunting horn was by no means a standard member of instrumental ensembles with strings. Furthermore, there are no known German precedents for the participation of horns in a concerto.

The horn first achieved stature in connection with the mounted hunt.[15] The size and grandeur of a nobleman's hunt became a symbol of his wealth and social status, for the expenses associated with the hunt were enormous. He had to purchase and maintain a respectable number of horses and hounds, weapons, musical instruments (one could live for a year on the price of a horn!), uniforms, and so on. Large amounts of money were paid to individuals who could play the horn as well as ride and shoot.

---

tute 23, no. 2 (Fall–Winter 1992): 31–46. Incidentally, there is also no secure evidence that Bach composed instrumental concertos of any sort before his encounter with Vivaldi's.

14. Pisendel and Prince Johann Ernst of Weimar, to name two. For a similar interpretation of Bach's application of Vivaldian concerto procedures to another piece in an ostensibly even more archaic style, see my "Relationships between Scoring and Structure in the First Movement of Bach's Sixth Brandenburg Concerto," *Music and Letters* 71 (1990): 494–504; trans. as "Beziehungen zwischen der Besetzung und dem Satzaufbau im ersten Satz des sechsten Brandenburgischen Konzerts von Johann Sebastian Bach," *Beiträge zur Bach-Forschung* 9–10 (1991): 104–28.

15. This account of the horn's place in the hunt and its affective connotations is taken from Horace Fitzpatrick, *The Horn and Horn-Playing and the Austro-Bohemian Tradition from 1680–1830* (London: Oxford University Press, 1970), 16–21.

As the hunt reflected a nobleman's social standing, the horn became a status symbol within the hunt. The musical skill of the mounted horn players came to be almost as important as their prowess in the field. Their elaborate systems of hunting calls turned the musical aspect of the hunt into a magnificent showpiece for their patron.

Beyond the strong associations with aristocracy and the outdoor life of the privileged classes, the hunt also embodied contemporary moral and philosophical principles. The mounted hunt ceremony was well suited for adoption into aristocratic life at the end of the seventeenth century, a time when the ancient courtly ideals inherited from the Middle Ages were seeking forms of expression more in line with the worldliness and prosperity of the late Baroque. The hunt was emblematic of *Tugend* (worldly virtue: a complex mixture of bravery, industry, honesty, and chivalry), signifying a new manifestation of the older *ritterlich-höfisch* (chivalrous-courtly) ideals central to aristocratic thought. Owing to its ceremonial and signal functions in the hunt, the horn emerged as an allegorical "figure" representing aristocratic values. The sound of the horn was therefore able to excite deep feelings in the aristocracy, in whose minds it symbolized the very essence of nobility.

Because of these associations, the original effect of horns in early eighteenth-century concerted music was probably much more evocative than we might suspect today. The fanfares in Reinhard Keiser's *Octavia* of 1705 provide an early example of the coloristic employment of horns for evoking the salubrity of the outdoors and the grandeur of aristocratic life. And in the Quoniam of Bach's B Minor Mass the horn's affective connotations highlight the image of God's entry into the world as a human being in the form of Christ the King.

To return to the First Brandenburg Concerto, in conjunction with the various returning episode blocks that are gradually less dependent thematically on the ritornello, it is possible to chart significant patterns in Bach's handling of the *Corni di caccia* within the first movement.

In the opening ritornello Bach assigns the horns their traditional role, going so far as to quote literally a greeting call familiar to contemporary Saxon huntsmen (see ex. 1).[16] But this is no genteel transfer of hunting-field music into the

16. This greeting call, as given in ex. 1, is illustrated (without citing its source) in ibid., 20; it is not found among the (few) horn signals in Hanns Friedrich von Fleming, *Der vollkommene Teutsche Jäger* (Leipzig, 1719–24), 1:311–12. There can be little doubt that Bach is quoting a hunting call, as the flourish appears in a number of other places; Fitzpatrick (*The Horn and*

EX.1 *a*, First Brandenburg Concerto, 1st mvt., horn 2, mm. 1-2.

b, Contemporary hunting-horn symbol

salon. Beyond considering the visual sensation that these outdoor instruments would probably have made inside the small and elegant chamber-music rooms used by Bach's ensemble, it is worth examining more closely the aural impression that they create within the structure of the First Brandenburg Concerto. In the ritornello the horns clash rather strongly with the rest of the ensemble, by means of three-against-four rhythms (mm. 2-3, 8-10, and 12) and conflicting harmonies (m. 12). (Apparently disturbed by these conflicts, many conductors today instruct their horn players to perform the ritornello as quietly as possible.) The rest of the ensemble, a choir of oboes and a choir of strings, "cooperates" closely in the ritornello, either proceeding essentially in unison or alternating with briefer gestures. Thus, by the very calling up of their traditional, aristocratic associations, the horns disrupt the surface "order" of Bach's otherwise complete, double-choir ritornello. And, in spite of their striking "presence," the horn parts could be removed from the ritornello without affecting its formal coherence or contrapuntal integrity.

Horn-Playing, 60-62) suggests that Bach may have come across it in Johann Joseph Fux's overture to the ballet music he set for Marc'Antonio Ziani's opera *Meleagro*. The same fanfare, scored for horn, has regal associations in the aria "Der Herr ist König ewiglich" from *Lobe den Herrn, meine Seele*, BWV 143 (for the purposes of the present discussion, questions regarding the authorship of this cantata are unimportant) (see Charles Sanford Terry, *Bach's Orchestra* [London: Oxford University Press, 1932], 46). The fanfare also appears with the same associations, this time scored for trumpet, in the aria "Grosser Herr und starker König" from Part 1 of Bach's Christmas Oratorio as well as in the earlier version of this aria, "Kron und Preis gekrönter Damen" from *Tönet, ihr Pauken, Erschallet, Trompeten*, BWV 214 (see Edward Tarr, "Monteverdi, Bach und die Trompetenmusik ihrer Zeit," in *Bericht über den internationalen musikwissenschaftlichen Kongress Bonn 1970*, ed. Carl Dahlhaus [Kassel: Bärenreiter, 1971], 595). More curious is the fanfare's (slightly altered) appearance in the string parts to Gavotte II from Bach's Orchestral Suite in C Major, BWV 1066.

Just as the episodes gradually become less dependent thematically on the ritornello, so the horn writing for these episodes gradually becomes less akin to the idiomatic horn writing of the ritornello. Already in the episode of mm. 13–18 (episode i) the horns move away from their hunting signals in favor of material loosely related at first to the oboe figuration of the *Vordersatz* segment. For the remainder of the episode, the horn parts stay thematically distinct from the ritornello-derived material of the accompanying string and oboe choirs. Nonetheless, the presence of the horns remains inessential to the structure. That is, here, as in the ritornello, the horn lines could be removed without any formal or contrapuntal damage (apart, perhaps, from the second half of m. 14). When the horns do become contrapuntally and formally essential, in m. 20, they no longer dissociate themselves from the rest of the ensemble but instead participate in the refined alternation of group gestures familiar from the second *Fortspinnung* segment of the ritornello (Fb 1, mm. 6–8). This gradually approached assimilation with the material shared by the rest of the ensemble is then maintained in episodes ii and iii (mm. 24–27 and 33–36), where treble pairings of horns, oboes, and violins alternate with the same episode material. The return of episode iii in m. 53 carries this instrumental assimilation even farther by pairing the treble instruments from different choirs. The process borders on caricature in episode iv (mm. 36–43): proceeding at first in dissonant fourth-species counterpoint – a style of writing entirely foreign to eighteenth-century brass instruments [17] – the horns for the first time assume unambiguously the principal voice throughout an entire episode. As in the ritornello, they are strikingly differentiated from the ensemble, but, unlike in the ritornello, they are now contrapuntally indispensable.

Although these procedures might be attributed wholly to Bach's musical ingenuity or rational inclination, it is difficult to ignore their social implications. Just as the episodes only gradually gain a formal "identity" by becoming less dependent on the ritornello, the horns lose their social "identity" by becoming gradually assimilated into the more neutral instrumental style of the rest of the

17. To my knowledge, the only (somewhat) similar example from roughly contemporary brass parts occurs in the occasionally independent trumpet parts to the first chorus of Bach's cantata *Wir danken dir, Gott, wir danken dir,* BWV 29 (more familiar from Bach's reuse of the movement as the "Gratias" and "Dona nobis pacem" in the B Minor Mass; note, however, that this entire chorus is in *stile antico*). Later examples include the opening period of Mozart's Piano Concerto in E♭ Major, K. 482.

ensemble. That is, the string and oboe choirs are not contrasted by "violinistic" or "oboistic" treatment; instead both choirs play counterpoint that is not instrument specific. And the horns reach their greatest prominence contrapuntally only when, at the end of the process, they adopt a style utterly unidiomatic to the instrument. (As if in recognition of having "gone too far," Bach closes this episode with more conventional clarino-style writing; see mm. 38–43.)

This bridging of the "social distance" between the horns and the rest of the ensemble in the First Brandenburg Concerto would have been more readily apparent to the early eighteenth century's musical connoisseurs than today's, who are likely to be unaware of the "figuration," to employ Norbert Elias's useful term, of performing organizations in Bach's time.[18] In this work Bach juxtaposes three groups of instruments (the pair of horns, the oboe choir, and the string choir) that are somewhat disparate from a social perspective. In the way Bach initially uses them, the horns would doubtless have been associated with the nobleman's mounted hunt, thus referring to a rather high social status within the musical hierarchy. Bach's string choir would have been most readily associated with the ripieno of the court instrumental ensemble, pointing up a highly respectable status within the hierarchy, but one beneath the horns and the other soloists within the court instrumental ensemble (court soloists carried the distinguishing title of *Cammermusiker* and were paid a much higher salary than musicians who were used only as ripienists). The oboe choir might have been associated with military bands or with the *Stadtpfeifer* (municipal musicians), reflecting a respectable status within the musical hierarchy but one somewhat lower than that of court musicians.[19]

In this interpretation, rather than employing various families of instruments

18. Norbert Elias, *The Court Society*, trans. Edmund Jephcott (Oxford: Blackwell, 1983).

19. Although sometimes there was a *Cammermusiker* in the court ensemble who played the oboe, court conductors would have had to engage city musicians in the uncommon event that a piece required as many as three oboes. On the social position of oboists in the eighteenth century, see Werner Braun, "The 'Hautboist': An Outline of Evolving Careers and Functions," in *The Social Status of the Professional Musician from the Middle Ages to the 19th Century*, ed. Walter Salmen (New York: Pendragon Press, 1983), 132–33. Court conductors would also have had to engage city musicians in the uncommon event that a piece required a large ripieno string section. The musically respected *Stadtpfeifer* and related *Kunstgeiger* employed for cantata performances by Bach in his subsequent tenure at Leipzig had no *Cammermusiker* to compete with, for Leipzig was not a court city. On the structural significance of prestige in eighteenth-century Europe, see Elias, *Court Society*, chap. 3.

merely for their coloristic effect, Bach worked out a concerto movement in which implied extramusical associations for the instruments are brought into significant relationships via an unorthodox application of Vivaldian ritornello procedure. By means of this relationship between scoring and structure, Bach is able to achieve in music what was not possible in the "real" world: by having the groups within the ensemble of his concerto movement gradually function as and thus become "equals," Bach neutralizes social distinctions that at the time would normally have been taken for granted.[20] It was therefore perhaps not fortuitous that Bach reused this movement in Leipzig at the head of a church cantata contrasting the world's speciousness with God's loyalty (*Falsche*

20. There are, of course, many eighteenth-century pieces in which the instruments are treated "equally," but I am not aware of any other composer than Bach who manipulates instrumental writing in such a socially significant way. That is, other composers, like Telemann and Vivaldi, either employ instruments "equally" from the start in a way that does not seem extramusically significant or use them "unequally" in a manner that, if interpreted socially, would reflect rather than challenge uncritically held social assumptions.

Evidence has recently surfaced documenting the interest that Prince Leopold of Cöthen (Bach's employer at the time the Brandenburg Concertos were assembled) had in analogies between political and musical structures (see Günther Hoppe, "Köthener politische, ökonomische und höfische Verhältnisse als Schaffensbedingungen Bachs [Teil 1]," *Cöthener Bach-Hefte* 4 [1986]: 13-62; Hoppe cites Staatsarchiv Magdeburg, Abt. Köthen. A1 NR.2211, fol.18, which transmits a lecture pointing out correspondences between politics and music that was given during Leopold's coronation ceremonies). Relationships between politics and music were discussed in a general way by various Baroque music theorists (see, e.g., the quotations from, among others, Athanasius Kircher's *Musurgia universalis* [Rome, 1650], Giovanni Andrea Angelini Bontempi's *Historia musica* [Perugia, 1695], Zaccaria Tevo's *Musico testore* [Venice, 1706], Johann Mattheson's *Vollkommener Capellmeister* [Hamburg, 1739], Johann Gottfried Walther's *Musicalisches Lexicon* [Leipzig, 1732], and John Hawkins's *General History of the Science and Practice of Music* [London, 1776] provided in Volker Scherliess, "Musica Politica," in *Festschrift Georg von Dadelsen zum 60. Geburtstag*, ed. Thomas Kohlhase and Volker Scherliess [Neuhausen-Stuttgart: Hänssler, 1978], 270-83; see also Richard Leppert, "Music, Representation, and Social Order in Early-Modern Europe," *Cultural Critique* 12 [1989]: 25-55; and Jacques Attali, *Noise: The Political Economy of Music*, trans. Brian Massumi [Minneapolis: University of Minnesota Press, 1985]). For similar interpretations of other Brandenburg Concertos, see my "Relationships between Scoring"; "Organological Questions and Their Significance in J. S. Bach's Fourth Brandenburg Concerto," *Journal of the American Musical Instrument Society* 17 (1991): 5-52, and "J. S. Bach's Brandenburg Concertos as a Meaningful Set," *Musical Quarterly* 77 (1993): 193-235. This last essay also explores, via Bach's documented reading of Lutheran theology, some indications that he considered the figuration of his orchestra in terms similar to the contemporary social hierarchy.

Welt, dir trau ich nicht, BWV 52): the aristocratic elements become the world's vainglory.

* * *

If the interest in the opening movement centers on the horns and their relationship to Bach's application of Vivaldian concerto procedure, the focus in the remaining movements shifts to the role of the "violino piccolo" (a small violin, in this case, tuned a minor third higher than the normal violin). As with the discussion of the first movement, I will consider formal aspects before interpreting Bach's scoring socially in terms of court-ensemble figuration.

Only the third movement of the concerto appears to have been conceived with the violino piccolo in mind.[21] There is no part whatever for the instrument in the early version of the work (the sinfonia BWV 1046a, formerly BWV 1071), which lacks both the third movement and the Polonaise.[22] In the Brandenburg

21. Bach used this movement again, in D major, as the opening choruses to the secular cantatas *Vereinigte Zwietracht der wechselnden Saiten*, BWV 207 (in 1726), and *Auf, schmetternde Töne der muntern Trompeten*, BWV 207a (in the 1730s). Malcolm Boyd (*Bach* [London: J. M. Dent & Sons, 1983], 81) suggests that the cantata choruses and the Brandenburg Concerto movement may have originated in some still earlier vocal composition in D major, now lost. According to Boyd, this would help explain the (D-major) tuning of the violino piccolo and the unusual (chordal) nature of Bach's writing for the instrument. It is common among Bach scholars to attribute his unusual writing to lost originals with different scorings. The inference from this approach, it often seems, is that we are relieved of having to come to terms with such works in the form in which we know them. Besides calling attention to this methodological problem, however, I would mention that in some cases a mundane examination of Bach's personal scores will straightforwardly counter the skillfully reasoned arguments for the lost originals. In the case of Boyd's suggestion on the First Brandenburg Concerto, the original score of *Vereinigte Zwietracht* (SBB MUS. MS BACH P 174) contains a number of Bach's corrections to readings that he had originally entered a third too high (e.g., m.13/oboe 1/notes 11–12, m.22/oboe 2/notes 1–5, m.22/oboe 1/note 8, m.41/violin 2/note 2, m.71/oboe 2/♮ sign, and m.72/taille/note 2), which suggests that his exemplar was notated in F major. In a rather different sort of attempt to account for Bach's use of a small violin tuned a third higher than the ensemble, Andreas Moser suggests that the First Brandenburg Concerto may have been composed for a performance by Bach's oldest son, Wilhelm Friedemann, who was only a child at the time and therefore perhaps too small to handle a normal violin (see "Der Violino piccolo," *Zeitschrift für Musikwissenschaft* 1 [1918–19]: 377–80).

22. The earliest surviving manuscript for the sinfonia BWV 1046a (SBB MUS. MS BACH P 1061, copied in 1760 by Christian Friedrich Penzel) does not, strictly speaking, transmit the early version of the First Brandenburg Concerto. Rather, as Ulrich Siegele explained already in his

version the violino piccolo line is mostly borrowed note for note from the first violin part of the early version. In the first movement and in the tutti minuet of the Brandenburg version Bach has the violino piccolo double the first violin. And in the second movement he gives to the violino piccolo what was originally the first violin part of the early version and writes new filler material for the first violin. (The instrument is not called for in any of the three trios to the minuet.)

The violino piccolo thus plays a marginal role in the first movement. The only place it is independent from the first violin part is in mm. 54–57. The instrument is here neither a real soloist (thus contradicting the *concertato* in Bach's title for the margrave of Brandenburg's score)[23] nor an integral member of the ripieno ensemble. In the second movement – a sort of triple-concerto movement in which the first oboe, the violino piccolo, and the continuo instruments compose the concertino – the violino piccolo is a true member of the concertino; yet it is the first oboe that is treated as if it were the central soloist in the ensemble, as evinced by its cadenza in m. 34.

To focus briefly on other aspects of the second movement, consider that in slow movements in Italian concertos ornamented melodies are presented in an extended episode that is typically set against two tutti statements almost perfunctorily opening and closing the movement.[24] In this slow movement, however, Bach dispenses with a framing tutti and opens directly with highly ornamented melody (played initially by the first oboe), placed in a passacaglia-like setting. And, while in Italian concertos the solo melody has a quasi-improvisatory character, Bach's ends up far from improvisation: it gets subjected to sophisticated contrapuntal treatment in the form of a quarter-note canon at

---

1957 dissertation (University of Tübingen), published as *Kompositionsweise und Bearbeitungstechnik in der Instrumentalmusik Johann Sebastian Bachs* (Neuhausen-Stuttgart: Hänssler, 1975), the sinfonia BWV 1046a, the sinfonia from BWV 52, and the First Brandenburg Concerto are all revised versions separately based on the original. The sinfonia BWV 1046a, however, is apparently the only version preserving Bach's original sequence of movements (see ibid., 146–50).

23. "Concerto 1 mo á 2 Corni di Caccia. 3 Hautb: è Bassono. Violino Piccolo concertato. 2 Violini, una / Viola è Violoncello, col Basso Continuo" (SBB AM.B.78; published in facsimile as *J. S. Bach: Brandenburgische Konzerte: Faksimile nach dem im Besitz der Staatsbibliothek in Berlin befindlichen Autograph*, ed. Peter Wackernagel [Leipzig: Peters, 1947]).

24. For an example of a Bach concerto following this pattern, see the slow movement of the E-major harpsichord concerto BWV 1053.

the unison (see mm. 12–14 and 23–25). Here, then, is a further indication – to add to those already pointed out in the first movement – that the First Brandenburg Concerto is a far more complex composition than its Italian models.

Only in the third movement does the violino piccolo seem to have achieved the function of central soloist. But even here its status appears problematic when the relationship between Bach's scoring and his structure is explored. The opening tutti comes as close as one will get in the Brandenburg Concertos to textbook Vivaldi ritornello structure.[25] It consists of *Vordersatz* (mm. 1–4; hereafter "V"), a double *Fortspinnung* segment (mm. 5–7 and 8–11; "F1" and "F2"), and a double *Epilog* (mm. 12–15 and 15–17; "E1" and "E2"). The first episode, mm. 17–20, is modeled very closely on the V segment of the ritornello. The second episode, mm. 25–35, consisting of two extended sequential passages, is related thematically to the F1 and F2 segments of the ritornello. And the brief third episode, mm. 38–40, provides a clear cadence in the newly established tonality. Considered collectively, the three episodes conform rather closely to the syntax of the opening ritornello (opening statement, two consecutive sequences, and a cadence). In fact, when joined together in a continuous series, mm. 17–20, 25–34, and 39–40 form a musically coherent entity. If these episodes are labeled with lowercase letters to indicate their affinity with the segmentation of the ritornello, the run of mm. 1–53 could be summarized as: V–F1–F2–E1–E2 / v / V / f1–f2 / V / e / F1–F2–E1–E2.

Although in the first episode the violino piccolo adopts material that is closely related to the head of the ritornello's V segment, the instrument attempts to distinguish itself through virtuosic multiple stops in every measure. It continues to strive in this manner through the return of the V segment in mm. 21–24. Bach even instructs all the other members of the ensemble here to play *piano sempre* and *pianissimo sempre*, presumably to ensure that they will not drown out the chords of the (solo) violino piccolo. In the second episode the violino piccolo is overshadowed first throughout f1 by the first oboe and the first violin and then throughout f2 by the first horn. So in spite of a great deal of "flailing" by the violino piccolo – the instrument at this point has even thicker textures than in the first episode, with numerous triple stops and even one quadruple stop – it does not quite emerge as a genuine soloist presenting

25. While scholars have generally considered the first movement to be un-Vivaldian, they agree on the Vivaldian style of the third movement.

95

its own thematic material. It does stand out properly for the first time in the third episode, where it has its own material and is accompanied only by the continuo, but here it turns out that the apparently purposive move of cadencing in the dominant may be formally "redundant," for, if this two-measure, interruptive solo were removed, the concerto would proceed, beginning in m. 35, with a syntactically complete quotation of the ritornello in the dominant (V–F1–F2–E1–E2).

The violino piccolo abandons the syntax of the *Fortspinnung*-type ritornello and presents its own thematic material for its episodes in the B section of this da capo movement (mm. 53–83). Nonetheless, its solo status remains problematic. Right at the outset, in mm. 53–55, the first oboe and the two horns appear to remind the violino piccolo of its straying from the true path of the ritornello, as it were, by providing in the (*piano*) accompaniment fragmentary quotations from the V segment of the ritornello. Coming out of this, the first oboe immediately assumes the principal voice in a trio-sonata texture with violino piccolo – marked by stock "pathetic" gestures of slurrings by twos – and continuo (mm. 55–60). And, with its fragmentary V and f1 quotations, the ensemble, particularly the horns, completely overshadows the violino piccolo in a second approach to the A-minor cadence (mm. 60–63). On the other side of the A-minor ritornello (F2–E1; mm. 63–70) this procedure recurs in reverse order (mm. 70–80), with one subtle difference: in the passage of trio-sonata texture the first violin part assumes the principal voice (mm. 74–80), thus approximating the timbre of the struggling violino piccolo soloist. And Bach marks the first violin part of the ensemble *pia[no]* at m. 74 even though he had already marked this part *p[iano].* at m. 70. He seems intent on having the solo violino piccolo line, which again is merely a secondary voice consisting primarily of stereotypical slurred couplets, performed more loudly than the principal voice.

At m. 82 it appears that the violino piccolo will finally achieve some semblance of its long-denied genuine solo status. Bach's fermatas in all parts except the violino piccolo and his *Adagio* marking provide the traditional context within concerto style for the improvised cadenza, a prerogative belonging to the soloist. But by the violino piccolo's third note in the mini-Adagio the ensemble appears already to be bringing the written-out cadenza to a quick close. The continuo adopts specifically the hemiola rhythm and the intervallic content of the closing (*Epilog*) segment of the ritornello. In this interpretation a performance will best reflect the sense of the cadenza by accelerating from

96

the second half of m. 82 until the initial tempo of the movement is resumed in the second half of m. 83. (Note in this connection that neither the double bar nor the *Allegro* indication found at m. 84 in several modern editions appears in Bach's own score.)[26]

The structure of the seven dances following the Allegro is a quasi-symmetrical one in which a tutti minuet contrasts with trios performed by various subsets of the ensemble. Bach designates them as *Menuet–Trio á 2 Hautbois è Bassono. Corni è Viole tacet.–Menuet–Poloinesse. Tutti Violini è Viole. mà piano. Violino piccolo tacet.–Menuet–Trio à 2 Corni & 3 Hautbois in unisono–Menuet*. Having explored several Italian concerto styles in the first three movements, Bach now turns from the Italian style altogether by presenting a series of French, Polish, and German dances. He does not entirely abandon concerto principles, however, for the continually returning tutti minuet acts as a sort of "ritornello" in relation to the three trios with reduced textures.

For these dances the violino piccolo resumes the marginal role in the ensemble that it had adopted in the opening movement of the concerto. In fact, Bach appears to have organized the style of the dances to emphasize this diminished role. In the "ritornello" (the tutti minuet) the violino piccolo merely doubles the first parts in the string and oboe choirs. The style of the tutti minuet conforms closely to the French court minuet, which was designed for dancing in carefully prescribed step patterns (note the characteristic two-measure phrases and the twelve- rather than sixteen-measure strains).[27] In keeping with the French style, Bach sets the first trio as a minuet for the first and second oboes and bassoon, a scoring commonly referred to today as the *Lullian trio.* The second trio is a polonaise, an aristocratic Polish dance, scored for the string choir, minus violino piccolo, and the continuo group. And the third trio is a piece of Germanic hunt music scored for the two horns (constituting the upper two parts) and the three oboes playing in unison. It is worth pointing out that in court dances only individuals of the highest status were given the privilege of comprising the smaller groups who danced the trios while the larger group looked on. Intriguingly, in Bach's series of dances all the

26. Interestingly, this passage and what precedes it read differently in the choral versions of the movement in Cantatas 207 and 207a.

27. For specific information on the step patterns in the French minuet, see Meredith Ellis Little, "Minuet," in *The New Grove Dictionary of Music and Musicians*, ed. Stanley Sadie (London: Macmillan, 1980), 12:353–58.

instruments except for the putative soloist (the "Violino Piccolo *concertato*") have an opportunity to "participate" in trios while the ensemble "looks on."

The trio most likely to have included the violino piccolo is the string-choir Polonaise, the center of Bach's seven-movement dance series. Bach appears to have composed the Polonaise at around the same time that he copied the new version of this concerto for the margrave of Brandenburg,[28] and therefore he could very easily have accommodated a violino piccolo part. Even as the trio stands it would require the changing of only a few low notes in m. 28 to make the first violin line playable on the violino piccolo. (Bach had made similar changes for the instrument in the first two movements of the concerto.) Perhaps it was because of this very ease of adaptation that Bach went to the trouble of inserting *Violino piccolo tacet* below the title to the trio. His similarly squeezed *Tutti* indication between *Poloinesse.* and *Violini è Viole* further emphasizes the exclusion of the violino piccolo.

In connection with this apparent snubbing of the soloist for a Polish dance movement, there is evidence that German musicians of the day considered the violino piccolo to be a "Polish" instrument. The following comments on Polish tavern music appear in the Telemann autobiography that was published in 1740:

> Als der Hof sich ein halbes Jahr lang nach Plesse, einer oberschlesischen, promnitzischen Standesherrschaft, begab, lernete ich so wohl daselbst als in Krakau, die polnische und hanakische Musik, in ihrer wahren barbarischen Schönheit kennen. Sie bestund, in gemeinen Wirtshäusern, aus einer um den Leib geschnalleten Geige, die eine Terzie höher gestimmet war, als sonst gewöhnlich, und also ein halbes Dutzend andre überschreien konnte; aus einem polnischen Bocke; aus einer Quintposaune; und aus einem Regal. An ansehnlichen Oertern aber blieb das Regal weg; die beiden erstern hingegen wurden verstärckt: wie ich denn einst 36. Böcke und 8. Geigen beisammen gefunden habe. Man sollte kaum glauben, was dergleichen Bockpfeiffer oder Geiger für wunderbare Einfälle haben, wenn sie, so offt die Tantzenden ruhen, fantaisiren. Ein Aufmerc-

---

28. The Polonaise is not fully autograph, which suggests that Bach had recently composed the movement and therefore did not "need" to copy the music himself. (In the opening movements, presumably composed somewhat earlier, he would have wanted to do the copying himself so that he could immediately enter revisions as he went along.) On the identification of the non-autograph handwriting, see Georg von Dadelsen, *Beiträge zur Chronologie der Werke Johann Sebastian Bachs* (Trossingen: Hohner-Verlag, 1958), 84.

kender könnte von ihnen, in 8. Tagen, Gedancken für ein gantzes Leben er-
schnappen. Gnug, in dieser Musik steckt überaus viel gutes; wenn behörig
damit umgegangen wird. Ich habe, nach der Zeit, verschiedene grosse Concerte
und Trii in dieser Art geschrieben, die ich in einen italiänischen Rock, mit ab-
gewechselten Adagi und Allegri, eingekleidet.[29]

When the court [of Count Erdmann von Promnitz at Sorau (now Zary in
Poland)] removed to Pless [now Pszczyna] for six months, one of Promnitz's
estates in Upper Silesia, I heard there, as I had done in Cracow, the music of
Poland and the Hanaka region of Moravia in its true barbaric beauty. In the
country inns the usual ensemble consisted of a violin strapped to the body and
tuned a minor third higher than ordinary, which therefore could out-shriek
half a dozen normal violins; a Polish bagpipe [an instrument made of goatskin
with the head, horns, and all left intact on the bag]; a trombone; and a regal [a
small portable organ with snarling reed pipework]. In respectable places, however, the regal was omitted and the number of the first two instruments listed
was increased; in fact I once heard thirty-six [Polish] bagpipes and eight [pic-
colo] violins playing together. One would hardly believe the inventiveness with
which these pipers and fiddlers improvise when the dancers take an intermis-
sion. An observer could collect enough ideas in eight days to last a lifetime. But
enough; this music, if handled with understanding, contains much good material. In due course I wrote a number of grand concerti and trios in this style,
which I clad in an Italian coat with alternating Allegri and Adagi.[30]

At any rate, if Bach did associate the violino piccolo with Poland, its exclusion
from the only "Polish" movement in the concerto is nothing if not ironic.

The violino piccolo seems also to have been "excluded," in a less obvious
manner, from the final trio. In the early version of the concerto, BWV 1046a,
the trio is scored for two horns, with the lowest line written for violins instead
of oboes. Bach appears to have composed the oboe version of the trio at the
last minute, for in the margrave's dedication score the music to this trio is not
in Bach's handwriting,[31] suggesting that he had just composed it and therefore

29. See Johann Mattheson, *Grundlage einer Ehren-Pforte* (Hamburg, 1740), quoted in Werner
Rackwitz, ed., *Georg Philipp Telemann: Singen ist das Fundament zur Music in allen Dingen – Eine
Dokumentensammlung* (Leipzig: Philipp Reclam jun., 1981), 202.

30. This translation is adapted slightly from the one found in Richard Petzoldt, *Georg Philipp
Telemann*, trans. Horace Fitzpatrick (New York: Oxford University Press, 1974), 25.

31. This is pointed out in Dadelsen, *Beiträge*, 84.

did not "need" the copying process as an opportunity for on-the-spot entering of minor revisions, something he would more likely have wanted if the piece were one he had pulled from his drawer of older pieces.[32] Since it is far from clear that one version represents a compositional improvement over the other, Bach may have had some other reason to go to the trouble of writing the alternate version – such as to ensure the participation in the trios of every player from the ensemble except the violino piccolo (remember that the other violins had already played in the Polonaise and that the third oboe had not yet appeared in a trio).

The treatment of the *Violino Piccolo concertato* throughout the concerto takes on additional interest when Bach's scorings and structures are interpreted socially. A *concertato* part for solo violin would have been most readily associated in the early eighteenth century with the principal violinist in the court instrumental ensemble. In reference to the ensemble he would have carried the designation *Konzertmeister* (concert master), or in reference to the group of *Cammermusiker* he would have enjoyed a title like *Premier Cammermusicus*.[33] The Kapellmeister (conductor) was typically the only person in the court musical establishment to receive a higher salary.[34] Accordingly, the solo violinist enjoyed a relatively elevated social status within the court ensemble. In this concerto Bach appears to be deflating this status both quite literally by writing for "Violino *Piccolo* concertato" and musically by preventing the *Violino Piccolo concertato* from achieving true solo character.[35]

32. Furthermore, a close look at the trio's heading, which is in Bach's hand, reveals that the ampersand between *2 Corni* and *3 Hautbois in unisono* may have been carefully revised from an uppercase *V*, suggesting that Bach initially intended to copy out the version of the trio with the *Violini* (hence the *V*). But it seems unlikely that Bach would at the first instance have omitted a conjunction or a period between *Corni* and *Violini*.

33. This was the title, e.g., of the violinist Joseph Spiess, the concertmaster at the Cöthen court while Bach was employed there (see NBA VII/2, KB, 20).

34. The only musicians who might have been better remunerated than a Kapellmeister were opera singers. At those few courts that boasted opulent opera establishments, the (mostly foreign) singers were paid fabulous sums, often well more than ten times what an average Konzertmeister received.

35. To recapitulate, in the opening Allegro the violino piccolo merely doubles the first violin part; in the slow movement it constitutes only one member of a group of soloists drawn from the ensemble; in the third movement it vainly strives for independence from the ensemble or

* * *

Interpreting the First Brandenburg Concerto in terms of extramusical implications of relationships between form and scoring exposes a rather didactic character in Bach's court-entertainment music, music that has come to be considered "pure" of the sorts of external references confronted in his more obviously "applied" music such as the cantatas written for the Lutheran liturgy.[36] With its strong social implications this work would effectively counter the view of Bach's contemporaries that concertos "lacked moral and laudable purpose" when not connected with some specifically text-related situation such as introducing an opera or enhancing a church service.[37] Bach had, I am suggesting, a much broader view of what would constitute "texts," and he had the requisite skill and imagination to produce instrumental music that referred to them.

---

fails to sustain being the principal voice when it is independent; and in the dances it either merely doubles the soprano voice of the ensemble or remains silent in places where its presence would most readily be expected. Eric Chafe describes the progression from movement to movement as a dialectical one, proceeding from the unusually pompous and external opening movement, to the unusually plaintive and inward slow movement, to the synthesis in the third movement where both the full court ensemble and the violino piccolo as central soloist are heard for the first time (see *Tonal Allegory in the Vocal Music of J. S. Bach* [Berkeley and Los Angeles: University of California Press, 1991], 182).

36. I use the word *extramusical* because of its currency in the musicological literature. It is important to be aware, however, that in the premodern understanding what we call extramusical ideals were regarded as constitutive of the musical. For a clear, historical treatment of the aesthetic issues revolving around this idea, see Lydia Goehr, *The Imaginary Museum of Musical Works: An Essay in the Philosophy of Music* (Oxford: Clarendon Press, 1992), chap. 5.

37. See Arthur Hutchings, *The Baroque Concerto* (London: Faber, 1959; rev. ed., 1973), 175, quoting, without page reference, Johann Mattheson, *Der musicalische Patriot* (Hamburg, 1728). What Hutchings says seems to fit with the contents of at least this book of Mattheson's, but I have not succeeded in locating the quotation. Views of several contemporary writers questioning the value of concertos on account of their typically nonreferential character are discussed in Bellamy Hosler, *Changing Aesthetic Views of Instrumental Music in 18th-Century Germany* (Ann Arbor, Mich.: UMI Research Press, 1981).

Anfang und Ende: Cyclic Recurrence in Bach's Cantata *Jesu, nun sei gepreiset*, BWV 41

Eric T. Chafe

ANFANG/ENDE SYMBOLISM
IN THE LITURGICAL YEAR

In four of Bach's church cantatas Jesus is referred to as the "A" and "O" – that is, the Alpha and the Omega, the beginning and the end – a metaphor used in three passages from the book of Revelation to express God's all-encompassing nature and, more particularly, Jesus' control over life and death.[1] In two of these passages the resurrected Jesus refers to himself as "the first and the last," and in one he speaks of holding the "keys of death and death's domain." The Bach cantata in which the "A" and "O" idea derives most directly from its scriptural source is the Easter cantata *Die Himmel lacht! Die Erde jubilieret*, BWV 31 (text by Salomo Franck). Its first recitative begins:

Erwünschter Tag!	Awaited day!
Sei, Seele, wieder froh!	Soul, rejoice again!
Das A und O,	The A and O,
Der erst und auch der letzte,	The first and also the last
Den unsre schwere Schuld	Whom our heavy guilt

---

1. Those three passages are Rev.1:8 ("'I am the Alpha and the Omega,' says the Lord God, who is and who was and who is to come, the sovereign Lord of all"), 21:6 ("I am the Alpha and the Omega, the beginning and the end"), 22:13 ("I am the Alpha and the Omega, the first and the last, the beginning and the end"). The last of these refers to Jesus; in addition, other passages in Revelation (1:17 and 2:8) refer to the resurrected Jesus as "the first and the last." All biblical references are to Samuel Sandmel, M. Jack Suggs, and Arnold J. Tkacik, eds., *The New English Bible* (Oxford: Oxford University Press, 1976).

In Todeskerker setzte,	Placed in death's prison,
Ist nun gerissen aus der Not!	Is now torn from peril!
Der Herr war tot,	The Lord was dead,
Und sieh, er lebet wieder!	But see, he lives again!
Lebt unser Haupt, so leben auch	If the head lives, so then do
die Glieder!	the members!
Der Herr hat in der Hand	The Lord has in his hand
Des Todes und der Höllen Schlüssel!	The keys to death and hell!

Of the other direct references to the "A" and "O" in Bach's cantatas, only that in Cantata 41, *Jesu, nun sei gepreiset*, was authored specifically for the work in question (the libretto to this cantata may have been written by Bach himself). This reference will be discussed in the second part of the present essay. The other two references were the result of the librettist's appropriation of the final verse of Philipp Nicolai's chorale "Wie schön leuchtet der Morgenstern," which begins "Wie bin ich doch so herzlich froh, dass mein Schatz ist das A und O, der Anfang und das Ende." Both Cantata 1, *Wie schön leuchtet der Morgenstern*, and Cantata 49, *Ich geh und suche mit Verlangen*, end with that verse, the latter work assigning it to the soprano solo of a soprano/bass dialogue. The remaining lines of the *Stollen* anticipate the believer's being received in paradise by Jesus, while the *Abgesang* expresses longing for that event. The *Abgesang* alone (without, therefore, any direct reference to the "A" and "O") served as the final movement of Cantata 61, *Nun komm, der Heiden Heiland*.

Besides these direct references to the "A" and "O," indirect references to the idea also appear in a few of Bach's cantatas. Not surprisingly, some of these are found in cantatas for New Year's Day, the day for which Cantata 41 was composed. Since the gospel reading for New Year's Day (Luke 2:21) centered on the circumcision and naming of Jesus, Bach's cantatas for that day generally focus on the person and name of Jesus. Several of Bach's cantatas for New Year's Day bring out such ideas as the believer's beginning and ending the year (and even ending his life) with the name *Jesus*. The first such cantata, *Singet dem Herrn ein neues Lied*, BWV 190 (1724), follows a recitative that ends "so fang ich dieses Jahr in Jesu Namen an" with a duet aria ("Jesus soll mein alles sein") that contains the lines "Jesus soll mein Anfang bleiben" and "Jesus macht mein Ende gut" (every line of the aria begins with the word *Jesus*). Cantata 41 (1725) features an aria that begins "Lass uns, o höchster Gott, das Jahr vollbringen, damit das Ende so wie dessen Anfang sei." Cantata 171, *Gott, wie dein Name, so ist auch dein Ruhm* (1729 or later), contains a soprano aria ("Jesus soll mein erstes Wort in dem neuen Jahre heissen") that ends "und in meiner letzten Stunde ist Jesus auch mein letztes Wort." Its extraordinary solo violin part continually sweeps upward and downward through the entire range of the instrument in arpeggio patterns symbolizing Jesus' all-encompassing nature.[2]

The all-encompassing quality expressed by the Alpha and Omega idea derives, of course, from the beginning and ending of the Greek alphabet; translated into the German or Latin alphabet, the symbolism involved the letters from one to fourteen, or from A to O. In this connection we may note that the number fourteen, widely associated nowadays with the name *Bach* as spelled according to the number alphabet, had long-standing Christological associations borrowed from the Alpha/Omega idea. That particular association served Paul Speratus, for example, as a means of ordering the fourteen verses of his early doctrinal chorale "Es ist das Heil uns kommen her." Speratus headed each of the verses of his chorale with one of the letters from A to O and added fourteen paragraphs headed from A to O identifying the scriptural basis of the theological ideas expressed in the chorale verses. Drawing heavily on the books that Luther named as the most important in the Bible, particularly Romans, Speratus summarized all the main tenets of Lutheranism, including the Christocentric nature of scripture.[3]

On the basis of these associations with the number fourteen, I have suggested elsewhere that a symbolism of this kind was present in the first two cantatas produced by Bach for his first annual Leipzig cantata cycle of 1723–24, *Die Elenden sollen essen*, BWV 75, and *Die Himmel erzählen die Ehre Gottes*, BWV 76.[4] These two cantatas were created with striking similarities in their "ground plans" that are unique in all Bach's cantata œuvre, and they offer an unmistak-

2. On the association of Bach's violoncello piccolo parts with this quality, see n. 22 below.

3. On Speratus's "Es ist das Heil uns kommen her," see Klaus Duwel, ed., *Epochen der deutschen Lyrik*, vol. 3, *Gedichte 1500–1600* (Munich: Deutscher Taschenbuch Verlag, 1978), 71–75. On Luther's Christocentric view of scripture, see Paul Althaus, *The Theology of Martin Luther*, trans. Robert C. Schulz (Philadelphia: Fortress Press, 1966), 74, 79–81.

4. See Eric T. Chafe, "Bach's First Two Leipzig Cantatas: A Message for the Community," in *A Bach Tribute: Essays in Honor of William H. Scheide*, ed. Paul Brainard and Ray Robinson (Kassel: Bärenreiter; Chapel Hill, N.C.: Hinshaw, 1993), 71–86.

able continuity in their theological messages. With fourteen movements each, they are the longest of all Bach's church cantatas as well as obvious candidates for numerological interpretation.[5] Most important, however, their texts develop theological themes that derive more from the *epistles* than the Gospels for the two Sundays in question (the first and second Sundays after Trinity, respectively), an unusual occurrence in Bach's cantatas. Those themes, centering on love, lead to a remarkable emphasis on brotherly love in Cantata 76, a theme not only well suited to Bach's beginning a position in a new community but reverberating with Bach's well-known expressions of the purpose of music on the title page of the *Orgelbüchlein* and in a set of rules for the thoroughbass: the glory of God (as in Part 1 of Cantata 76) and the edification of one's neighbor (as in the emphasis on brotherly love in Part 2 of Cantata 76).[6]

If Cantatas 75 and 76 do indeed utilize their fourteen-movement designs to articulate a beginning/ending symbolism related either to the name *Bach* or to the "A" and "O" idea (or to both), that symbolism would also be connected

5. Thus Friedrich Smend suggested that the use of fourteen-movement sequences represented the composer's "announcing his presence" numerologically to the congregations of St. Nicholas and St. Thomas in turn, by the spelling of his name according to the number alphabet (see *Joh. Seb. Bach: Kirchen-Kantaten vom Trinitatis-Fest bis zum 7. Sonntag nach Trinitatis*, 2d ed. [Berlin: Christlicher Zeitschriftenverlag, 1950], 24). If there is any truth to my suggestion that Bach associated the number fourteen with the "A" and "O" idea in Cantatas 75 and 76, we might consider that the design of each of the two cantatas features a division into two parts of seven movements each, with close parallels between the two parts. According to *The New English Bible*, "The structure of Revelation is dominated by series of sevens, the biblical number of fullness or completeness" (p. 313). In view of the related association between the fourteen letters and the "A" and "O" idea, it may be significant that Cantatas 75 and 76 form multiples of seven, that Bach's cantata setting of "Es ist das Heil uns kommen her," BWV 9, reduces the fourteen strophes of the chorale to seven movements, and the like.

6. Günther Stiller interprets Bach's well-known 1708 statement regarding his goal of a "well-regulated church music" in the light of his later statements regarding the purpose of music and the thoroughbass (trans. in BR, 21, 32–33, 60–61) (see Günther Stiller, *Johann Sebastian Bach and Liturgical Life in Leipzig* [St. Louis: Concordia, 1984], 208–11). One such statement (as translated in BR, 32–33) reads: "The thorough bass is the most perfect foundation of music, being played with both hands in such manner that the left hand plays the notes written down while the right adds consonances and dissonances, in order to make a well-sounding harmony to the Glory of God and the permissible delectation of the spirit; and the aim and final reason, as of all music, so of the thorough bass should be none else but the Glory of God and the recreation of the mind."

to the fact that Cantata 75 marks the turning of the year insofar as Bach's cantata cycles were concerned.[7] The first arias of the two cantatas, "Mein Jesus soll mein Alles sein" and "Hört, ihr Völker, Gottes Stimme" (the latter containing the line "Aller Dinge Grund und Ende ist sein eingeborner Sohn"), recall texts from the New Year's Day cantatas mentioned above. And quite possibly the first cantata of Bach's second Leipzig cycle, *O Ewigkeit, du Donnerwort*, BWV 20, alludes to the *Anfang/Ende* symbolism as well. The chorale verses with which it begins and ends contain the line "O Anfang sonder Ende," an expression intended to induce fear of eternal damnation (very nearly the opposite of the theological message of the year before). These cantatas all come at the beginning of the Trinity season since, owing to the timing of his arrival in Leipzig (May 1723), Bach's cantata cycles reverse the ordering of the two "halves" of the year. Toward the end of the Trinity season in his first Leipzig cycle Bach had mounted a cantata, BWV 60 (for the twenty-fourth Sunday after Trinity), that began with the text "O Ewigkeit, du Donnerwort" and therefore also contained the line "O Anfang sonder Ende"; and two weeks later he had produced a cantata, *Wachet! betet! betet! wachet!* BWV 70 (for the twenty-sixth Sunday after Trinity), in which other forms of *Anfang/Ende* imagery appear.[8]

7. Alfred Dürr makes the point that Bach's Leipzig cantata cycles shift the ordering of the year by six months, noting also that Bach's librettist Picander dated the preface to his 1728 cycle of cantata texts 24 June (the feast day of John the Baptist, which was the closest immovable feast to the first Sunday after Trinity) (see *Die Kantaten von Johann Sebastian Bach*, 2 vols., 5th ed. [Kassel: Bärenreiter; Munich: Deutscher Taschenbuch Verlag, 1985], 1:40-41). The division of the liturgical year into two halves, the first occupied with the time of Christ (the *Proprium Temporale*) and the second constituting the Trinity season, emerges also in the ordering of the *Orgelbüchlein*, which Charles Sanford Terry grouped under the broad headings of "Church seasons and festivals" and "the Christian life" (see *Bach's Chorals*, vol. 3, *The Hymns and Hymn Melodies of the Organ Works* [Cambridge: Cambridge University Press, 1921], 41-46). The *Orgelbüchlein* follows, of course, the ordering of the liturgical year, beginning with Advent, but, owing to the date of Bach's arrival in Leipzig (May 1723), his cantata cycles reversed the ordering of the two halves of the year.

8. The *Anfang/Ende* idea in Cantata 70 centers on the gospel theme of the last judgment and the end of the world, on the one hand, and the epistle's theme of the expectation of a "new heaven and a new earth," on the other. Thus the first chorus advocates preparation for the time when "der Herr der Herrlichkeit dieser Welt ein Ende machet," while the first recitative juxtaposes the judgment and fear of the "verstockten Sünder" with the "Anfang wahrer Freude" that God will show to the "erwählte Gotteskinder."

It may seem that, coming as they do at different points in the year, the works introduced above have little in common with each other beyond their various forms of *Anfang/Ende* symbolism.[9] In fact, though, they share sets of associations arising from a common element in their placement in the liturgical year, for all twelve occur at points related to the turning of the seasons of the geophysical, liturgical, and/or civil years. Following the organization of Bach's cantata cycles into a sequence that shifts the beginning of the year by six months, Cantatas 75, 76, and 20 represent the beginning of the "year" that comes with the Trinity season. Cantatas 49, 60, and 70, on the other hand, come toward the end of the Trinity season and therefore at the end of the liturgical year (the twentieth, twenty-fourth, and twenty-sixth Sundays after Trinity), a time when the Lutheran cycle of weekly readings is completely absorbed with eschatological concerns in preparation for the turning of the year.[10] Cantata 61 comes on the first Sunday of Advent, the beginning of the liturgical year, and Cantatas 41, 190, and 171, as previously mentioned, are for New Year's Day, the beginning of the calendar year.

In the context of the turning of the seasons, the role played by Cantatas 1 (for the Annunciation) and 31 (for Easter Sunday) is rather more complex. Advent, Christmas, and New Year's Day celebrate three separate turning points – the liturgical year (Advent), the geophysical year (Christmas, aligned with the winter solstice), and the civil year on 1 January – that the character of the Christmas season (Advent through Epiphany) weaves into a single, rich tapestry symbolizing the turning of the ages. The connection between Advent and the Annunciation echoed in the appearance of the final verse of "Wie schön leuchtet der Morgenstern" in Cantatas 61 and 1 arose in the very early history of the liturgical year, when the date of the Annunciation was equated with that of the Passion (set, like Passover, according to the lunar cycle following the spring equinox); the Annunciation became fixed at the date of the spring equinox on the Julian calendar (25 March), while the Passion and Easter fluctuated according to the lunar month that followed the equinox. As a result of

9. With the exception of the wedding cantata BWV 195, in which the single allusion to *Anfang* and *Ende* is incidental, the cantatas cited are the only ones to take up the subject.

10. The cantata that comes between Cantatas 60 and 70, e.g. (*Es reisset euch ein schrecklich Ende*, BWV 90), deals, like that of the following week (see n. 8 above), with the end of the world; now the "schrecklich Ende" is juxtaposed with the idea that God's blessings are renewed from day to day ("des Höchsten Güte wird von Tag zu Tag neu").

this symbolic alignment of the dates of Jesus' conception and his death (so that his life would circumscribe a "perfect" time span), Christmas followed nine months later, on 25 December (the winter solstice on the Julian calendar).[11] Advent and the Annunciation both look ahead to the birth of Christ.[12] The Annunciation is therefore related to Advent, Christmas, and the New Year, as evinced by the fact that the New Year was observed in England on 25 March until the first half of the eighteenth century. The symbolism of a new era that Nicolai's chorale projects, including the "A" and "O" reference, made it especially appropriate for the Annunciation. And, as is well known, Nicolai's chorale was published at the turning of the sixteenth century (1599) along with a companion chorale, "Wachet auf, ruft uns die Stimme," employed by Bach in Cantata 140 for the twenty-seventh Sunday after Trinity, the latest possible point in the liturgical year. Nicolai's chorales belong to the ancient category of watchman's songs, marking the turn between night and day and vice versa, a symbolism that Nicolai, following the customary reliance on multiple levels of interpretation (hermeneutics), relates to the turning of the ages in Jesus' birth, the turning of the century that saw the Reformation, the turning of the liturgical year, and the inner turning point of faith.[13] The beginning/ending sym-

11. See Thomas J. Talley, *Origins of the Liturgical Year*, 2d ed. (Collegeville, Minn.: Liturgical Press, 1986), 91–99. Similarly, the feast of John the Baptist, who was born six months before Jesus, was set at 24 June, corresponding to the summer solstice. Like the Annunciation and Christmas, but unlike Easter and Pentecost, its date is fixed.

12. A further link is that the gospel readings for Palm Sunday, which sometimes coincides with the Annunciation, and the first Sunday in Advent are the same, the account in Matthew of Jesus' entry into Jerusalem.

13. This kind of interpretation, one according to the four senses of scripture supplied by medieval hermeneutics, is clearly evident in Bach's earliest Advent cantata, *Nun komm, der Heiden Heiland*, BWV 61, whose final movement utilizes, as previously mentioned, the *Abgesang* of the last verse of "Wie schön leuchtet der Morgenstern." I have discussed this feature of the work in *Tonal Allegory in the Vocal Music of J. S. Bach* (Berkeley and Los Angeles: University of California Press, 1991), 142–43. To that discussion may be added the fact that the text of Cantata 61, by the Hamburg theologian Erdmann Neumeister, follows principles set forth by Neumeister in his book *Christlicher Unterricht wie die h. Adventszeit, das h. Christ-Fest und das neue Jahr gotgefällig zu feiren sey*, according to which, as Jaroslav Pelikan remarks, at the beginning of the church year "the threefold advent of Christ – in the flesh at his birth, in the means of grace through word and sacrament, and in judgment at the end of time – provided the topics for the Scripture readings and sermons on three Sundays of the Advent Season" (*Bach among the*

bolism that Nicolai's chorales celebrate is echoed in the appropriateness of the instinct, if such it was, that caused the editors of the Bachgesellschaft to place *Wie schön leuchtet der Morgenstern* at the head of their edition of Bach's works as Cantata 1. *Wachet auf, ruft uns die Stimme*, on the other hand, is in a sense the "last" of Bach's cantatas, that is, the only one for the very rare twenty-seventh Sunday after Trinity. Liturgically contiguous, but separated chronologically by almost the whole of Bach's cantata output, Cantatas 140 (1731) and 61 (1714) are linked by a beginning/ending symbolism whose origins trace back to those of the liturgical year itself.

It is appropriate that an Easter cantata (Cantata 31) should feature the most direct of the "A" and "O" references in Bach's work since the Passion and Easter, even more than Christmas, articulate the meaning of the work that Jesus came into the world to do: they celebrate completion of the victory over sin and death. The celebration of Jesus' death and resurrection originated the liturgical year, determining not only the placement of the other principal feast days but the overall perspective of the year itself, indeed of Christian life as a whole.[14] That perspective – of the Resurrection as a completed event – presents the Easter message as the change from old to new, from the first man of the creation (Adam) to the "new man" who is born in Christ, and so forth. Easter is the greatest of turning points; it is followed by the "great fifty days" – the period that formed the earliest core of the Western liturgy – that lead through the Ascension (forty days after Easter) to Pentecost (fifty days after Easter) and that are followed by Trinity Sunday and the "time of the church" (the Trinity season). The Passion and Easter climax the liturgical year, precipitating the conclusion of the liturgical cycle that comprises the half of the year known as the *Proprium Temporale* or "proper of the time (of Christ)"; Bach's cantata cycles mirror that aspect of the liturgical year by dividing the year at Trinity Sunday, which becomes in a sense a kind of "doxology" to the year as a whole.

Theologians [Philadelphia: Fortress Press, 1986], 4). In thus setting forth the basic principles of scripture interpretation, Bach's cantata marks the beginning of the church year just as clearly as his inscribing of the order of the Leipzig Advent *Hauptgottesdienst* on its title page (and that of the Advent cantata of the following year, BWV 62) (see Dürr, *Kantaten*, 1:102).

14. Thus Bach's Christmas and New Year's Day cantatas often bring out the defeat of the devil, a theme directly appropriate to Easter (see, e.g., Cantata 40, *Darzu ist erschienen der Sohn Gottes*, for the second day of Christmas; the final cantata of the Christmas Oratorio; or Cantata 41).

Salomo Franck's text for the first recitative of Cantata 31, whose beginning was cited at the outset of this essay, makes an association between the resurrected Jesus as "A" and "O" and St. Paul's description of Jesus as "head" of a "body" (the church), of which the community of believers are the "members."[15] The bond that Franck perceived between the Alpha/Omega and *Haupt/Glieder* metaphors was their association with the resurrected Jesus. The latter metaphor appears in several Bach cantatas (e.g., Cantatas 95 and 128), usually in connection with the believer's certainty of his own resurrection. Within Cantata 31 as a whole that certainty enables Franck to emphasize the believer's longing for death, so that the ending of his life, the "letzte Stunde" referred to in the penultimate movement, becomes the entranceway to the beginning of eternity. Within the present life the change from old to new is expressed in terms of the passing of the "old man" (Adam) to make way for the new ("Adam muss in uns verwesen, soll der neue Mensch genesen, der nach Gott geschaffen ist!"). The sequence of ideas in Cantata 31 thus emphasizes various different levels of beginning/ending imagery, expressing God's control of time and history, Jesus' originating and ruling over the church, the believer's inner change from the "old" to the "new" man, and, finally, the end of life and the onset of eternity. In this respect it expresses the meaning that the liturgical year celebrates in its entirety.

ANFANG/ENDE SYMBOLISM IN CANTATA 41

From the foregoing outline it is clear that in Bach's cantatas the "A" and "O" idea and its broader form, the *Anfang/Ende* symbolism, relate to the changing seasons and the turning points of the liturgical year. It perfectly expresses through the cyclic character of the year and the year's seasonal renewals the meaning of Jesus' work. Further, it expresses the bond between the liturgical, geophysical, and civil years as it does that between the great scale of events known as salvation history (the turning of the ages) and the various forms of cyclic recurrence that are more readily experienced by humanity (the changing seasons, change between night and day, etc.). All such turning points were analogous to the inner dynamic of faith. A number of the cantatas mentioned above might be studied in closer detail for the purpose of understanding how

15. The *Haupt/Glieder* metaphor is developed in several of Paul's epistles; see esp. 1 Cor. 12:12–27; Eph. 1:22, 5:24–30; and Col. 1:18.

those qualities operate in individual works. I have chosen Cantata 41, *Jesu, nun sei gepreiset,* because it reflects the idea of cyclic closure in a very purposive, rhetorically conceived manner involving various levels of musicotheological symbolism.

Each of the three New Year's Day cantatas previously cited (Cantatas 190, 41, and 171) features one or more verses of a New Year's chorale by Johannes Herman, "Jesu, nun sei gepreiset," whose fourteen-line strophes perhaps symbolized the "A" and "O" idea. The text of Cantata 41 adds the notion of the "A" and "O" to the aria and recitative (mvts. 2 and 3) that paraphrase the second of Herman's three verses (the first and third verses begin and end the cantata). In fact, a great deal of the theological meaning of Cantata 41 is bound up with the idea of *Anfang/Ende* equivalence, which Bach seems to have associated with this chorale. Thus in all his settings of the chorale Bach contrives that the music of the last two lines duplicates that of the first two (to a repetition of the text of lines 13 and 14). In the first and last movements of Cantata 41, however, he makes additional adjustments to the lines that precede the last two, so as to enhance the sense of return (see ex. 1).

Bach's interaction with chorale melodies is often a profound one. For instance, his various treatments of "Dies sind die heilgen zehn Gebot" (the so-called Ten Commandments chorale) draw much from the substantial modal inflection at the end of the tune (the pitch B♭ in a G mixolydian melody). In Cantata 77 that detail undoubtedly determined the "descending" tonal plan of the entire cantata, in which the final movement ends on the dominant of G minor (the cantata begins in C major and moves to A minor and D minor successively for the other tonally closed movements).[16] Many other examples of Bach's seizing on the "structural" and symbolic potential of his chorales could be cited just as readily. In the case of "Jesu, nun sei gepreiset" the original chorale melody (anonymous) is unusual in two respects: it ends a step higher than it begins (usually F major/G minor and C major/D minor are Bach's equivalents), and it changes from duple to triple meter for the final two

---

16. Whether or not the modal inflection in the original melody mirrored the role of the law in Lutheranism – spiritual humiliation, bringing the individual "down," so to speak – Cantata 77 outlines a progression of that kind in which the final aria acknowledges the "lauter Unvollkommenheit" of human love. Bach never fails to bring out something of this quality in his settings of this chorale, a testimony to his interpretation of the significance of the modal inflection.

phrases. These two features were probably intended to symbolize the change from the old to the new year. Throughout the seventeenth century the chorale was apparently sung in that form, in which there is a certain resemblance between the first and the last two lines, but by no means a straight transpositional relationship. In the eighteenth century, however, modifications were sometimes introduced to end the chorale in its original mode. No other version is identical to Bach's, which is the only one to retain something close to the original tune and at the same time use the repeat of the first two lines to return it to the original mode.[17]

In the form used by Bach, the anonymous chorale melody itself has basically only seven different melodic phrases, but through repetition they are extended to accommodate the entire strophe: in the *Stollen*, phrases 1 and 2 repeat as 5 and 6 and phrases 3 and 4 as 7 and 8; in the *Abgesang*, phrases 9 and 10 are identical, and 11 and 12 repeat as 13 and 14; finally, phrases 1 and 2 reappear as 15 and 16 (see ex.1). The only repeated lines of *text*, however, are 13 and 14 (to the music of phrases 1 and 2). In the opening chorus Bach sets the two *Stollen* (phrases 1–4 and 5–8) in common time, then the first two phrases of the *Abgesang* (phrases 9–10) in $\frac{3}{4}$, and the following four (phrases 11–14) in cut time, marked *presto*. Although these last phrases complete the fourteen lines of the text of the strophe, they cannot serve to end it since they end with a cadence to D minor rather than the key of the melody, C major. The repetition of the text of lines 13 and 14 to the music of phrases 1 and 2 therefore restores both the key of C major and the original time signature, causing the setting as a whole to have sixteen rather than fourteen phrases. The design is similar to that used for the verse that ends the cantata, except that there Bach introduces only one time signature change – to $\frac{3}{4}$ for phrases 11–14 (the two pairs of phrases that

---

17. The principal melody as cited in Johannes Zahn's *Die Melodien der deutschen evangelischen Kirchenlieder* ([Gütersloh, 1892; reprint, Hildesheim: Georg Olms, 1963], 5:191) is basically the same in outline as Bach's would be without the repeat of the beginning lines at the end; the most common modification of the melody was simply to end the final phrase a step lower. Another form (ibid., 5:192) introduced a clear ABA form into the tune, the four phrases of the *Stollen* (lines 1–4 and 5–8) returning to end the chorale (lines 11–14); in that form the G minor/ F major relationship was shifted to the cadences of phrases 2 and 4, respectively (and their repetition as 6 and 8 and as 12 and 14). Both those versions, like Bach's, interpret the "dorian" cadences as displaced forms of the basic "ionian" cadence – i.e., as the second scale degree, which returns to the tonic at the end.

EX.1. *a*, Cantus firmus in BWV 41/1.
b, Cantus firmus in BWV 41/6

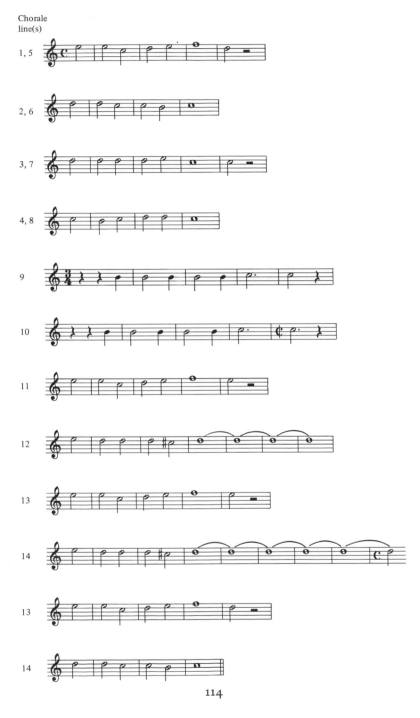

114

115

close in D minor, setting lines 11–14) – before returning to set the last two lines with the music of the first two phrases (this time significantly modified in their harmonization, as we will see). Since in both cases phrases 13 and 14 repeat the music of 11 and 12 to the final lines of the text, it would have been a simple matter to bring back the music of phrases 1 and 2 at that point, ending the chorale after fourteen lines and phrases as well as restoring the meter and key with the return of the music of phrases 1 and 2 for the final lines. That Bach did not do this and that all his settings of this chorale extend a chorale of already unusual length still further must express a particular intent. The most obvious effect of his settings of the final phrases is to increase the impact of the return to C major by delaying it for two additional phrases. Since the four phrases that precede the return of the first two at the end resemble the first two a step higher, the effect of the delay and return is a very palpable one.

But this is not the only means that Bach devised to project the *Anfang/Ende* symbolism in Cantata 41. The first and last movements are also related in that Bach utilizes the first two measures of the ritornello of the first movement as an interlude between the chorale phrases of the final movement, sounding it five times: after phrases 2, 4, 6, and 8 of the two *Stollen*, then after the *Abgesang*. The entire cantata therefore ends as it began. The two measures themselves, which center wholly around the principal tones of the C-major triad, sound a brief ABA pattern, so that they too end as they begin (see ex. 2).

From these details it appears likely that Bach intended the return to C as the principal level of *Anfang/Ende* symbolism in Cantata 41, perhaps a reflection of the role of C within the circle of keys, mediating between the sharps and the flats.[18] In any case, when Bach (or whoever the unknown librettist is) added the *Anfang/Ende* imagery to the two movements of the cantata that paraphrase the middle verse of Herman's chorale (which did not contain that imagery), he included additional details that point to his association of that idea to C. For example, the A section of the second movement, "Lass uns, o höchster Gott, das Jahr vollbringen, damit das Ende so wie dessen Anfang sei," a G-major soprano aria in pastorale style, prays that the ending (of the year) be the same as its beginning. And the beginning of the recitative that follows responds by fore-

18. That sense is clearly present in the first printed circle of keys, in Johann David Heinichen, *Neu-erfundene und gründliche Anweisung* (Hamburg, 1711). Heinichen places C, which he calls "the easiest key in music," at the top of the circle, calling the sharps and flats the *genus chromaticum* and *genus enharmonicum*, respectively (see pp. 261–67).

EX. 2. BWV 41/1, mm. 1–2

117

shadowing the key in which the cantata ends. Its first line, "Ach! deine Hand, dein Segen muss allein das A und O, der Anfang und das Ende sein," begins in A minor, then turns at the text "das A und O" to a C^6 chord that was obviously introduced to enable the voice to sing the notes for "A" and "O" to the octave c''/c'.[19] The remainder of the line moves to a cadence in C major for "der Anfang und das Ende sein." Since in this recitative the key of C major appears only in the passage just cited, it seems likely that Bach intended a reference to the key of the first and last movements. The C octave is conceptually related to the ending of the ritornello of the first movement, where the first trumpet and continuo play the simple C scale in contrary motion, reaching to the normal upper and lower limits of the pitch spectrum. Bach's intent was undoubtedly to suggest the all-encompassing nature of God that the Alpha/Omega idea signifies in Revelation.[20]

This recitative bridges between the two arias of Cantata 41, forming a sequence of three movements (mvts. 2–4) that are not in C major. The soprano aria's B section had referred to the presence of God's hand as the source of "an overflow of blessings" in the soon-to-come end of the year that is now beginning ("Es stehe deine Hand uns bei, dass künftig bei des Jahres Schluss wir bei des Segens Überfluss wie itzt ein Halleluja singen"). The joining of the *Hand/Segen* imagery of the aria in connection with the "A" and "O" idea at the beginning of the recitative just described ("Ach! deine Hand, dein Segen muss allein das A und O, der Anfang und das Ende sein") introduces a description of God's hand as a symbol for God's control over life and death, God's eye as watching over "Stadt und Land," and God's full knowledge of and control over human happiness and suffering. The conjunction of God's *Hand* and *Segen* with the Alpha and Omega resonates with those passages in Revelation (such as 1:17–18 and 2:8) where Jesus' description as the "first and last" is linked to his power over death and life as manifested in the Resurrection.[21] The recita-

19. In Cantata 31 Bach's reference to the "A" and "O" idea is preceded by a cadence to C, following which the "A" sounds during a shift to A minor.

20. Quite possibly, Bach thought of these devices in terms similar to Andreas Werckmeister's various "allegorical" interpretations of the intervals and tones of the harmonic series, in which the unison fundamental tone represents God the Father, the octave the Son, the fifth the Holy Spirit, and so forth (see the "Anhang von der allegorischen und moralischen Music" in Werckmeister's *Musicae mathematicae hodegus curiousus* [Frankfurt and Leipzig, 1686], 141–54).

21. In Rev. 1:17–18 Jesus lays his right hand (a well-known symbol of power) on John and says,

tive ends with a prayer that God will dispense both *Wohl* and *Leiden* according to his wisdom and mercy ("du zählest unser Wohl und kennest unser Leiden, ach! gieb von Beiden, was deine Weisheit will, wozu dich dein Erbarmen angetrieben").

This recitative also creates very much the sense that God's all-encompassing nature and wisdom, symbolized in the "A" and "O" idea, are the means by which the antitheses of human life are overcome. The following aria, "Woferne du den edlen Frieden vor unsern Leib und Stand beschieden," for the unusual combination of tenor solo, violoncello piccolo, and continuo, maintains this idea by associating God's gift of peace with the qualities of "Leib und Stand," that is, with physical life (echoing the "Stadt und Land" of the preceding recitative) and by petitioning for the gift of God's "selig machend Wort" for the soul or spiritual life. Its B section alerts itself to the distinction between earthly and spiritual spheres, adding "Wenn uns dies Heil begegnet, so sind wir hier gesegnet und Auserwählte dort." The association of the *Segnen* idea with the blessings of present life (especially peace, as in Jesus' post-Resurrection benediction, "Der Friede sei mit dir") has as its counterpart in the life to come the promise that the believer will be among the elect (*Auserwählte*). The assonance between *Seele, selig,* and *gesegnet* suggests that no sharp antithesis between the worldly and the spiritual spheres is intended. Rather, we might infer that God's *Hand*, represented here by the wide-ranging violoncello piccolo part, binds the two into the necessary union.[22]

"Do not be afraid, I am the first and the last, and I am the living one; for I was dead and now I am alive for evermore, and I hold the keys of Death and Death's domain."

22. The violoncello piccolo part of this aria is notated in treble and bass clefs, the former transposing down an octave, but in other movements such parts utilize alto and/or tenor clefs. That the instrument, despite its name, is held on the arm perhaps alludes to the *Hand* imagery of the preceding movements. Its appearance in an aria from Cantata 175 might have been associated by Bach with the reference to Jesus' *Schützarm* in the text of that aria. The violoncello piccolo, which Bach himself may have invented, exhibits a considerable degree of consistency in the theological associations of the nine movements in which it appears (in Cantatas 6, 41, 49, 68, 85, 115, 175, 180, and 183), all but one of which belong to the 1724–25 cycle and five of which appear in the post-Easter cantatas of that year. Close musicotheological study of all the cantatas for the spring of 1725 reveals that in them the violoncello piccolo bears a striking association with the presence and person of Jesus, in particular with his protective, "good shepherd" side. The part of the liturgical year represented by these works has a special, triumphant character arising from the relatively close conjunction of two of the three principal feasts of the liturgical

A number of features of the second aria that are bound up with the violoncello piccolo are of interest in this regard. One of the most prominent is the wide-ranging pitch spectrum of the instrument, which is reflected in the notation that Bach uses for it in several arias from his church cantatas, including this one: the upper register is notated in treble clef, sounding an octave lower than written, while the lower is written in bass clef, sounding at pitch (alto and tenor clefs may be used as well). The visual disparity in the notation both amplifies the impression of registral disparity – that Bach utilizes in this aria to a degree greater than in any other of his with this instrument – and masks the smooth progression from register to register in long scalar passages (in m. 23 the two-octave descending scale from d′ to D is notated with a change from treble to bass clefs, giving the appearance of an octave leap in the middle). The difference between what is seen and what is heard, between disjunct and conjunct melodic styles, and between treble and bass registers can be considered a mirror of the *Leib/Seele* and *hier/dort* antitheses in the text, while the continuity in register from the low C of the violoncello piccolo upward through three octaves to b′ binds them into a higher union.[23]

---

year (Easter and Pentecost) as well as Ascension Day and Trinity Sunday. The predominance of gospel readings from John in this period ensures that the theological themes center around the benefit of the Resurrection for humanity. Bach's cantatas from the spring of 1725 bring out this idea with particular reference to the dual image of Jesus as *Christus victor* and "good shepherd." That is, they develop the theological qualities that underlie mvts. 2–4 of Cantata 41. The questions surrounding the theological associations of these works are too detailed to take up here; I have discussed them fully in a forthcoming book on the Bach cantatas. The most recent and well-argued treatment of the violoncello piccolo is Winfried Schrammek, "Viola pomposa und Violoncello piccolo bei Johann Sebastian Bach," in *Bericht über die Wissenschaftliche Konferenz zum III. Internationalen Bach-Fest der DDR 18.–19. September 1975*, ed. Werner Felix, Winfried Hoffmann, and Armin Schneiderheinze (Leipzig: VEB Deutscher Verlag für Musik, 1977), 345–54. It appears likely that the instrument called *violoncello piccolo* by Bach was the same referred to in 1790 in Ernst Ludwig Gerber's famous account of Bach's invention of the *viola pomposa* in 1724. Laurence Dreyfus holds this view, suggesting that Bach invented the instrument "for his experimental set of demanding solos in the cantatas" (*Bach's Continuo Group: Players and Practices in His Vocal Works* [Cambridge, Mass.: Harvard University Press, 1987], 174). While Schrammek views the *viola pomposa* principally as a chamber instrument, he also admits that it might have been the violoncello piccolo of the cantatas ("Viola pomposa," 347–48).

23. In the lowest octave the violoncello piccolo plays all the diatonic pitches from C to B, in

Bach's aria develops these features in its overall design, bringing out qualities of juxtaposed ascent and descent in the principal musical ideas. The ritornello divides into two segments, the first of which (mm. 1–4) comprises two phrases in an antecedent-consequent relationship. The first phrase is built on the descending tetrachord a–g–f–e, and its sequential descent in the violoncello piccolo part features jagged leaps between high and low notes, the last of which (only) is notated in bass clef. The second phrase then ascends over A/a, B/b, and c, with its last note again changing to bass clef and sinking now to the lowest pitch available on the violoncello piccolo, C. The second part of the ritornello (mm. 5–10) introduces a melodic idea in still more florid style; its wide-ranging violoncello piccolo line returns in the final measures to the style of the first idea but remains within the treble clef. Its first three measures ascend sequentially to the highest pitch that Bach assigns the violoncello piccolo in this movement, b′ (notated b″).

These qualities of low and high registers then reappear in the violoncello piccolo part in the two principal vocal sections of the aria. The A section, based chiefly on the first and second melodic ideas of the ritornello, subdivides into three segments, the first of which outlines in the violoncello piccolo part the a–g–f–e descent of the ritornello (A–G–F–E, at mm. 11–12) and the second and third of which extend the scalar descent first from A to D (mm. 15–17), then from A to C (mm. 22–24). The low C on the violoncello piccolo is its only appearance outside the ritornello; it caps a progressive descent in register that involves two two-octave descending scales. Conversely, the close of the B section utilizes the ascending melodic sequences of the second segment of the ritornello to ascend to the highest available pitch on the instrument, b′, which sounds twice in close succession just before the sectional cadence (but, like the low C, nowhere else in the aria outside the ritornello). To this ascent the immediate return of the opening ritornello then juxtaposes the descending character of its first phrase and the downward leap to the low C. Bach seems therefore to have intended the idea of registral opposition and bonding as the central pictorial device of this aria, a mirroring of God's control of human affairs, both physical and spiritual.

In this context we may note that iconographical representations of the ges-

---

the next octave it plays all the chromatic pitches from c to b but one (d♯), and in the uppermost octave it plays the full chromatic spectrum from c′ to b′.

ture of benediction underlying the meaning of the word *Segen* in this three-movement sequence are legion. They frequently represent Christ in victory bearing an emblem of the Resurrection (a banner bearing the cross).[24] We need look no further than the frontispieces of two books from Bach's own library for examples of the kinds of imagery that lie behind these three movements of Cantata 41.[25] Johann Christian Adami's *Güldene Aepffel* represents God the Father in heaven giving such a benediction, beneath which a banner bears the inscription from John, "also hatt Gott die Welt geliebet," and beneath that again the resurrected Christ with a banner of the cross places a crown on the head of one of the faithful, who bears a large basket full of fruit, symbol of the *Überfluss* referred to in the first aria of Cantata 41. The imagery is stocked with symbols of bounty: a fountain (Jesus is often described in Bach's cantatas as the fountain [*Brunnquell*] of grace or blessings), a rosebush, a tree bearing fruit (apples?), a palace garden with another fountain, animals (sheep and watchdogs?), a vine laden with grapes, and the like. Beneath the whole is another inscription: "Herr Gott Vater mein starcker Held du hast mich ewig vor der Welt in deinem Sohn geliebet." Subtly conveyed in this picture, and reflected in the title of the work and the name *Adami*, is a link between the bounty of the Garden of Eden and the present and future benefits of Jesus' redemptive work, motivated by love (the basket of fruit represents the present and the crown the future).[26]

24. According to Elke Axmacher (*"Aus Liebe will mein Heyland sterben": Untersuchungen zum Wandel des Passionsverständnisses im frühen 18. Jahrhundert* [Neuhausen-Stuttgart: Hänssler, 1984], 79–84), the theological background to the imagery of Jesus' outstretched arms in the dialogue aria "Sehet, Jesus hat die Hand uns zu fassen ausgespannt" from the St. Matthew Passion involves two interpretative traditions, one emphasizing the gesture as Jesus' blessing (*Segen*) of the faithful, arising from his priesthood, the other (and the one followed in Picander's text to the St. Matthew Passion) deriving from scriptural representations of Jesus' protective nature (the good shepherd). The two traditions often complement one another, of course. They both underlie the meaning of mvts. 2–4 of Cantata 41.

25. For facsimiles of the two title pages discussed in this and the following paragraph, see Robin A. Leaver, *Bachs theologische Bibliothek* (Neuhausen-Stuttgart: Hänssler, 1983), 115 and 132.

26. The allegorical detail is richer than I have indicated, of course; e.g., the fountain behind the figure of Jesus has a cracked base, and the fruit tree that balances it on the other side of the picture is growing from a stone sphere atop a stone or mortar pedestal that is similarly cracked.

Johannes Müller's *Atheismus devictus* reveals another side to the meaning of the sign of benediction. The frontispiece to this more aggressively polemical work divides into three levels. The uppermost level depicts the resurrected Christ in heaven, one hand outstretched with the banner of victory and the other with the sign of benediction, above which a banner bears the inscription "Herrsche unter deinen Feinden"; Jesus' feet rest on the heads of a group of atheists. The middle level places Jesus on the left, again giving the sign of benediction, and a priest on the right, each bearing a biblical inscription (from the Old and New Testaments, respectively) that refers to God's rejection of Satan. Beneath their feet in the lowermost level the artist has depicted Satan as a serpent from whose mouth emerge more serpents, while the inscription below is a negation not only of God but also of the word of God, Providence, the Resurrection, and hell. As Jesus in his earthly form and the priestly symbol of the church tread Satan under their feet, so the resurrected Jesus in glory treads the atheists under his, both representations making the sign of benediction to the faithful. In this picture the image of Jesus as *Christus victor* dominates, whereas in the one described above it is rather the depiction of the good shepherd that underlies the meaning.

The pastoral character of the first aria of Cantata 41 derives, as does that of the dialogue "Sehet, Jesus hat die Hand uns zu fassen ausgespannt" from the St. Matthew Passion, from the representation of Jesus as good shepherd, even though that idea is not stated directly in its text. The portrayal of Jesus as the protective "good shepherd" is inevitably bound up with that of the *Christus victor*; the two emerge very prominently in the post-Easter cantatas of the year (1725) whose beginning Cantata 41 celebrates. The *Christus victor* idea is also present in Cantata 41, especially in the trumpet sonorities of the outer movements. In this connection the final recitative is particularly revealing, especially since it sets the final return to C that ends the cantata in the context of the overcoming of some highly contradictory tonal ideas. Set for bass solo, it is divided at the midpoint by three measures in which the remaining three voices enter above the bass with a litany-like chanting of the line "Den Satan unter unsre Füsse treten." The six measures that precede the litany describe the con-

---

The meaning intended was undoubtedly the insecure nature of life "below" as opposed to the bounty that springs from that "above."

stant threat of the *Feind* (i.e., Satan) to the peace of the faithful (as if in contradiction to the beginning of the preceding aria) and the community's prayer
to God; the six that follow it expand on the meaning of the *Auserwählte:* "So
bleiben wir zu deinem Ruhm dein auserwähltes Eigentum und können auch
nach Kreuz und Leiden zur Herrlichkeit von hinnen scheiden." The image of
treading Satan underfoot is based on God's promise to Eve in the Garden of
Eden after the Fall (Gen. 3:15); associated widely with the Resurrection, it is
represented graphically in other Bach cantatas, just as it is on the title page of
Müller's *Atheismus devictus.*[27]

Since this movement effects the return to C for the final chorale, the symbolism of which was indicated above, Bach's association of the devil with
tonal qualities that resist and undermine C is interesting. The recitative begins as if on the dominant of C, but its "resolution" to a $^{4\natural}_2$ chord above B♭
introduces both vertical and horizontal tritones (*diabolus* symbols) that turn
the tonality away from C; the tendency toward F deflects the third measure
toward the dominant of D minor, but that harmony "resolves" in turn to a $^{4\sharp}_2$
chord above C. These restless harmonies set the text "Doch weil der Feind bei
Tage und Nacht zu unserm Schaden wacht und unsre Ruhe will verstören."
The chromaticism in the continuo part (mm. 3–5: c♯, c, B) leads briefly to C,
cadencing there momentarily to offset Satan's tonally destructive work with
God's hearing the prayer of the faithful ("so wollest du, o Herre Gott, er-
hören"). But additional tritones between the voice and the continuo above
another chromatic descent in the continuo (mm. 5–7: e, e♭, d, setting the words
"wenn wir in heiliger Gemeine beten") lead to the sounding of the dominant-
seventh harmony of E♭ for most of the two measures that begin the litany
"Dem Satan [unter unsre Füsse treten]." In effect, from m. 3 of the recitative
the harmonies move through a segment of the circle of fifths from A^6 to E♭$^{+7}$,
the distance of a tritone, with the cadence to C as its "center" (A^6, D$^{4\sharp}_2$, G^6, C^6,
C^7, F$^4_2$, B♭$^6_{5♭}$, E♭$^{+7}$); circle-of-fifths progressions are a device that Bach uses
elsewhere to represent the devil's attempts to cause the downfall of the faithful.[28] With the entrance of the upper voices on the dominant of E♭, the bass

27. The aria "Höllische Schlange" from Cantata 40, e.g., depicts this idea in its B section (see
Helene Werthemann, *Die Bedeutung der alttestamentlichen Historien in Johann Sebastian Bachs
Kantaten* [Tübingen: J. C. B. Mohr, 1960], 16–18).

28. In the fourth movement of Cantata 42, e.g., Bach utilizes such a progression to illus-

represents the winding of the snake beneath the "feet" of the chorus. The bass (and continuo) alone sound the pitch Ab, which threatens to lead the passage to an Eb cadence. The upper voices, though, hold to their Bb triad for seven successive iterations, and, when the bass finally reaches Eb, Bach draws it into the key of Bb instead, on which the litany cadences.

After the litany the continuo notes duplicate those of mm. 2, 3, and 4 (Bb, E, c#, c♮), as if to underscore the change of meaning ("So bleiben wir zu deinem Ruhm dein auserwähltes Eigentum"); an intensification of the tritones and chromaticism in the continuo now underlies the words "und können auch nach Kreuz und Leiden," with the harmonies on "Kreuz und Leiden" constituting the sharpest harmonic dissonances of the piece. Then the harmonic aura suddenly brightens for a secure final cadence to C ("zur Herrlichkeit von hinnen scheiden").

These events, which are rather detailed in a verbal description, resolve in the listener's ear into the final return of the C major that represents, as I have argued, the all-encompassing *Anfang/Ende* symbolism of the work. The exact nature of that symbolism is, of course, open to question; we may dispute, for example, whether the C somehow represents the center of the circle of fifths (midway between the A and the Eb chords that constitute the flat/sharp "boundaries" of the circle-of-fifths progression in mm. 3–9), whether the C might bear a Christological association, and the like. The main point is that the return to C is an *audible* signal of return, both at the end of the recitative and in the final chorale. Absolute pitch would help, of course, with the linking of the final C to the C of the first, third, and fifth movements, but Bach has given the sensitive ear plenty of clues. The unusually long and variegated chorale fantasy that begins the work is of particular interest in this respect, not only because of its musical relationship to the final chorale, but because in it Bach sets up an allegorical association for one of the most fundamental levels of cyclic recurrence in his music, that of the single key that is to serve as the "tonic" of a multimovement work.

---

trate the text "obschon die Feinde willens sein, dich gänzlich zu verstören, und suchen deinen Untergang." In the chorus "Sind Blitze, sind Donner in Wolken verschwunden" from the St. Matthew Passion Bach initiates a powerful circle-of-fifths motion for the opening up of hell ("Eröffne den feurigen Abgrund, o Hölle"), and in the final cantata of the Christmas Oratorio he utilizes a similar circle for the recitative "Was will der Höllen schrecken nun?"

One of the most "natural" sounding aspects of the elaborate opening movement is the ease with which its initial two-measure "motto" idea leads to a dominant-seventh chord on C in m. 3 (the violas introducing the bb), after which the first trumpet extends up to the fourteenth partial, bb″, in m. 4. This event initiates a circle-of-fifths harmonic motion that, as we will see, is central to Bach's conception of the movement. Bach utilizes a compressed version of this gesture on the next appearance of the motto (mm. 25–26), introducing the bb″ and the harmonic-fifth motion into the motto itself. All appearances of the motto in this movement feature a downward-rushing C scale in the continuo. This detail, which is significantly missing from the reappearance of those measures at the end of the cantata, fulfills an important role in Bach's intention in that it reinforces our perception of the circle-of-fifths harmonic motion as a form of descent. This is particularly clear in m. 3, by which point the circle-of-fifths harmonies have caused the continuo scale to descend from bb to Bb (then, in m. 6, from a to A), thereby preparing a bass descent of c′–bb–a–g–f over the first eight measures of the ritornello. The most salient harmonic feature of the ritornello, however, is its employment of a circle-of-fifths motion that is bound up with the gestures just described. The harmonies of the first ten measures of the ritornello – C, F, Bb, e, a, d, G, C, F (in simplified root-position spelling) – describes a diatonic circle that breaks off only to articulate the dominant/tonic relationship for the cadential measures (mm. 11–12: f♯°, G, C, G, C). At the cadence the descending C scale of the continuo moves into the lowest register (c–C). Its inversion by the trumpet (leading upward through the fifteenth partial, b♮″, to the opposite end of the pitch spectrum, c‴) symbolizes how the secure C major of the cadence overcomes the "weakening" tendency of the circular fifth motion, subsuming its individual members as the harmonic "ambitus" of the key.

If Bach's basing the ritornello of this movement on the circle of fifths is remarkable, even more so is his immediately drawing the first two phrases of the chorale and the interlude between them into another extended circle. Bach incorporates the first phrase of the chorale into the twelfth measure of the ritornello, thus overlapping its first word, *Jesu*, with the contrary-motion C scale of the ritornello cadence (perhaps another device to represent the equivalence of ending and beginning in terms of Jesus' all-encompassing nature). Taken on its own, the melody of the phrase itself very much suggests a C-major harmonization in which the final tone, d″, would sound to a half cadence. Instead,

Bach allows the pitch B♭, entering in several successive voices immediately after the word *Jesu*, to cause the harmonies of the phrase to initiate another circle-of-fifths progression: C (C^7), F (with momentary F^7), B♭. By m. 16 the C scale has changed to a B♭ scale in the bass (this time with e♭). The music then continues with the circle of fifths as it did in the ritornello. The first break comes with the entrance of the second phrase of the chorale in mm. 21–22; Bach switches from G to E$^6_5$ and continues the circle to F from the latter harmony, the F-major chord forming part of the plagal cadence to C with which the chorale phrase ends. After the pronounced subdominant emphasis within the first chorale phrase, the second one confirms C by utilizing a circle-of-fifths harmonic progression drawn now from the "sharp" or dominant side of the key: (D, G) E, a, D, G, C, F, C (again, in simplified root-position spelling). The effect of the two phrases is what is commonly known as a "weakening" of the tonic by motion to the subdominant (phrase 1) followed by an affirmation of the tonic by means of greater emphasis on the dominant (phrase 2).

Following phrase 2 Bach immediately initiates yet another such circle of fifths, this time shifting it up a fifth so that it arrives on the dominant of G for the beginning of the third chorale phrase. The shift of transposition level is easily audible from Bach's return to the motto of the ritornello (beginning in m. 25), first stated in C and then immediately transposed up a step. The resultant circle, sounding the harmonies (D^7/G) C, F, b, e, a, D, G, is "closed" now by the tritone-related F major and B minor harmonies. Thus the first thirty-five measures of the movement are permeated almost entirely by the circle of fifths. The degree of emphasis on the dominant, however, and hence the security of C as tonic, progressively increases throughout the three approximately equal length segments.

The eleven measures (mm. 35–45) that span the third and fourth phrases of the chorale and the brief interlude between them do not follow a circle-of-fifths pattern. Instead, Bach allows phrase 3 to cadence on F (although the melody suggests C) and introduces flat-minor harmonies (G minor and F minor in particular) to color and weaken the C-major cadence of phrase 4 in keeping with its text ("in aller Not und Gefahr"). From this point on the lengthy opening section of the movement (mm. 1–102) makes use only of music that has already been heard; a full repeat of the ritornello (mm. 46–57), followed by the music of the first four phrases (lines 5–8; mm. 57–91), leads into a third full statement of the ritornello (mm. 91–102). Remarkably, as a result of the design of this segment, some 80 of its 102 measures are occupied with circle-of-fifths harmonic progressions, a unique situation in Bach's work.

And yet Bach extends the focus on the circle of fifths still further. After the articulation of C that closes the part of the movement just described (corresponding to the two *Stollen*), he makes the change to $\frac{3}{4}$ meter and adagio tempo mentioned above. The textual motivation is obvious; the preceding segment ended with thanks to God for the "neu fröhliche Zeit," whereas the one now beginning thanks him for the peaceful completion of the old year ("dass wir in guter Stille das alt Jahr hab'n erfüllet"). Fulfilling or completing the old year "in guter Stille" (with its obvious undertone of death and rebirth) led Bach to a tremendous slowing of the harmonic rhythm to articulate what we might almost call an archetypal circle-of-fifths progression – that is, a representation of the basis of harmonic motion as defined by the eighteenth-century circle of keys. The passage in question begins from a minor-ninth chord on E and slowly returns to C, its harmonies outlining a segment of the circle: E^9, a, A^9, d, D^9, g, G^9, c, C (see ex. 3). The style details, such as the five-measure d in the bass on "Stille," are too obvious for comment. Their effect is to reveal in the most explicit manner imaginable the harmonic procedures that had dominated the preceding segment of the movement. At the same time, these sixteen measures constitute a kind of "prelude" to the setting of the next four phrases of the chorale (phrases 11–14), now marked *presto* in cut time. The fugal passage that begins that segment of the movement, preparing the entrance of the chorale in the soprano, continues the circle-of-fifths motion of the "prelude" in its initial harmonies, F major and Bb major, and moves on to set up a cadence to G minor (with a Picardy third) after briefly sounding an Eb^{+7} chord. Accompanied by the continuing circle-of-fifths motion, the text of this segment ("Wir wollen uns dir ergeben itzund und immerdar") expresses the idea of continuity with the old year in terms of the community's relinquishing control to God in the present and future. From this point (m. 128) the harmonic character of the movement is freer (i.e., less systematically patterned). Nevertheless, a similar motion in the subdominant direction occurs between the two chorale phrases; and, of course, the entire passage, from the fugal entrance that follows the adagio circle of fifths in m. 119 through the cadence to the dominant of D minor in m. 152, repeats (with the text of the last two chorale lines) as mm. 153–83 (now slightly modified and shortened in the last four measures, which close with a plagal G minor/D major cadence). In terms of the

EX.3. BWV 41/1, mm.103–19

guter Stil -

movement as a whole this segment represents an elaboration of the above-mentioned delaying of the return to C major within the chorale melody.

Immediately following the return of the original time signature, Bach effects the return to C major for the final segment of the movement (mm. 183–213) by means of a six-measure transition based on the second measure of the ritornello motto. From the entrance of the chorus (for the reiteration of lines 13 and 14 of the chorale text), the final section reintroduces the music of the first two chorale phrases (i.e., mm. 12–24 repeated as mm. 188–201, with minor modifications) followed by a full reprise of the ritornello (mm. 201–13 = mm. 1–12), both passages, as we saw, based on the circle of fifths. By such means the solid restoration of C acquires an emblematic character linked to God's control of human affairs.

Within the opening movement of Cantata 41 Bach strove to represent the quality of beginning/ending equivalence by several means: the ABA shape of the opening measures; the "weakening" and subsequent "strengthening" of C in the ritornello, in the music of the first two chorale phrases, and in the ritornello ending of the *Stollen*; the extension of that quality to the tonal relationship between the "prelude and fugue" section and the return of the first two chorale phrases; and, of course, the departure from and return to the style, tempo, and metrical qualities of the opening section. In the first recitative he associated the *Anfang/Ende* symbolism with the key of C. In the second recitative he brought in a striking circle-of-fifths progression to B♭ within a movement that again makes a symbolic return to C. Finally, in the chorale setting that brings back the opening measures of the cantata (minus the descending scales in the bass) to end the work, he modifies the harmonization of the first two chorale phrases on their final reappearance. In the *Stollen* the first phrase (= the fifth) closes on B♭ as before; and in the *Abgesang* phrases 12 and 14 close in D minor as usual. But now, for the first time in the work, the final phrases contain no B♭ at all; and Bach puts a walking, eighth-note bass beneath them, dropping out the pause that articulates the phrase division, so that they form a continuity (in addition, the bass sequence of mm. 41 and 42 spans the two phrases, eliminating any possibility of their separation). The security of the C that resounds in the trumpets for the final reiteration of the opening (= closing) measures of the work mirrors that at the beginning of the work before the entrance of B♭.

In Cantata 41 Bach created a multifaceted reflection on what the beginning/ending symbolism of the New Year meant. The work utilizes the commonest aspect of tonal design in Bach's cantatas – beginning and ending in the same key – to symbolize the idea of cyclic return, as if delineating the background against which the variegated events of the year would be measured. The keys of the individual movements – C major, G major, and A minor – represent a contiguous segment on the circle of keys, while circle-of-fifths patterns operate at the harmonic level, either to weaken or to reaffirm the tonic key; in particular, progressions in the subdominant direction tend to represent human weakness, especially in the sequence that leads to B♭ in the final recitative. The halting of the circular modulations in that recitative with the B♭ of the litany and the subsequent restoration of C link up conceptually with the points of return to C in the opening movement and their association with God's control of human affairs. Cantata 41 thus draws a fundamental part of its musical mirroring of representational-theological qualities from the eighteenth-century circle of keys and its first principle: the measuring of tonal relationships in terms of the circle of fifths, which, like the liturgical year itself, is a symbol of cyclic closure.

It is not necessary, of course, to believe that Bach thought of the design of *Jesu, nun sei gepreiset* in terms of a direct correspondence between the cyclic character of the year and the circle of fifths. His rhetorical play with the idea of beginning/ending equivalence and return simply spread throughout the work at a variety of levels. Nevertheless, that Bach viewed his work as a whole as a gift whose purpose was to pay tribute to the glory of God and to aid in the edification of his fellow man demanded that he think of each composition in all its uniqueness as existing within a larger framework from which it, like the individual within the community or the feast day within the year, drew much of its meaning and sustenance. In articulating the simple idea of a progression from beginning to end, followed by starting over again, Bach's cantata cycles, and many of the individual works that came at their turning points, mirrored the most fundamental pattern of life, one that served not only as a bond between the sacred and the secular, the past, present, and future, but as a model for how the scriptures were interpreted – as a progression from the literal and physically present to the spiritual, which involved doctrinal and faith-transformational qualities and extended ultimately to understanding according to the light of eternity (in the eschatological sense). Acceptance of the cyclic round of life and death was, and is, the most natural and inevitable of human responses to existence. For us, having lost much of the close experience of the liturgical year, coming to an understanding of how Bach's cantatas fit into such a perspective is one of our greatest challenges.

The Question of Parody in Bach's Cantata *Preise dein Glücke, gesegnetes Sachsen*, BWV 215

Stephen A. Crist

In the fall of 1734, Johann Sebastian Bach faced an unexpected challenge. Evidently without any advance notice, the elector of Saxony, Friedrich August II, his wife, Maria Josepha, and their twelve-year-old son, Friedrich Christian, had arrived in Leipzig on the afternoon of 2 October. It was announced that the royal family had made the trip to visit the city's renowned trade fair and that they would be staying until the sixth. The Leipzig university students then hastily planned a musical celebration for the first anniversary of August's election as king of Poland on 5 October.[1] Bach was enlisted to compose a serenade, and the work that he furnished was the congratulatory cantata *Preise dein Glücke, gesegnetes Sachsen*, BWV 215.

The presentation of Cantata 215 was one of the more colorful events of Bach's career, and far more is known about the historical circumstances surrounding this piece than most of his other vocal works. The elaborate torchlight procession around 9:00 P.M. through the streets of Leipzig by some six hundred students and the performance of the cantata beneath the balcony of the building where the royal family was staying are described vividly in an ac-

I am grateful to Professor Robert L. Marshall and Dr. Hans-Joachim Schulze for their comments on earlier versions of this essay. I also wish to thank the University Research Committee of Emory University for partial support of this project.

1. The student who probably spearheaded this effort – the eighteen-year-old Ludwig Siegfried, Count Vitzthum of Eckstädt – was himself a member of the nobility (see Hans-Joachim Schulze, *Studien zur Bach-Überlieferung im 18. Jahrhundert* [Leipzig: Edition Peters, 1984], 91). For additional information regarding the financing of this event, see Werner Neumann, ed., NBA I/37 (*Festmusiken für das Kurfürstlich-Sächsische Haus II*), KB, 67.

count by the town chronicler Salomon Riemer.[2] Reports also appeared shortly after the fact in newspapers in Hamburg and Dresden, in the Leipzig publication *Eröffnetes Cabinet Grosser Herren*, and three years later in a biography of the king by Johann Gottfried Mittag.[3] The title page of the libretto, seven hundred copies of which were printed by Johann Christian Langenheim, provides further documentation.[4] In addition, a manuscript copy of the text, in the hand of its author, the Leipzig schoolmaster Johann Christoph Clauder (1701–79), is bound with the autograph score.[5] We have as well Bach's handwritten receipt for fifty thalers, dated 14 October 1734, for his honorarium.[6] Finally, we even know the identities of some of the performers. From his application for a position at the Latin School in Plauen, we learn that Johann Christoph Hoffmann (who had been a student at the university in Leipzig) sang bass in the performance.[7] And Riemer reports the tragic news that the next day Bach's principal trumpeter Gottfried Reiche "suffered a stroke not far from his lodging in the *StadtPfeiffer Gässgen*, as he was on his way home, so that he collapsed and was brought dead into his house. And this is said to have occurred because on the previous day he had been greatly fatigued by playing in the royal music and had suffered severely from the smoke of the torches."[8]

While the external circumstances concerning the composition and perfor-

2. BDOK 2, no. 352; BR, 433–34.

3. BDOK 2, no. 353.

4. BDOK 2, no. 351; BR, 132. A facsimile of the entire print appears in Werner Neumann, ed., *Sämtliche von Johann Sebastian Bach vertonte Texte* (Leipzig: VEB Deutscher Verlag für Musik, 1974), 412–13.

5. See NBA I/37, KB, 60, 67; and Hans-Joachim Schulze, "Bemerkungen zu einigen Kantatentexten Johann Sebastian Bachs," *Bach-Jahrbuch* 46 (1959): 169–70.

6. BDOK 1, no. 119; BR, 133.

7. BDOK 2, no. 356.

8. BDOK 2, no. 352, commentary; trans. taken from Timothy A. Collins, "Gottfried Reiche: A More Complete Biography," *Journal of the International Trumpet Guild* 15, no. 3 (February 1991): 16. According to Arnold Schering ("Zu Gottfried Reiches Leben und Kunst," *Bach-Jahrbuch* 15 [1918]: 139–40), Reiche's stroke was more likely precipitated by smoke inhalation than by the trumpet part itself, which was not especially difficult. For evidence that members of the collegia musica regularly participated in performances of Bach's vocal music, including Cantata 215, see Don L. Smithers, "Bach, Reiche and the Leipzig Collegia Musica," *Historic Brass Society Journal* 2 (1990): 1–51, esp. 38–40.

mance of Cantata 215 are richly documented, its "internal" history is not entirely clear. To judge from the ample documentation, the work's gestation
period was no longer than three days – from about the time the king and queen
arrived to the time of the performance – which has led to the widespread assumption that Bach based much of it on previously composed music.[9] There
has never been any doubt that the recitatives (mvts. 2, 4, 6, and 8) were newly
composed; this can be readily inferred from the noncalligraphic script and the
relatively large number of corrections in the autograph score.[10] But there has
been no unanimity about the rest of the piece.

Arnold Schering believed (for reasons unstated) that the elaborate opening
double chorus demanded new music but that preexistent material could have
been used for the arias and the final chorus.[11] W. Gillies Whittaker speculated,
on the other hand (also for reasons unstated), that the opening chorus could
have been derived from an earlier composition, that the tenor aria was also
borrowed, and – following Charles Sanford Terry's lead – that the soprano aria
was based on a lost instrumental work, possibly a movement of a flute sonata.[12]

Werner Neumann's ideas about the origins of the individual movements are
informed by the appearance of the autograph score. In Neumann's words, "As
always, the character of the handwriting reflects the structure of the movement in that, as a rule, reversions back to preceding parts of a movement are
paralleled by a lack of corrections and smoothness of script."[13] On this basis,

9. See, e.g., Philipp Spitta, *Johann Sebastian Bach*, 2 vols. (Leipzig: Breitkopf & Härtel, 1873–
80; reprint, Wiesbaden: Breitkopf & Härtel, 1979), 2:461–62; and Alfred Dürr, *Die Kantaten von Johann Sebastian Bach*, 2 vols. (Kassel: Bärenreiter; Munich: Deutscher Taschenbuch
Verlag, 1971), 2:670.

10. SBB MUS. MS BACH P 139. I am grateful to Dr. Wolfgang Goldhan, director of the Music
Division of the former Deutsche Staatsbibliothek, Berlin (now Staatsbibliothek zu Berlin-
Preussischer Kulturbesitz), for allowing me to examine the original manuscripts of Cantata 215.

11. Arnold Schering, *Johann Sebastian Bach und das Musikleben Leipzigs im 18. Jahrhundert*
(Leipzig: Fr. Kistner & C. F. W. Siegel, 1941), 143–44.

12. W. Gillies Whittaker, *The Cantatas of Johann Sebastian Bach: Sacred and Secular*, 2 vols.
(London: Oxford University Press, 1959), 2:666–69.

13. NBA I/37, KB, 35 (unless otherwise noted, all translations are my own). Alfred Dürr has recently argued that "drafts with few corrections [*korrekturenarme Niederschriften*] from Bach's
later years do not necessarily indicate reuse of earlier compositions, but also … could have been
composed with the help of sketches" (see "Schriftcharakter und Werkchronologie bei Johann

he argues convincingly that the first half of the opening chorus was modeled on an older work. A glance at the autograph score makes this clear: the A section is a fair copy and relatively free of corrections, while the B section is in Bach's "composing" hand and is quite heavily corrected. Neumann suggests that the music of the A section was borrowed from the first movement of *Es lebe der König, der Vater im Lande*, a cantata (BWV ANH.11) that Bach had composed two years earlier (3 August 1732) for the name day of August the Strong. (The same music was later reincarnated as the Osanna of the B Minor Mass.)[14] Using similar evidence, Neumann argues – contrary to the views of Schering, Terry, and Whittaker – that the soprano aria was newly composed but that the tenor and bass arias could be parodies.[15]

More recently, Klaus Häfner has resurrected Schering's view that the three arias and the concluding chorus are all parodies.[16] Häfner suggests specific models for these movements and even offers reconstructions of what he believes might have been their original versions.

Although it is tempting to address Häfner's lengthy arguments point by point, Hans-Joachim Schulze's blistering review makes this unnecessary.[17] Instead, I will show that, contrary to the conclusions of Häfner and others, Bach appears to have used relatively little material from earlier works in composing Cantata 215. I will then broaden the scope of the inquiry to consider how it was possible for Bach to compose such a large-scale work in an extraordinarily short period of time. Finally, I will offer some thoughts on the implications of these observations for our view of Bach's genius.

* * *

Sebastian Bach," in *Bericht über die Wissenschaftliche Konferenz zum V. Internationalen Bachfest der DDR in Verbindung mit dem 60. Bachfest der Neuen Bachgesellschaft*, ed. Winfried Hoffmann and Armin Schneiderheinze [Leipzig: VEB Deutscher Verlag für Musik, 1988], 288). In the case of Cantata 215, however, the use of sketches is out of the question, given the short period of time within which it was prepared.

14. NBA I/37, KB, 70–73.

15. Ibid., 69, 73–74. Neumann ventures no opinion about the final chorus.

16. Klaus Häfner, *Aspekte des Parodieverfahrens bei Johann Sebastian Bach* (Laaber: Laaber-Verlag, 1987), 213–39.

17. *Bach-Jahrbuch* 76 (1990): 92–94.

It is well known that the soprano aria "Durch die von Eifer entflammeten Waffen," BWV 215/7, served as the model for a parody; in fact, it is more familiar in its later guise as a bass aria. Just a few months after the composition of Cantata 215, the music for this movement was incorporated into Part 5 of the Christmas Oratorio (for the Sunday after New Year's Day, 2 January 1735) with the text "Erleucht auch meine finstre Sinnen" (BWV 248/47). Bach changed not only the text and the voice type but several other fundamental aspects as well: the aria was transposed from B minor to F♯ minor; a normal continuo line was substituted for the unusual *bassetto* (a high bass line), played by the violins and viola ("Violetta") in the earlier version; and even the musical substance was revised, particularly in the B section.

Although Häfner and others believe that the version of this aria in Cantata 215 is also a parody, this notion is not at all supported by philological evidence. We are exceptionally well informed about Bach's parody procedures in the last quarter of 1734 through the autograph score of the Christmas Oratorio,[18] a work that contains no fewer than eight arias based on known models. In the parodies (mvts. 4, 8, 15, 19, 29, 39, 41, and 47) the script is calligraphic, and there are relatively few corrections. Most of the corrections that do exist are aimed merely at rectifying copying errors or improving the continuo line; the majority of the remaining corrections are concentrated in the vocal lines and appear to be connected with retexting.

The appearance of the autograph score of the soprano aria in Cantata 215 contrasts sharply with the parodies in the Christmas Oratorio and provides clear testimony that this is a composing score rather than a copy (see pl. 1). The general character of the handwriting is hasty: the notes are usually slanted instead of perpendicular to the staves, and more often than not the downward stems are set to the right rather than to the left of the note heads. Moreover, formative corrections are found in all three lines, and many of them belong to the categories of corrective gestures that appear quite commonly in composing scores but rarely in copies. There are, in addition, two other features of the autograph that virtually prove that this aria was newly composed.

First of all, at the bottom of the first page (fol. 16r) there is a lengthy con-

18. SBB MUS. MS BACH P 32; facsimile reproduction with a commentary, ed. Alfred Dürr (Kassel: Bärenreiter, 1960).

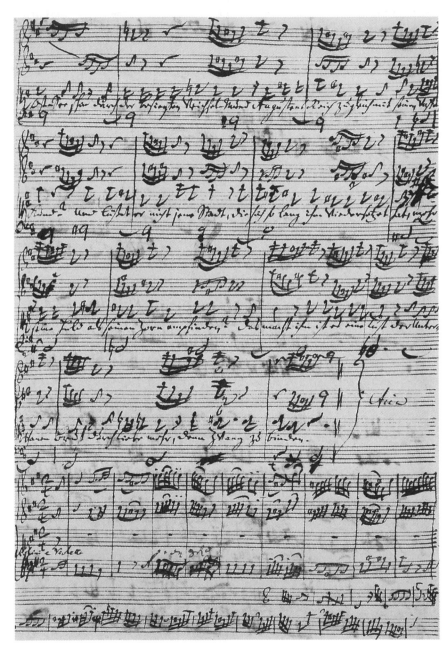

141

tinuation sketch for the second half of the ritornello. As Robert Marshall has described Bach's continuation sketches:

> [They] are found on recto pages in the autograph scores and record the continuation of the music that was to be written on the following verso once the ink had dried. One can consider such sketches – which are usually found on the bottom of the page on any spare staff or staves – to be essentially extended custodes. ... Such sketches ... were necessary only when the page turn interrupted the free invention of new musical material. Therefore, they do not appear in recitatives or in simple four-part chorales ... where the melodic material, rhythm, and texture were predetermined. ... But in the freer forms, the choruses and arias, there are also relatively few continuation sketches. If a page turn occurred while Bach was writing out a major repetition of an earlier passage ... continuation sketches were rarely necessary, for such a passage normally involved literal copying or perhaps mechanical transposition of "preexistent," i.e., earlier, material.[19]

Since the making of a parody entailed "literal copying" or "mechanical transposition of ... earlier material," it stands to reason that continuation sketches would not normally be found in parodies – and, conversely, that movements containing continuation sketches are not parodies.[20]

Comparison of the sketch with the final version of the ritornello (see ex.1) reveals several significant aspects about the genesis of this melody and corroborates the view that the autograph score represents the earliest written stage in the compositional history of this movement. The first difference concerns the first note of m.12, the cadential pitch of the first phrase. In the sketch, the pitch is d', the lowest note on the Baroque flute. This note completes a step progression downward from f♯'. But it also is preceded and followed by large leaps, which would have been difficult to play. In the final version, the cadential pitch is an octave higher. The revised form preserves the stepwise approach to the cadence; it is merely shifted to the upper octave. By altering just one note, Bach eliminated the awkwardness of the leaps and avoided using a weak low note at the end of the phrase.

19. Robert Lewis Marshall, *The Compositional Process of J. S. Bach: A Study of the Autograph Scores of the Vocal Works*, 2 vols. (Princeton, N.J.: Princeton University Press, 1972), 1:141–43.

20. At fourteen measures, the sketch in BWV 215/7 is by far the longest of the 110 continuation sketches in the autograph scores of Bach's vocal works, most of which are no longer than a measure or two.

EX.1. BWV 215/7, mm.10–23, flute (after Marshall
The Compositional Process, vol.2, no.147): *a*, sketch (P 139, fol.16r);
b, final version (P 139, fol.16v)

The second spot where the final reading diverges from the sketch also involves a small change with significant implications. In the sketch, the beginning of the second phrase is harmonically stagnant: mm.13–15 merely prolong the D-major harmony (III) that had been the goal of the first phrase. In the final version, the d″ in m.14 is changed to d♯″. This introduces a new element into the harmony: D♯ is the third of a chord (B–D♯–F♯–A) that functions in mm.14–19 as V^7 of E minor (iv). The inflection of D♮ to D♯ leads away from the mediant toward the subdominant, thereby relieving the harmonic inactivity of the first version.

This alteration, in turn, prompted a change of pitch from a′ to b′ for the first three notes of m.15. Having outlined in descending sequence the top three pitches of the secondary dominant, it was only natural for Bach to complete the sequence with the root of the chord, rather than duplicating the seventh at the lower octave. The change of pitch also eliminated the awkward tritone leap from a′ to d♯″ in mm.15–16 of the sketch and effected a much smoother modulation from D major to E minor.

Originally, the beginning of the second phrase suffered from thematic stasis, too: indeed, in the sketch, mm. 14 and 15 are virtually identical to mm. 12 and 13. By recasting m. 15, Bach eliminated the circularity. More important, however, in the final version the sequence of Lombard figures is a beat longer than in the sketch. This revision, together with a change of the first beat of m. 18 from ♫ ♩ to the Lombard rhythm, helps integrate this distinctive rhythmic figure more fully into the fabric of the melody.

These details show that several basic features of the opening ritornello were not yet fully worked out when Bach penned the sketch, thus demonstrating that BWV 215/7 was the first draft of a new composition rather than a reworking of an older one.

A second clue that the soprano aria was newly composed concerns an important change in its texture. The layout of the autograph score indicates that Bach originally planned for it to have two independent flute parts and a basic four-part texture (flutes 1 and 2, soprano, and *bassetto*): the first five systems have four staves each; the upper two staves of the first system share the same flute theme; and, in the remaining four systems, the second staff is blank (save cue notes in mm. 10 and 19).[21] By the time he began the sixth system, Bach had abandoned this plan in favor of unison writing for the flutes and three-part texture. What this means is that Bach did not settle on the present texture of the movement until he had composed the entire ritornello and over half the A section. Such revisions are occasionally found in Bach's composing scores. But it is impossible to reconcile such evidence with the notion that this aria is a parody.

In this connection, it is worth mentioning that the soprano aria later experienced a change of instrumentation that is not reflected at all in the autograph score. The addition of an oboe d'amore to double the soprano line is indicated only in the original performing parts.[22] The *tacet* marking in the oboe 1 part was amended, and to this part was added an extra leaf in Bach's hand.[23] I suspect that both revisions of the scoring – the decision to lead the flutes in unison

---

21. Marshall, *The Compositional Process*, 1:221–22. The clef on the bottom staff of the first system (fol. 16r) was corrected from bass to alto, suggesting that Bach's decision to use a *bassetto* instead of a normal basso continuo was an afterthought. This does not exclude the possibility, however, that Bach inadvertently drew the bass clef for the bottom staff here, just out of habit (cf. similar corrections in systems 7 [fol. 16v] and 15 [fol. 17r]).

22. SBB MUS. MS BACH ST 77.

23. NBA I/37, KB, 51–52, 58.

rather than independently and the doubling of the soprano line by the oboe d'amore – were connected with the location of the first performance. Without the doubling, the flutes and (boy) soprano might have been barely audible in the open air beneath the king's balcony – the excellent acoustics of the Leipzig market square notwithstanding.[24]

It was mentioned earlier that various corrections and other notational details in the autograph of BWV 215/7 support the view that it is a composing score. This evidence accumulates from many different quarters:

1. From the spacing of the notes and the different sizes of the note heads in mm. 3, 4, and 8 (as well as the position of the second sharp in m. 8), it is evident that the rhythm of the ritornello was originally simpler and that it was subsequently embellished with additional sixteenth and thirty-second notes (see ex. 2).[25] Corrections of this type are much more likely to be found in composing scores than in parodies.

2. The rhythmic figure that first occurs in m. 3 as ♩ ♪♪♪ ♩ ♩ is inconsistently notated. It appears as ♩ ♪♪♪ ♩ ♩ in mm. 41 and 53, then reverts back to the earlier form in m. 87. Similarly, the rhythm of a brief descending scalar passage that occurs twice in close proximity in each of three statements of the ritornello is not uniform. In the continuation sketch, the first beats of mm. 18 and 20 are notated as ♫ ♩. But, when Bach copied it onto the next page, he changed the rhythm of the first figure to ♫ ♩·. The incongruous coupling of the plain and the dotted forms is maintained in mm. 66 and 68, while in mm. 109 and 111 both members have the dotted form (apparently because of the sequential extension of the passage). Of particular interest is the standardization of these rhythms (with only one exception) in the Christmas Oratorio version (BWV 248/47) to ♩ ♪♪♪ ♩ ♩ in the first set of passages and ♫ ♩· in the second.[26] The rhythmic inconsistencies, which were smoothed out in the par-

24. Arnold Schering mentions that the rapt attention of the crowd as well as the acoustics would have contributed to the audibility of the performance (see *Johann Sebastian Bachs Leipziger Kirchenmusik* [1936], 2d rev. ed. [Leipzig: Breitkopf & Härtel, 1954; reprint, Wiesbaden: Breitkopf & Härtel, 1968], 119).

25. The parallel passages later in the movement are inconsistent. The original reading is retained in the vocal line (mm. 28, 32, 34) and in the flute part at mm. 54 and 56, while the embellished version appears in the flute at mm. 42 and 92 (uncorrected) and 88 (corrected from eighth notes).

26. Curiously, the ♩ ♪♪♪ ♩ ♩ rhythm crept back into m. 87 of BWV 248/47. This can be seen in the facsimile edition of the Christmas Oratorio but not in the NBA, where the rhythm is

a)

b)

ody, provide further evidence that the soprano aria was composed in extreme haste and that it represents the earliest form of the movement.

3. In several spots in the flute part where portions of the ritornello are quoted, the material preceding the quotation was added later. For instance, Marshall has shown that m.38 originally contained the eighth-note anacrusis for the ritornello quotation and that the sixteenth-note passage leading up to it was entered afterward.[27] Similarly, the correction of the last note of m.50 from a separate note to a member of a beamed pair of notes (as well as the calligraphic script in mm.51–54) reveals a similar order of events. And, from the unusual shape of the beam in the second half of m.103, it is clear that the first four notes were appended to the second phrase of the ritornello, presumably to increase the rhythmic thrust of the passage. The fact that the notation of the autograph score did not proceed in a wholly linear fashion testifies that BWV 215/7 was not based on preexistent material.

4. Extreme crowding, such as is found in m.84 of the *bassetto* (fol.17r, system 3), is unlikely to have occurred if the movement was a parody. Here the

normalized (see Walter Blankenburg and Alfred Dürr, eds., NBA II/6 [*Weihnachts-Oratorium*], KB, 305).

27. Marshall, *The Compositional Process*, 1:217.

Table 1. The Form of BWV 215/9

mm. 1–16	=A	I
mm. 1–4	= a (orchestra)	
mm. 5–8	= a (orchestra and choir)	
mm. 9–12	= b (orchestra)	
mm. 13–16	= b (orchestra and choir)	
mm. 17–24	= B (orchestra and choir) → vi	
mm. 25–40	= A	I
mm. 41–48	= C (orchestra and choir) → iii	
mm. 49–64	= A	I

voice part – a quarter note followed by a quarter rest – was obviously entered first and fit quite comfortably in the small amount of space left at the end of the system. But, when Bach subsequently entered the *bassetto*, he had to write the eight sixteenth notes so close together that they were almost illegible and had to be clarified with tablature letters. If he were copying from an exemplar, he would have seen that the *bassetto* part would exceed the available space and entered the entire measure or part of it at the beginning of the next system.

5. The high density of formative corrections in the soprano line toward the end of the B section (mm. 105–13) – many of which are illegible – would be highly unusual in a parody but is typical of composing scores.

The combined testimony of these details and others – as well as the evidence adduced earlier – leaves no doubt that the soprano aria was newly composed.

* * *

Let us turn now to the final movement of the cantata, the chorus "Stifter der Reiche, Beherrscher der Kronen," BWV 215/9. Its A section consists of two four-measure phrases, each of which is presented first by the orchestra alone, then by the orchestra and choir together (see table 1). Häfner observes that in the choral statements (mm. 5–8, 13–16, etc.) the melody previously played by the treble instruments is sung by the altos instead of the sopranos (see ex. 3). He feels that this creates "an unsatisfactory aural impression" resulting from the transposition of a preexistent model from some other key into D major.[28]

28. Häfner, *Aspekte des Parodieverfahrens*, 235–36.

The question of whether it sounds good for the altos to sing this melody is, of course, open to disagreement. I do not find this aspect of the movement to be problematic, especially since the melody is doubled by trumpet 1, both flutes, oboe 1, and violin 1. At any rate, the fact that the treble instruments and the sopranos do not have the same melody is insufficient evidence that BWV 215/9 is a parody – especially in view of the appearance of the autograph score (see pl. 2). From the first page alone, one can see that the manuscript contains a large number of formative corrections. Moreover, the corrective activity is not concentrated in the vocal lines – as is usually true of parodies – but extends to the instrumental parts as well.

Although many of the corrections provide evidence that this movement was newly composed, I shall focus on just one. At the beginning, the upper number of the meter signature in the staves for violins 1 and 2 is corrected from "9" to "6" (see pl. 2, staves 9 and 10).[29] According to Bach's normal modus

29. This correction is missing from the list in NBA I/37, KB, 45.

PL. 2. Autograph MS of the chorus "Stifter der Reiche, Beherrscher der Kronen,"
BWV 215/9, mm. 1–7 (Staatsbibliothek zu Berlin–Preussischer Kulturbesitz,
Musikabteilung, MUS. MS BACH P 139, fol. 19r)

operandi, these two lines would have been the first to be entered. Therefore this revision represents a fundamental shift in the metrical conception of the chorus from $\frac{9}{8}$ to $\frac{6}{8}$. This occurred at a very early stage of composition, before the meter signatures for the other instruments were entered. Of course, the dactylic meter of the text suggested the use of compound meter for the musical setting. As ex. 4 shows, the choice of $\frac{6}{8}$ instead of $\frac{9}{8}$ entailed the elimination

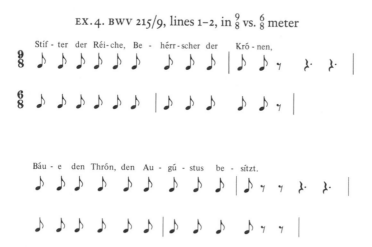

EX. 4. BWV 215/9, lines 1–2, in $\frac{9}{8}$ vs. $\frac{6}{8}$ meter

of a lengthy caesura between lines 1 and 2 of the text. If the autograph were a copy, it certainly would not contain a correction involving a basic alteration of the movement's metrical structure. On the other hand, such corrections are not uncommon in Bach's composing scores.[30]

It is worth noting also that the manuscript lacks the type of correction common in movements involving the transposition of a preexistent model – such as the arias "Schlafe, mein Liebster, geniesse der Ruh" (BWV 248/19) and "Ich will nur dir zu Ehren leben" (BWV 248/41) from the Christmas Oratorio. The former was transposed down a third from B♭ to G major; accordingly, the autograph contains a number of spots where Bach accidentally followed the readings of the model and entered a note or a group of notes a third too high.[31] The latter movement was shifted down a second from E to D minor;

---

30. See Marshall, *The Compositional Process*, 1:120–25.

31. See NBA II/6, KB, 36–37. This movement is a parody of Pleasure's aria "Schlafe, mein Liebster, und pflege der Ruh" (BWV 213/3) from the "Hercules" Cantata, composed for the eleventh birthday of the electoral prince, Friedrich Christian, on 5 September 1733.

accordingly, there are several corrections in which the original reading was a step too high.[32] If the concluding chorus of Cantata 215 were based on a movement in A major, as Häfner suggests,[33] why are there no passages in which a reading was originally entered a fourth too low?

The composition of this movement was surely an easy task for Bach. Its form is highly repetitive: not only does the choir join the orchestra in repeating each of the four-measure phrases in the A section, but rondeau form is used (see table 1 above). This means that only twenty-four of the chorus's sixty-four measures represent new composition; through the judicious use of repetition, Bach managed to stretch a small amount of music into a complete movement. Moreover, the eight-part, double-chorus texture of the opening chorus is here telescoped into four parts, and elaborate polyphony is replaced by a prevailingly homophonic texture. It would undoubtedly have been as much trouble for Bach to transpose an older piece as to compose a relatively simple movement such as this.[34]

* * *

The compositional history of the bass aria "Rase nur, verwegner Schwarm," BWV 215/5, has long been a riddle. On the one hand, the calligraphic script and the paucity of corrections on the first three pages (fols.14r–15r) raise the suspicion that it is a parody – especially considering the extreme time pressure under which this manuscript was penned. On the other hand, "several crucial changes, particularly a concentration of corrections at the close of the B section and the presence of a sketch," led Marshall to conclude that "the movement is a composing score."[35] The apparent contradiction vanishes, however, with the possibility that the second vocal period of the B section (mm.133–61) was newly composed and that the rest of the movement is based on an un-

32. See NBA II/6, KB, 59. The model for this movement is Virtue's aria "Auf meinen Flügeln sollst du schweben" (BWV 213/7), also from the "Hercules" Cantata (see n.31 above).

33. Häfner, *Aspekte des Parodieverfahrens*, 236–39.

34. Compare the statement by Hans-Joachim Schulze ("The Parody Process in Bach's Music: An Old Problem Reconsidered," *Bach: The Journal of the Riemenschneider Bach Institute* 20, no.1 [Spring 1989]: 18) that "sometimes the expenditure of effort for a reworking [was] greater than that for a new composition."

35. Marshall, *The Compositional Process*, 1:20.

known model. This view is supported by the contrasting appearance of fols. 15r and 15v (see pl. 3). The former (like fols. 14r and 14v) is notated in Bach's calligraphic hand and contains only a few corrections. The latter is more heavily corrected and is in Bach's "composing" script: the note heads are smaller, the stems slanted, and the downward stems set to the right of the note heads. Furthermore, the brief continuation sketch – normally an unmistakable sign of new composition (see above) – appears at the bottom of fol. 15r (after m. 133), precisely at the point where the B² section begins. And the crowding of the string parts – which often extend over the bar lines – on fol. 15v (a clear indication that the vocal line was entered first) contrasts sharply with the rest of the movement, where the bar lines were drawn so that the groups of sixteenth notes fit comfortably in the allotted space. Finally, the fact that a number of corrections in the vocal line in earlier parts of the movement concern details of text declamation (e.g., mm. 19, 30-31, 43)[36] increases the likelihood that these sections, at least, are based on older material.

Two larger implications follow from these observations. First, if the end of the B section represents new composition, the unusual *dal segno* form[37] was probably conceived specifically for BWV 215/5 and was not present in the model. Second, from the shorthand notation of the oboe part in mm. 1-7,[38] it seems likely as well that the model did not include the oboe and that Bach did not decide to add it until sometime after he wrote out the first system – perhaps not until after he had notated the entire movement.

There would seem to be little doubt that the last remaining movement to be discussed, the tenor aria "Freilich trotzt Augustus' Name," BWV 215/3, is a parody. As Marshall notes, "The opening ritornello is almost flawless, and the occasional revisions are mostly restricted to the inner parts and to details of declamation and beaming in the tenor part."[39] Yet at the end of the A section is a brief continuation sketch, which would normally indicate that the movement was newly composed. A closer look at the sketch (see pl. 4), though, reveals

36. See NBA I/37, KB, 41. The correction of m. 43 from ♫ ♪ ♪ to ♫♫ ♪ is not noted.

37. The second period of the B section is elided with A¹, and the ritornello that normally appears between the end of B and the beginning of A is omitted.

38. The oboe part is indicated on the staff for violin 1 by extra note stems and the abbreviation *Hautb.* (see NBA I/37, KB, 64).

39. Marshall, *The Compositional Process*, 1:19.

154

155

that it defies the usual raison d'être for continuation sketches; oddly enough, it apparently was a by-product of the parody process. The primary purpose of the sketch was not to preserve pitches at this important cadential point but rather to remind Bach of the way the new text was to be underlaid to the pre-existent melody.

* * *

To compose, copy the performing parts of, and rehearse such a large-scale work as Cantata 215 in three days is an extraordinary feat of musical prowess.[40] Indeed, the point of departure for those who hold that the piece consists largely of parodies is the unspoken assumption that it would otherwise have been humanly impossible to prepare it on such short notice. Just how was Bach able to accomplish this?

To begin with, there is reason to believe that Cantata 215 was performed with a minimum of rehearsal. Our main clue is the unusually large number of uncorrected errors in the performing parts. According to the Neue Bach-Ausgabe, there are about one hundred incorrect pitches in the instrumental parts alone. Occasionally, entire measures were left out. There is even a four-measure passage at the end of the final chorus where the wrong lines of the text were entered in five of the eight vocal parts.[41]

In preparing the performing parts, Bach was assisted by a total of nine copyists[42] – roughly three times the number that he normally had for his Leipzig

40. The feat becomes all the more extraordinary considering that the king and queen arrived during the weekend (on a Saturday afternoon), which was presumably the most hectic time of the week for a church musician with such a wide range of duties as Bach. Assuming that on Saturday most of Bach's time was devoted to finalizing music for Sunday morning worship, and assuming that he did indeed perform his duties on the following Sunday morning, he would have had little more than two days – from Sunday afternoon to Tuesday afternoon – to complete the project.

41. NBA I/37, KB, 59, 68.

42. NBA I/37, KB, 55–58. The principal scribe of the vocal parts ("Hauptkopist E" in Alfred Dürr, *Zur Chronologie der Leipziger Vokalwerke J. S. Bachs*, 2d ed. [Kassel: Bärenreiter, 1976]) was probably Joh. Gottl. Haupt (see NBA I/37, KB, 57, n.8; and NBA II/6, KB, 124, n.19). The principal scribe of the instrumental parts ("Hauptkopist F") was the twenty-one-year-old Johann Ludwig Dietel (see Andreas Glöckner, "Neuerkenntnisse zu Johann Sebastian Bachs Aufführungskalender zwischen 1729 und 1735," *Bach-Jahrbuch* 67 [1981]: 57–69). Two other copyists were the seventeen-year-old Rudolph Straube ("Hauptkopist G"; see Schulze, *Bach-*

church cantatas. Since the score consisted of a series of eleven sheets of paper, the copying work could have begun as soon as Bach had filled all four pages of a folded sheet. And, by sharing the individual sheets of the score, it was possible for several copyists to work at once.

In order to understand how Bach was able to compose Cantata 215 so quickly, however, we must consider a constellation of other factors. First of all, he is known to have completed similar tasks in brief periods of time. For instance, the first cantata that Bach composed after arriving in Leipzig in May 1723, *Die Himmel erzählen die Ehre Gottes*, BWV 76, was evidently created very rapidly, as can be seen from the extremely high density of corrections and other signs of haste in the autograph score. As I have argued elsewhere, this work (which is comparable in length to Cantata 215) may have been composed in "as few as three days during a particularly busy week."[43] Likewise, the cantata *Tönet, ihr Pauken! Erschallet, Trompeten!* BWV 214, apparently was finished at the last minute. This work was composed for the birthday of the electoress, Maria Josepha, just ten months before Cantata 215. Since the autograph is dated 7 December 1733 and the first performance was on the eighth, the copying of the parts and any rehearsing that may have taken place must have been packed into a single day.[44]

Consider also the incredible pace of production during Bach's first few years in Leipzig. As Schulze has written, "Bach's productivity in his second year in the job [1724–25] is almost unbelievable; in addition to the forty known chorale cantatas, he wrote the Sanctus of the later B-minor Mass, a town council cantata, along with compositions for out-of-town commissions and for guest performances. … Never again did he venture such a compositional tour de force, and never again did he saddle himself with such a burden. Possibly, a creative crisis resulting from fatigue caused the early demise of the chorale cantata cycle and prevented its completion."[45] In this light, the creation of Cantata 215 was

---

Überlieferung, 120) and Friedrich Christian Samuel Mohrheim ("Anonymous Vg"; see NBA II/6, KB, 124). The identities of the other scribes are unknown.

43. Stephen A. Crist, "Bach's Début at Leipzig: Observations on the Genesis of Cantatas 75 and 76," *Early Music* 13 (1985):215.

44. See Werner Neumann, ed., NBA I/36 (*Festmusiken für das Kurfürstlich-Sächsische Haus I*), KB, 107.

45. Schulze, "Parody Process," 18–19.

Table 2. Bach's Congratulatory Cantatas for
the Saxon Royal Family, 1733–34

3 August 1733, name day of elector, Friedrich August II: "Frohes Volk, vergnügte Sachsen," BWV ANH.12

5 September, birthday of electoral prince, Friedrich Christian: "Lasst uns sorgen, lasst uns wachen," BWV 213 ("Hercules" Cantata)

8 December, birthday of electoress, Maria Josepha: "Tönet, ihr Pauken! Erschallet, Trompeten," BWV 214

19 February 1734, coronation of Friedrich August II as king of Poland: "Blast Lärmen, ihr Feinde! verstärket die Macht," BWV 205a

5 October, first anniversary of the election of Friedrich August II as king of Poland: "Preise dein Glücke, gesegnetes Sachsen," BWV 215

surely much less taxing for Bach than what he had done in the 1720s. After all, it is easier to endure an isolated creative burst – no matter how intense – than a relentless succession of such moments over a period of years.

In addition, Bach must have been motivated to complete the cantata so that he could perform it in the presence of the king and queen. A little over a year earlier (27 July 1733), after the death of August the Strong, Bach had sent to the new elector, Friedrich August II, a *Missa* that later became the Kyrie and Gloria of the B Minor Mass; this was accompanied by a letter requesting that he be granted a court title.[46] Immediately thereafter, he began a series of congratulatory cantatas clearly intended to support his application (see table 2). A cantata for the name day of the elector (3 August 1733) was followed by works for the birthday of the eleven-year-old heir on 5 September, the birthday of the electoress on 8 December, and the coronation of the elector as king of Poland on 19 February of the next year. Although the royal family had surely received news of these performances from their home in Dresden, their visit to Leipzig provided the occasion to hear some of Bach's music at firsthand. Bach was, no doubt, anxious to make the most of this opportunity, in hopes that a court title might soon be conferred.[47]

Finally, as we have seen, Bach did incorporate some earlier material into

46. BDOK 1, no. 27; BR, 128–29.

47. Dürr, *Kantaten*, 2:661.

Cantata 215. Therefore, his true compositional work (i.e., new composition, as opposed to parody) included just the B section of the opening chorus (fifty-six measures), four recitatives,[48] the soprano aria, about thirty measures of the bass aria, and a simple concluding chorus.[49] Doubtless his most challenging

48. Some of the most interesting and suggestive corrections are found in the recitatives. For instance, the revision of the instrumentation in the heading for the tenor recitative "Wie können wir, grossmächtigster August," BWV 215/2, from *Travers.* to *Hautb. accomp.* (see Marshall, *The Compositional Process*, 1:244) indicates that Bach planned to use one or two flutes before settling on the present scoring with a pair of oboes. Similarly, a series of corrections in the vocal and continuo lines of the soprano recitative "Ja, ja! Gott ist uns noch mit seiner Hülfe nah," BWV 215/6, reveals that Bach reworked the ending – visible in pl.1, fol.16r, end of system 4 – so that the cadence would occur in B minor (the key of the following aria) instead of D major (see ibid., 1:94, 98). Two other revisions, not noted by Marshall, in the recitative "Lass doch, o teurer Landesvater, zu," BWV 215/8 (for tenor, bass, soprano, and the full instrumental ensemble), show Bach grappling with details of the relationship between text and music. Two brief trumpet fanfares, in mm.14 and 17, were crossed out (see NBA I/37, KB, 44, 65), apparently because they contradicted the sense of the word *gedämpfet* (muted, subdued). This seems to have occurred fairly late in the compositional process (perhaps at a rehearsal) since these passages were copied into the performing parts and deleted there, too. Likewise, the correction of notes 4–6 of the bass part in m.15 from c′–d♯–d♯ to a–d♯′–d♯′ (see NBA I/37, KB, 44) evidently was made to bring the melodic line into conformity with the upward direction implied by the word *Norden* (north).

49. If one considers the proportion of old and new music solely from the perspective of the number of measures filled in the autograph score (see below), it turns out that about 60 percent of Cantata 215 was based on earlier material and 40 percent was newly composed:

Movement 1 (chorus)
    Old: 20 staves × 181 measures = 3,620 score measures
    New: 20 staves × 56 measures = 1,120 score measures
Movement 2 (recitative)
    New: 4 staves × 16 measures = 64 score measures
Movement 3 (aria)
    Old: 5 staves × 98 measures = 490 score measures
Movement 4 (recitative)
    New: 2 staves × 28 measures = 56 score measures
Movement 5 (aria)
    Old: 5 staves × 132 measures = 660 score measures
    New: 5 staves × 29 measures = 145 score measures
Movement 6 (recitative)
    New: 4 staves × 18 measures = 72 score measures

assignment was the completion of the opening chorus, with its complex poly-phonic texture. But he faced this task early on, when his energy was high. As was mentioned earlier, the composition of the final chorus was surely unprob-lematic. And, since Bach had composed hundreds of recitatives and arias in the past, the creation and adaptation of a few more could not have cost him more than a day's work.

The ability to compose new music quickly and on demand was an essential qualification of composers in the eighteenth century. Who has not marveled at the enormous quantity of music created by Telemann, or the extraordinary number of concertos composed by Vivaldi, or the rapidity with which Han-del's oratorios are said to have been written? Although we have known for nearly forty years that Bach wrote the majority of his cantatas at the rate of one per week, his amazing facility as a composer has not yet fully penetrated our picture of his genius. Perhaps the consistently high quality of his music has misled us into thinking that it could not have been composed quickly. But an examination of the evidence surrounding the composition of Cantata 215 has demonstrated that Bach was able to create an enduring work of art almost as quickly as he could move his pen.

Movement 7 (aria)

   New: 3 staves × 120 measures = 360 score measures

Movement 8 (recitative)

   New: 5 staves × 9 measures = 45 score measures

   8 staves × 14 measures = 112 score measures

   6 staves × 4 measures = 24 score measures

   4 staves × 14 measures = 56 score measures

Movement 9 (chorus)

   New: 16 staves × 48 measures = 768 score measures

Total number of score measures in BWV 215 = 7,592

Number of score measures based on earlier material = 4,770 (63 percent)

Number of newly composed score measures = 2,822 (37 percent)

My thanks to Robert Marshall for suggesting this approach to the question.

The Perfectability of J. S. Bach, or Did Bach Compose the Fugue on a Theme by Legrenzi, BWV 574a?

James A. Brokaw II

They have all a lively faith in the perfectability of man ... and they admit that what appears to them today to be good, may be superseded by something better tomorrow. – Alexis de Tocqueville, *Democracy in America*

Arrangement, as a manner of perpetuating musical discourse, has lost much of its former validity for us. Only a few generations ago, the now-scorned arrangements of Bach by Stokowski and Busoni were regarded as effective and even valuable amplifications of Bach's little-known work, effective because they brought out the essential though subtle beauties of their objects, valuable because, for the uninitiated, they transcended the esoteric and revealed the original. If this seems distant from de Tocqueville's phrase quoted above, there was another feature of such arrangements: they transformed their objects in the course of a process whose aim was to reveal the objects' hidden perfection. In a very real sense, the intent to reveal perfection, to clarify, could not be separated from the intent to perfect, to transform. Perhaps it is in part a loss of idealism that causes us to prefer the objects in their "authentic" state to the sometimes gaudy raiments of a modern arrangement. The point of this essay is to explore an arrangement that is remarkable not only for its early date (before 1792) but for its very pronounced intent to perfect its original, to render the Bachian work more truly Bachian in style.

An earlier version of this study was read at the fifth triennial meeting of the American chapter of the Neue Bachgesellschaft, Harvard University, 29 April–1 May 1988.

The arrangement in question is of Bach's Fugue in C Minor on a Theme by Legrenzi, a uniquely significant work among Bach's fugues on borrowed subjects. Not only does the Legrenzi fugue represent Bach's only known borrowing from the works of Legrenzi, but it is the only Bach fugue on a borrowed theme in the form of a classic double fugue. That is, each of its two subjects is set forth independently, to be combined in the fugue's concluding section.[1] Moreover, its presence in the Andreas Bach Book, a source apparently dating from ca.1708-ca.1713,[2] suggests that the Legrenzi fugue may represent Bach's first essay altogether in the multiple-subject fugue, the genre that assumes so much importance in such later works as the Well-Tempered Clavier and the Art of Fugue.

Only recently have we begun to resolve fundamental issues regarding this important composition, such as the identity of the theme's source, now known to be Legrenzi's trio sonata op. 2, no. 11 ("La Mont Albana").[3] A question that remains is the number of different versions prepared by Bach. Four are known: BWV 574, the most frequently transmitted version; BWV 574b, published in the Neue Bach-Ausgabe as an early version; an unpublished and undoubtedly corrupt arrangement of BWV 574, most likely by the Nuremberg organist Leonard Scholz (1720-98); and BWV 574a, published in the Neue Bach-Ausgabe as a "variant" version.[4] Although certain sources present conflations of BWV 574 and 574b, there can be no question whatsoever about the authenticity of the two or their relative chronology (BWV 574b is clearly an early version of BWV 574). The unpublished arrangement is an utterly primitive, simplified version of BWV 574 that can have nothing to do with Bach. But whether BWV 574a plays any role in the evolution of the Legrenzi fugue has yet to be clarified. Although it is obviously adapted from BWV 574, not BWV 574b – it consis-

1. On the origins and development of the double fugue, see Joseph Müller-Blattau, *Geschichte der Fuge*, 3d ed. (Kassel: Bärenreiter, 1963); Imogene Horsley, *Fugue: History and Practice* (New York: Free Press, 1966), 344-54; and Alfred Mann, *The Study of Fugue* (Oxford: Oxford University Press, 1958), 42, 192-96.

2. See Robert Hill, ed., *Keyboard Music from the Andreas Bach Book and the Möller Manuscript* (Cambridge, Mass.: Department of Music, Harvard University, 1991), xxii-xxiii.

3. See Robert Hill, "Die Herkunft von Bachs 'Thema Legrenzianum,'" *Bach-Jahrbuch* 72 (1986): 105-7.

4. Dietrich Kilian, ed., NBA IV/5-6 (*Präludien, Toccaten, Fantasien und Fugen für Orgel*); NBA IV/5-6, KB, 508-9, contains a discussion of the unpublished arrangement.

tently reflects the revised readings of BWV 574 in those instances where BWV 574 and 574b differ – and is therefore the last of the three published versions, its authorship is still in doubt.

BWV 574a differs from the other two published versions in several significant ways. Most important, it transmits readings that in many cases are substantially different from those in the other two versions. It also lacks a single measure near the end of the fugue proper (m. 80) as well as the entire fourteen-measure coda that concludes the other two versions in most sources. And, whereas the other two versions survive in several authoritative sources dating from Bach's own lifetime, BWV 574a exists in a single manuscript, copied by an anonymous scribe at the end of the eighteenth century.

Despite the late date and unclear origins of its only source, BWV 574a is generally accepted today as authentic. In surveying the scant literature on the work, one senses that it has remained in the canon because of the convincing nature of the variant readings themselves. Ernst Naumann, who first published the work as a "variant" in the Bachgesellschaft edition, remarked that the voice leading is often more flowing and graceful than in BWV 574, and, noting the absence of the coda, he judged BWV 574a to be a late, "simplified" arrangement of BWV 574, probably by Bach himself.[5] Dietrich Kilian, who published BWV 574a in the Neue Bach-Ausgabe, concurred that BWV 574a was quite possibly authentic since many – though by no means all – of its variant readings appear to be improvements of readings in BWV 574.[6]

Other scholars have endorsed the authenticity of BWV 574a in more cryptic terms. Walter Emery, for example, once suggested that "by [1708] Bach would have made the Legrenzi fugue end convincingly in fugal style without tacking on an irrelevant toccata-like coda."[7] And Christoph Wolff has written that "the fact that the Legrenzi Fugue survives in three different versions strongly suggests that [Bach's] remaining fugues on themes by other composers also went through several stages of refinement."[8] Peter Williams, on the other hand, has

---

5. BG 38:xlix.

6. NBA IV/5–6, KB, 571.

7. Walter Emery, "Cadence and Chronology," in *Studies in Renaissance and Baroque Music in Honor of Arthur Mendel*, ed. Robert L. Marshall (Hackensack: Joseph Boonin; Kassel: Bärenreiter, 1974), 163.

8. Christoph Wolff, "Johann Adam Reinken and Johann Sebastian Bach: On the Context of Bach's Early Works," in *J. S. Bach as Organist: His Instruments, Music, and Performance Practices,*

been openly suspicious of Bach's authorship of BWV 574a, proposing that the work may be an arrangement by the copyist of its only source, who may have sought "to present, without the distraction of a toccata flourish, a fugue closely fitting its context [in the manuscript]."[9]

One glaring problem with the view that BWV 574a is Bach's own final version of the Legrenzi fugue – a problem that has gone unmentioned in the literature – is the mere fact that it is the shortest version. When Bach altered the length of one of his compositions while revising it, he almost always increased the size. To cite just one example, Bach altered the forms of no less than eighteen works as he prepared the two books of the Well-Tempered Clavier, and, in every case, he expanded the work in question.[10] Of course, one might argue that, with its "irrelevant" and "distracting" coda, the Legrenzi fugue was an exceptional case and that, by the time Bach carried out the final revision, he would indeed have found the coda extraneous. After all, such concluding flourishes are characteristic only of Bach's earliest keyboard fugues, works directly influenced in this respect by the north German organ school of the late seventeenth century (the thirty-second-note figuration in mm. 106–11 may be a direct imitation of Buxtehude). The excision of the coda, however, is not the only evidence against Bach's authorship, for it is the context of the work within its only source (but a different context than that alluded to by Williams) that supplies the most compelling argument regarding its authorship.

Let us first look closely at the three passages in BWV 574a that differ most extensively from BWV 574 (see exx. 1–3). It is surely not coincidental that all three end with structurally significant cadences: the arranger chose to strengthen certain cadences that are crucial to the work's form – including the final cadence (mm. 100–102), where the arranger added a three-measure pedal point – thereby sharpening its profile as a double fugue. Example 1 closes the first exposition in the fugue's second section, where the second fugue subject is set

---

ed. George Stauffer and Ernest May (Bloomington: Indiana University Press, 1986), n. 72; reprinted in Christoph Wolff, *Bach: Essays on His Life and Music* (Cambridge, Mass.: Harvard University Press, 1991), 56–71.

9. Peter Williams, *The Organ Music of J. S. Bach*, 3 vols. (Cambridge: Cambridge University Press, 1980–84), 1:241.

10. See my "Techniques of Expansion in the Preludes and Fugues of J. S. Bach" (Ph.D. diss., University of Chicago, 1986); and Herbot Hugo Riedel, "Recognition and Re-cognition: Bach and the Well-Tempered Clavier I" (Ph.D. diss., University of California at Berkeley, 1969).

forth; ex. 2 closes the second section altogether; ex. 3 closes the first exposition in the final section, in which the subjects are combined.

In ex. 1, the texture in mm. 50–51 is enriched in BWV 574a by the addition of a high bass voice. Furthermore, the rather monotonous alternation of tonic and dominant chords in root position in mm. 51–52 is relieved by conjunct motion in the pedal and soprano as well as by the interpolated subdominant seventh in the cadential gesture itself. The soprano and alto in m. 52 are reworked so as to avoid the anticipations in those voices and to maintain a steady sixteenth-note flow until the arrival.

In ex. 2, a new bass part is once again added in BWV 574a, in mm. 66–67, embellishing the subject statement in the pedal with a diminution of its head motive. The supertonic harmony on the last beat of m. 67 is changed to a Nea-politan; and the chordal texture in m. 68 is relieved by conjunct counterpoint in the manual parts and by the sustained tone in the pedal.[11] The rhetorical pause in m. 69 in the three lower voices is filled in with the inflection of a sec-ondary dominant (V/iv). At the arrival itself, the counterpoint in the manuals is enriched by the addition of neighbor and passing tones (note in particular the chromatic F♯, which creates a vii°⁷/V).

The principal change in ex. 3 is the elimination in BWV 574a of m. 80. In Kilian's view, the passage becomes "more direct" since the dominant harmony on the downbeat of m. 80 makes the inception of the cadence itself in m. 81 redundant.[12] The manual parts in mm. 79 and 80 (old m. 81) are reworked, pre-sumably to mediate the measure's removal. The harmony on the second beat of m. 80 has been changed from the tonic to the submediant. Finally, the manual parts (especially the alto) in m. 80 have been changed to avoid the anticipation in the alto and soprano.

There can be little doubt that in these three instances BWV 574a improves

11. The rhythmic makeup of the manual voices in m. 68 of BWV 574 – in which repeated-note ♫ rhythms in one voice (or, in this case, three voices) are complemented by ♪♫ rhythms in another voice, resulting in a continuous musical flow – is every bit as old fashioned an ele-ment as the free coda. This rhythmic configuration is a regular feature of the keyboard music of Bach's predecessors, such as Buxtehude, Böhm, Lübeck, and Pachelbel, as well as of Bach's earliest organ chorales, especially the so-called Neumeister Chorales, BWV 1090–1120. It is thus conceivable that the arranger's objectives in altering m. 68 also included modernizing the style somewhat by the removal of these rhythms (if only half of them).

12. NBA IV/5–6, KB, 571.

EX. 1. Fugue in C Minor on a Theme by Legrenzi, mm. 49–52

EX. 2. Fugue in C Minor on a Theme by Legrenzi, mm. 66–70

EX. 3. Fugue in C Minor on a Theme by Legrenzi, mm. 77–82

on BWV 574, and in a way compatible with Bach's own compositional style and revising procedure. The arranger has made the counterpoint more ornate, the harmony richer, the texture more dense. Only in the excision of m. 80 does he depart from Bach's well-documented tendency in revising his music to elaborate rather than to simplify.[13] But the realization that the music is written in a convincing and fluent late-Baroque contrapuntal style, in a manner that closely matches our general conception of Bach's own luxuriant counterpoint, should have no bearing on the question of authorship in BWV 574a, for one could argue with good reason that a talented imitator could have made these refinements just as easily as Bach himself, in hopes of transforming a youthful Bach composition into one more consistent with his mature fugal style – or at least *our* notion of this style – as represented by such works as the Well-Tempered Clavier.

The manuscript in which BWV 574a is contained, SBB MUS. MS BACH P 207 (Poelchau Collection), offers no incontrovertible philological evidence to confirm or deny its authenticity.[14] Its contents betray an acute interest in fugue. The source opens with some forty-two fugues and fifteen preludes from Bach's Well-Tempered Clavier, in the order of their appearance in the collection. BWV 574a follows, and it is followed in turn by three fugues of unknown authorship (BWV ANH.100, 98, and 96). The manuscript concludes with six movements from Handel's *Suites de Pièces pour le Clavecin* (first collection), HWV 426–33, here entitled "Praeludium" or "Fuga," and five of the *Six Fugues or Voluntarys [sic] for Organ or Harpsichord*, op. 3 (HWV 605–10). Only in the case of HWV 433 does the scribe provide a composer attribution for any composition in the manuscript, so the lack of an attribution to Bach in the case of BWV 574a should not be taken as any sign against Bach's authorship. (BWV 574a is given the generic title "Fuga a 4 Voc.," the formulation used for basically every four-voice fugue in the source, including, of course, many from the unquestionably authentic Well-Tempered Clavier.)

The manuscript's preparation seems to have been remarkably consistent. According to Yoshitake Kobayashi, a single watermark – an evergreen with or-

13. See George B. Stauffer, "Bach as Reviser of His Own Keyboard Works," *Early Music* 13 (1985): 185–98.

14. For data on this source, see NBA IV/5–6, KB, 43; and Paul Kast, *Die Bach-Handschriften der Berliner Staatsbibliothek* (Trossingen: Hohner-Verlag, 1958), 13.

namental design; countermark "GEIPEL" – is found in the musical text, and the watermark "IWI" (probably from the Johann Wolfgang Jaeger papermill in Niederreuth [Bohemia]) is found in the title page and back cover.[15] There are no changes to be found in the script at all, no gradual changes or distinct breaks; the entire manuscript appears to have been written out in a single, continuous process. There are relatively few emendations – merely a few corrections of scribal errors – and certainly no evidence that the source is anything other than a fair copy. The copy of BWV 574a – like all the entries in the manuscript – is free of "compositional" or "conceptual" revisions; it would never be confused with an arranger's working score. In other words, there is no hard evidence that the unknown scribe and the arranger are one and the same, although this possibility cannot be dismissed out of hand.[16] The scribe dated his copy of the first work in the manuscript, the C-major fugue from Book 1 of the Well-Tempered Clavier, with the note "den 21sten Aug.1791." That date is corroborated by the source's first documented owner, Georg Poelchau, the famous collector and librarian of the Berlin Singakademie, who signed the verso of the front cover with the note "G. Poelchau / Jena 1792." Poelchau, eighteen years old at the time, matriculated at the University of Jena in that year.[17]

It is the context of BWV 574a in P 207, as mentioned earlier, that is the key to its authorship: many if not most of the works from the Well-Tempered Clavier are preserved in P 207 in a corrupt state, as evidently are the several works by Handel, and, tellingly, there are stylistic links between these corruptions and the so-called variant readings in BWV 574a.

As Alfred Dürr has remarked, we know very few works by Bach whose text is so securely and unqualifiedly established as that of the first book of the

15. I wish to thank Dr. Kobayashi for sharing this information with me. Regarding the "IWI" watermark, see Wisso Weiss and Yoshitake Kobayashi, *Katalog der Wasserzeichen in Bachs Originalhandschriften* (= NBA IX/1), *Textband*, 49, 68.

16. As Dr. Kobayashi has informed me, whoever the scribe is, he is also responsible for copies of a G-minor fugue and an anonymous E-major fragment in SBB MUS. MS BACH P 247, also from the Poelchau Collection. For data on P 247, see NBA IV/5–6, KB, 46–47; and Kast, *Bach-Handschriften*, 17.

17. For a comprehensive discussion of Poelchau and his music collection, see Klaus Engler, "Georg Poelchau und seine Musikaliensammlung: Ein Beitrag zur Überlieferung Bachscher Musik in der ersten Hälfte des 19. Jahrhunderts" (Ph.D. diss., University of Tübingen, 1984).

Well-Tempered Clavier.[18] Much of this unparalleled authority resides in the autograph manuscript itself since it contains no fewer than three layers of corrections entered by the composer; the many copies of Book 1 made by others during Bach's lifetime can be collated with these corrections.[19] The exemplar for the works from Book 1 contained in P 207 is descended from the autograph during its third layer of corrections, evidently dating from the 1740s.[20] While the source situation for the second book of the Well-Tempered Clavier is more complicated, its various authentic readings are also well established.[21] The many variant readings found in P 207 reflect none of the authentic readings from either Book 1 or Book 2 as found in the holographs or copies by Bach's pupils and colleagues; they are unique to P 207 and obviously corrupt.

We are perhaps on somewhat less secure ground when considering the works of Handel contained in P 207, for it is difficult to know how the variant readings in P 207 are to be understood within the constellation of sources for these two collections. At the very least, there is no evidence to link the variant readings to any other sources – including the extant holographs – much less to the texts as established by the Hallische Händel-Ausgabe.[22] As in the case of the Well-Tempered Clavier, the variant readings are unique to P 207.

The most dramatic corruptions in P 207 are to be found in the preludes and fugues from the Well-Tempered Clavier. These involve breathtaking transformations of thematic material – as well as the consequences of those transformations for the form of the work in question. Having at first altered a fugue subject or countersubject or a prelude's opening theme, the unknown arranger never returns to the Bachian original but instead carries the consequences of

---

18. Alfred Dürr, *Zur Frühgeschichte des Wohltemperierten Klaviers I von Johann Sebastian Bach* (Göttingen: Vandenhoeck & Ruprecht, 1984), 5.

19. See Alred Dürr, ed., NBA v/6, pt.1 (*Das Wohltemperierte Klavier I*), KB, 142–78.

20. See Walther Dehnhard, ed. *J. S. Bach: Das Wohltemperierte Klavier I (BWV 846–869)* (Vienna: Wiener Urtext Edition, 1977), xvi–xxi; dating from NBA v/6, pt.1, KB, 192–95.

21. See Werner Breckoff, "Zur Entstehungsgeschichte des zweiten Wohltemperierten Klaviers von Johann Sebastian Bach" (Ph.D. diss., University of Tübingen, 1965).

22. See Rudolf Steglich, ed., *Georg Friedrich Händel: Klavierwerke I*, Hallische Händel-Ausgabe, IV/1 (Kassel: Bärenreiter, 1955); and Terence Best, ed., *Georg Friedrich Händel: Klavierwerke III*, Hallische Händel-Ausgabe, IV/6 (Kassel: Bärenreiter, 1970).

his changes through to their ultimate formal conclusions. The concern for form in these cases may be seen as a strong connection to the concern for projecting the double-fugue structure of BWV 574a, in which the arranger fortified a number of cadences most significant to the work's form.

Three examples of these extreme corruptions will suffice. In the D-major fugue from Book 1, the subject's elaborate, thirty-second-note flourish is reduced to sixteenths; the chief episodic motive is completely transformed as well (see exx. 4 and 5). In the E♭-minor prelude from Book 1, all the arpeg-

EX. 4. Fugue in D Major, BWV 850/2, subject

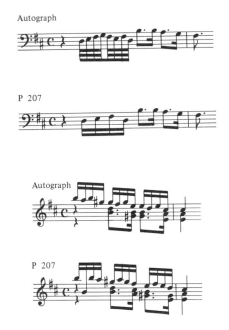

gio indications are omitted, and the elaborate, sixteenth-note flourishes are reduced to steady eighth-note motion. Even more interesting – especially for its patently Classical ideology – is the corruption of the B♭-major prelude from Book 2. This work is one of the several binary preludes from the Well-Tempered Clavier that have been described as protosonata forms.[23] In P 207, the arranger has replaced the contrasting material that initiates the "second key

23. See Karl August Rosenthal, "Über Sonatenvorformen in den Instrumentalwerken Joh. Seb. Bachs," *Bach-Jahrbuch* 23 (1926): 68–89.

area" (mm. 9–12) with a transposition of the opening theme; a corresponding change is made in the "recapitulation," at mm. 53–56. It is not too far-fetched to call the result a monothematic sonata form.

These corruptions appear to be the work of a skilled, knowledgeable composer, one, as characterized by Albert Schweitzer, whose Classical ideology is manifested in an openly patronizing approach to the Bachian style.[24] However, the arranger's overall approach does not easily reduce to a concrete and consistent set of specific values. The alteration of thematic material remains a relatively exceptional event; even as numerous as the corruptions are, the arranger let stand far more themes than he altered.

On the other hand, many of the corruptions reveal an intense dislike of repetition, especially of single notes or small groups of notes. In ex. 5, for instance, the D-major fugue's main episodic motive has been reworked to eliminate all repeated pitches. Similar changes are found in the F♯-major fugue from Book 1, where the main episodic motive is relieved of its characteristic repeated pitches (see ex. 6). And, in ex. 7, the arranger has altered the countersubject to the

EX. 6. Fugue in F♯ Major, BWV 858/2, episodic motive

E-major fugue from Book 1, ridding it of its repeated sixteenth-note motive (although the change does result in repeated f♯s between the countersubject and subject on beat 3). It is important to note, however, that even though thematic anticipations or struck suspensions are sometimes altered, as in exx. 4

24. "There was one copyist in particular who thought it his duty to improve Bach, and tried to do so in every prelude and fugue in both Parts [of the Well-Tempered Clavier]. His chief concern was to rid them of all unnecessary complexity, and to give them the form that Bach himself would have conferred on them had he lived in another epoch than that of the "Zopf" (pigtail) and had a more refined taste" (Albert Schweitzer, *J. S. Bach*, trans. Ernest Newman, 2 vols. [London: Breitkopf & Härtel, 1911; reprint, New York: Dover, 1966], 1:336).

EX.7. Fugue in E Major, BWV 854/2, countersubject

Autograph

P 207

and 5, the arranger more frequently allows them to stand – as in the counter-subject to the D-minor fugue from Book 1 or the highly repercussive subject to the B♭-minor fugue from Book 2. Despite his general aversion to repetition, the arranger's respect for thematic material and for its relation to overall form apparently often keeps him from changing thematic anticipations.

With respect to one matter of detail, however, the arranger is remarkably – even fanatically – consistent. Far more frequent than alterations to thematic material are altered *cadences;* specifically, the arranger has removed nearly every cadential anticipation from the works contained in P 207. While this often involves simple omission or minor alteration, as in the C-major fugue from Book 1 (see ex.8), there is just as often a fundamental reshaping of the ca-

EX.8. Fugue in C Major, BWV 846/2, mm.13–14

Autograph

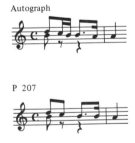

P 207

dence's rhythmic and/or melodic profile, as in the C-minor fugue from Book 1 and the F♯-major fugue from Book 2 (see exx.9 and 10). So thoroughgoing is the arranger's alteration of cadences and removal of anticipations that it is more useful to consider those cadential anticipations that have been allowed to stand. Only fifteen nonthematic anticipations remain among the fifty-seven

EX. 9. Fugue in C Minor, BWV 847/2, m. 29

Autograph

P 207

EX. 10. Fugue in F♯ Major, BWV 882/2, conclusion

Autograph

P 207

preludes and fugues from the Well-Tempered Clavier that appear in P 207; among the eleven movements from the keyboard works of Handel, only two nonthematic anticipations remain.

To return to the point at issue, BWV 574 contains seven cadential anticipations, all of which have been removed in BWV 574a. The arranger's acute distaste for anticipations appears to be a central component of his alteration of cadences, and this is what most clearly links BWV 574a to what are undoubtedly corruptions of movements from the Well-Tempered Clavier and, evidently, corruptions of Handel's keyboard works as well. Needless to say, this circumstance strongly implies that all these corruptions were made by the same skilled "composer," who unfortunately must remain nameless.

Other aspects are almost as suggestive. The final cadences of all five fugues from Handel's op. 3 contained in P 207 are altered in such a way as to imply the arranger's dislike of improvisatory ornamentation. As mentioned above, in the E♭-minor prelude from Book 1 of the Well-Tempered Clavier, the profuse arpeggio indications found in the holograph and all reliable copies are omitted altogether in P 207. With similar apparent intent, the arranger has filled

177

out the cadences of Handel's op. 3 fugues, preventing the ornamental arpeggiation that the skeletal, chordal textures call for. Note that in the G-minor fugue (ex. 11) he has omitted the *Adagio* marking – itself probably an open invi-

EX. 11. Handel, Fugue in G Minor, HWV 605, conclusion

tation to extemporaneous embellishment – as well as the arpeggio indication and that he has transformed the *freistimmig*, chordal texture into strict, four-part counterpoint with active inner voices. At the close of the B-minor fugue (ex. 12), not only has the arranger omitted the *Adagio* indication and changed the free, chordal texture to four-part counterpoint, but he has truncated the cadence, eliminating the rhetorical pause in the original cadence. This excision is highly reminiscent of the reworking of m. 69 in BWV 574a (see ex. 2 above), where a rhetorical pause is also eliminated, but filled in with newly composed material, so that the passage's original length is unchanged.

In view of these corruptions, it is tempting to conclude that the Legrenzi fugue's rhapsodic coda was omitted in P 207 because of the arranger's aversion to free ornamentation or bravura passagework in general. Another possible scenario – as suggested by Williams – is that the arranger cut the coda out of concern for structural uniformity among the fugues in the manuscript; none of the other fugues in P 207 conclude with material even remotely approaching a "toccata-like" nature, and in this respect the Legrenzi fugue in its unaltered state would have been decidedly anomalous.

EX.12. Handel, Fugue in B Minor, HWV 608, conclusion

Hallische Händel-Ausgabe

P 207

But there is probably a far more pragmatic reason for this omission, namely, that the coda was missing from the arranger's exemplar. The coda, after all, is omitted in two of the sources for BWV 574 – probably because the scribes felt it to be superfluous – and in one of them, MBLPZ MS 1 (Scheibner Collection), m. 80 is also absent.[25] Furthermore, it is clear from the many redundant A♭s in the copy of BWV 574a in P 207 that its exemplar – unlike P 207 itself, which uses the modern key signature of three flats – was in so-called dorian notation, a system whereby keys in the minor mode requiring flats were notated one flat short of modern practice;[26] the MS 1 copy of BWV 574, like most of the sources for BWV 574 and 574b, also uses dorian notation. Finally, the MS 1 copy was almost certainly in existence by 1790.[27] The only circumstance that speaks against the possibility that MS 1 was the direct exemplar for P 207 is that it lacks m. 83, which P 207 contains.[28]

25. According to NBA IV/5–6, KB, 505.

26. Ibid., 571.

27. See Russell Stinson, *The Bach Manuscripts of Johann Peter Kellner and His Circle: A Case Study in Reception History* (Durham, N.C.: Duke University Press, 1989), 40–44.

28. There is a further connection between P 207 and the Scheibner Collection involving Handel's op. 3, for in both P 207 and MBLPZ MS 2 (Scheibner Collection) the fugues appear in the same unusual order, radically different from that used in any other sources (see Bernd

I hope to have shown how formidable the evidence against the authenticity of BWV 574a is, despite the work's compelling representation of the mature Bachian style. In light of the fugue's context in P 207, it is very difficult to believe that Bach had anything whatsoever to do with the variant readings in BWV 574a, even with their adept and attractive counterpoint, or that BWV 574a plays any role in the evolution of the Legrenzi fugue. Franz Kroll, editor of the Bachgesellschaft edition of the Well-Tempered Clavier, concluded his discussion of those corruptions with rare sarcasm – sarcasm that might well be applied to the corruption known as BWV 574a: "In short, Bach is not always up to snuff; and, fortunately, the scribe is not affected by barren theoretical restrictions. Rather, he meets the problem head-on: make it better! is his motto. ... [But] we should not heap too much scorn on the clever man, so long as there are connoisseurs who do not reward such misdeeds with their applause."[29]

Baselt, *Thematisch-systematisches Verzeichnis: Instrumentalmusik, Pasticci und Fragmente*, Händel-Handbuch, vol. 3 [Kassel: Bärenreiter, 1986], 333). This striking correspondence only strengthens the view that the exemplar for the copy of the Legrenzi fugue in P 207 was a source from the Scheibner Collection.

29. "Kurz überall schreibt ihm Bach nicht recht zu Danke, und zum Glücke braucht er sich nicht auf unfruchtbare theoretische Plänkeleien einzulassen, sondern begegnet dem: Mach's besser! gleich als ein rechter Practicus. ... [Aber] fern sei es, den wackern Mann mit allzuviel Hohn zu überschütten, so lange es noch Kenner giebt, die nicht minder argen Versündigungen ihren Beifall zollen" (BG 14:xvii).

REVIEWS

Christoph Wolff. *Bach: Essays on His Life and Music.* Cambridge, Mass.:
Harvard University Press, 1991. xiv, 461 pp.

Although collections of essays by eminent scholars have been a feature of
the musicological landscape since the days of Spitta and Nottebohm,[1] they
have blossomed into a new literary genre in the 1980s and 1990s. For Bach
alone we have such collections by Georg von Dadelsen, Gerhard Herz, Alfred Dürr,
and Robert L. Marshall.[2] Christoph Wolff's recent anthology is an important addition to this list. It takes its place alongside similar books on Bach as well as within a
series that is gradually emerging from the Harvard University Press.[3]

While every Bach scholar has had contact with Wolff's research, I dare say that no
one has read *all* his articles on Bach. This is not only because they are so numerous
(in the twenty-five years from 1963 to 1988 there are about sixty!) but also because
they cover an extraordinarily broad range of topics and have appeared piecemeal in
a wide variety of places (some relatively inaccessible) in German as well as English.[4]
The publication of Wolff's book makes it possible for the first time to gain a comprehensive view of his work and to assess the significance of his contributions.

The five headings under which the thirty-two essays are grouped provide an indication of the scope of Wolff's interests. "Outlines of a Musical Portrait" includes
articles on aspects of Bach biography and the influence of other composers on Bach's
life and works. "New Sources: Broadened Perspectives" and " 'Old' Sources Revisited: Novel Aspects" contain the results of Wolff's examination of various manuscript and printed sources of Bach's music. A variety of issues involving works from

1. Philipp Spitta, *Zur Musik: Sechzehn Aufsätze* (Berlin: Paetel, 1892; reprint, Hildesheim: Georg Olms,
1976), and *Musikgeschichtliche Aufsätze* (Berlin: Paetel, 1894; reprint, Hildesheim: Georg Olms, 1976);
Gustav Nottebohm, *Beethoveniana* (Leipzig: J. Rieter-Biedermann, 1872; reprint, New York: Johnson
Reprint Corp., 1970), and *Zweite Beethoveniana* (Leipzig: J. Rieter-Biedermann, 1887; reprint, New
York: Johnson Reprint Corp., 1970).

2. Georg von Dadelsen, *Über Bach und anderes: Aufsätze und Vorträge 1957–1982* (Laaber: Laaber-Verlag,
1983); Gerhard Herz, *Essays on J. S. Bach* (Ann Arbor, Mich.: UMI Research Press, 1985); Alfred Dürr, *Im
Mittelpunkt Bach: Ausgewählte Aufsätze und Vorträge* (Kassel: Bärenreiter, 1988); Robert L. Marshall, *The
Music of Johann Sebastian Bach: The Sources, the Style, the Significance* (New York: Schirmer Books, 1989).

3. Other essay collections by distinguished musicologists recently published by the Harvard University Press include Alan Tyson, *Mozart Studies* (1987); Maynard Solomon, *Beethoven Essays* (1988); Leo
Treitler, *Music and the Historical Imagination* (1989); and Lewis Lockwood, *Beethoven: Studies in the Creative Process* (1992).

4. Wolff's extensive list of publications also includes important work on Mozart, Schubert, Brahms,
Hindemith, and many others.

the *Orgelbüchlein* to the B Minor Mass are discussed in "Concepts, Style, and Chronology." A final group of essays ("Early Reception and Artistic Legacy") investigates Bach's reputation, especially the ways in which the composer and his music were viewed by his contemporaries.

Throughout his career Wolff has single-mindedly pursued an integrated approach. Rather than aligning himself exclusively with any particular methodology, he has employed many different modes of inquiry – manuscript studies, style criticism, *Rezeptionsgeschichte*, and others – to grapple with a vast array of difficult and central problems. In the preface, Wolff calls attention to "the virtual omnipresence of philology, analysis, criticism, and interpretation" in his work and expresses his "hope that the reader will be able to detect and follow the 'red thread' running through all chapters: traces of a deliberately integrated examination whose aims are to uncover historical evidence of various kinds; to refine our understanding of Bach's creative life … and of his artistic development, work habits, and compositional intentions; as well as, finally, to illuminate the substance of his musical language and the significance of his œuvre" (p.x).

In addition to his numerous individual contributions, Wolff has both explicitly and implicitly pointed the way for future scholarship. Through his academic posts at Harvard, Columbia, and the University of Toronto, his coeditorship (with Hans-Joachim Schulze) of the *Bach-Jahrbuch*, and, most recently, his coauthorship (again with Schulze) of the new *Bach Compendium*, Wolff has decisively influenced the direction of scholarship on Bach's life and music. Taken as a whole, his work constitutes nothing less than a blueprint for Bach research at the end of the twentieth century.

BIOGRAPHICAL ISSUES

For over a decade music students have had their first contact with Wolff's research primarily through his contribution to the *New Grove* article on Bach.[5] In connection with the preparation of this important article (which is sure to shape initial perceptions of the composer for many years to come), Wolff had occasion to reflect deeply on our picture of Bach in the twentieth century. Many of his insights are distilled in "New Perspectives on Bach Biography," one of the key essays in the book.

Wolff offers a revisionist critique of the picture of Bach that was formulated by Philipp Spitta in the late nineteenth century[6] and that has shaped our modern view

---

5. Walter Emery and Christoph Wolff, "Bach, Johann Sebastian," in *The New Grove Dictionary of Music and Musicians*, ed. Stanley Sadie (London: Macmillan Publishing Co., 1980), 1:785–840; reprinted in Christoph Wolff et al., *The New Grove Bach Family* (New York: W. W. Norton & Co., 1983), 44–237. Wolff also wrote the *New Grove* articles on several other members of the Bach family.

6. Philipp Spitta, *Johann Sebastian Bach*, 2 vols. (Leipzig: Breitkopf & Härtel, 1873–80; reprint, Wiesbaden: Breitkopf & Härtel, 1979).

of the composer. Simultaneously, he sounds several of the themes that permeate his other essays. For instance, Wolff takes issue with Spitta's schematic periodization of Bach's life, according to which he slowly evolved through the stages of organist, Kapellmeister, and Kantor, composing works appropriate to these offices during the respective periods. He argues instead that Bach's compositional interests and professional duties were not nearly so synchronized and that "the borderlines of the emerging biographical phases are definitely more blurred than Spitta and traditional Bach biography suggested" (p. 7). Wolff also concurs with the emerging consensus that Bach's last decade was "a kind of self-styled retirement" (p. 11) during which he pursued compositional projects unrelated to his official duties and with a strong theoretical-historical bent (e.g., the Art of Fugue, the Musical Offering, the B Minor Mass).[7] And an important biographical perspective that weaves its way through the book is Wolff's conviction that throughout his career Bach "behaved a lot more like a free and emancipated person" than is generally thought – indeed, that "in every single case ... he himself was the prime mover acting in his own best interest" (pp. 6, 12). Such notions constitute a multifaceted view of Bach, one that takes into account the complexities of his personality and that is ultimately more convincing than Spitta's two-dimensional portrayal.

One of the most stimulating parts of this essay is Wolff's discussion of Bach's move from Cöthen to Leipzig in 1723. Scholars generally have taken at face value Bach's remarks in his 1730 letter to his childhood friend Georg Erdmann that the transition from Kapellmeister to Kantor represented a step downward and that it was motivated, in part, by the declining musical interest of Prince Leopold after his marriage with Princess Friederica Henrietta of Anhalt-Bernburg early in 1722.[8] Wolff, however, calls into question the story of the unmusical princess, citing evidence of Bach's desire to leave Cöthen even before Leopold's marriage (Bach's application for the position of organist at St. Jacobi in Hamburg in 1720 and his dedication of the score of the Brandenburg Concertos to the margrave of Brandenburg in 1721). He argues that Bach wanted to leave because of "the gradual reduction of the Cöthen Hof-Capelle after 1718, which had been built up only shortly before 1717 as a remarkably strong band of instrumental virtuosos" (pp. 7–8). This is reflected, above all, in the fact that most of the chamber and orchestral music dates from Bach's first three years in Cöthen, while the last three years are dominated by soloistic works such as the sonatas and partitas for unaccompanied violin, the *Clavierbüchlein* for Wilhelm Friedemann Bach, the first book of the Well-Tempered Clavier, the first *Clavier-*

---

7. Similar views are expressed in Gerhard Herz, "Toward a New Image of Bach," in *Essays*, 171–81; and in Rudolf Eller, "Thoughts on Bach's Leipzig Creative Years," trans. and annotated by Stephen A. Crist, *Bach: The Journal of the Riemenschneider Bach Institute* 21, no. 2 (Summer 1990): 40–47.

8. BDOK 1, no. 23; BR, 125–26.

büchlein for Anna Magdalena Bach, and the Inventions and Sinfonias. As for the other point, Wolff notes that "Bach's move into the university town and commercial metropolis of Leipzig and his appointment to one of the most respected and influential musical offices of Protestant Germany was definitely not a step downward" and that, moreover, his new job "was considerably more flexible than his Cöthen position" (p. 8).

At the end of the article, Wolff makes another important statement: "Especially in the case of Bach, we gain very little by merely collecting data and documents. Their messages remain for the most part very meager unless they are intellectually penetrated by critical questions with the aim of detecting inner connections that make historical sense" (p. 13). This is exactly what Wolff does, not only in the present essay but in the three that follow. Indeed, an exemplary "intellectual penetration," coupled with unparalleled mastery of the source material, is the strength of Wolff's biographical work.

"The Family," "Decisive Career Steps," and "Employers and Patrons" are reprinted from material that originally accompanied a series of Bach recordings issued by Archiv Produktion. But this is no mere liner-note fluff; Wolff consistently demonstrates his command of the documentary evidence bearing on Bach's life and his ability to weave these materials into a compelling biographical portrait. Aimed at a general audience, these chapters provide an excellent point of entry, especially for students and other readers who are less experienced with the intricacies of Bach research.

COMPOSITIONAL INFLUENCES ON BACH

Another locus in Wolff's intellectual journey has been the area of compositional influences on Bach. While many writers have made general comments about the alleged influence of certain figures, Wolff has been able to lift the veil in significant ways.

The essay "Bach and the Tradition of the Palestrina Style," a distillation of material from Wolff's widely praised dissertation,[9] attempts to define Bach's attitude toward the style of vocal polyphony associated with Palestrina's music, the *stile antico*. Almost all the movements in question are from liturgical works dating from Bach's late period (1739 or later), particularly *Clavierübung* III and the B Minor Mass. Fac-

9. Christoph Wolff, *Der stile antico in der Musik Johann Sebastian Bachs: Studien zu Bachs Spätwerk*, Beihefte zum Archiv für Musikwissenschaft, vol. 6 (Wiesbaden: Franz Steiner, 1968), discussed in Friedrich Blume, "The Present State of Bach Research," in *Syntagma Musicologicum II: Gesammelte Reden und Schriften 1962–1972*, ed. Anna Amalie Abert and Martin Ruhnke (Kassel: Bärenreiter, 1973), 290–92; Paul Henry Lang, "Editorial," *Musical Quarterly* 55 (1969): 545–58; Alfred Dürr, "Zu Christoph Wolffs 'Der stile antico in der Musik Johann Sebastian Bachs,'" *Die Musikforschung* 23 (1970): 324–28; and Robert L. Marshall's review in *Notes* 27 (1970): 33–34.

tors bearing on Bach's involvement with the *stile antico* include (1) his use of the rich collection of vocal polyphony in the library of the St. Thomas School, documented, for instance, by Bach's arrangement of the Sanctus from the *Missa Superba* by Johann Caspar Kerll (BWV 241);[10] (2) his personal copy of the original Latin edition of Fux's *Gradus ad Parnassum* (1725), the fundamental counterpoint manual based on the Palestrina style;[11] and (3) the remnants of his private library, including approximately thirty Masses, individual Mass sections, Magnificats, and other works by different masters, such as Palestrina's six-part *Missa sine Nomine*, two chorale Masses by Schütz's student Christoph Bernhard, a six-part *Missa* by Bernhard's student Johann Christoph Schmidt, an anonymous Magnificat (BWV ANH.30), and Bach's parody of Pergolesi's *Stabat Mater* on the text "Tilge, Höchster, meine Sünden." [12]

Particularly illuminating is Wolff's discussion of two little-known Bach compositions and their relationship to the B Minor Mass. In his copy of Giovanni Battista Bassani's *Acroama Missale* (a collection of six Masses), there is a choral intonation in *stile antico* by Bach that shares several stylistic features with the Credo of the B Minor Mass. Wolff views the interpolation into the Bassani Mass as a study for the later Credo. Similarly, he sees in Bach's six-part arrangement of the original four-part setting of "Suscepit Israel" from Caldara's Magnificat in C Major (which involved the addition of two obbligato violin parts) a parallel with the treatment of voices and instruments in the Credo from the B Minor Mass.

"Buxtehude, Bach, and Seventeenth-Century Music in Retrospect" examines the question of Buxtehude's influence on Bach. Wolff notes a number of striking parallels between the two musicians. Buxtehude, like Bach, pursued a multifaceted career as church organist, traveling virtuoso, teacher, composer of both sacred and secular works, impresario, and publisher of his own works. Moreover, both demonstrated

---

10. This composition is the subject of an essay by one of Wolff's former doctoral students at Harvard (see Peter Wollny, "Bachs Sanctus BWV 241 und Kerlls 'Missa Superba,'" *Bach-Jahrbuch* 77 [1991]: 173–76).

11. Wolff notes that Bach must have been involved with the first German translation of Fux's treatise, too, since it was edited by one of his students, Lorenz Christoph Mizler, and published in Leipzig in 1742.

12. More recent studies of this repertory include Kenneth Nott, "Johann Sebastian Bach's Arrangement of Pergolesi's *Stabat Mater:* A Critical Edition and Commentary" (D.M.A. essay, University of Hartford, 1988), and "'Tilge, Höchster, meine Sünden': Observations on Bach and the *Style Galant*," *Bach: The Journal of the Riemenschneider Bach Institute* 23, no.1 (Spring/Summer 1992): 3–30; Kirsten Beisswenger, "Bachs Eingriffe in Werke fremder Komponisten: Beobachtungen an den Notenhandschriften aus seiner Bibliothek unter besonderer Berücksichtigung der lateinischen Kirchenmusik," *Bach-Jahrbuch* 77 (1991): 127–58, and *Johann Sebastian Bachs Notenbibliothek* (Kassel: Bärenreiter, 1992).

their extensive theoretical knowledge not by writing treatises but by composing works with a strong theoretical orientation (e.g., Buxtehude's canons BUXWV 123-24 and Bach's Art of Fugue); both explored a wide variety of styles and genres, old and new, from many different national traditions; and both were experts in organology. Above all, Buxtehude embodied "all the distinguishing features of a powerful integrating figure" (p. 47); he was to the seventeenth century what Bach was to the eighteenth.

Beyond his function as role model, Wolff points to some specific compositional influences that Buxtehude may have had on Bach. He argues convincingly that Bach not only heard but actively participated in the performance of Buxtehude's oratorio *Templum honoris*, BUXWV 135, on 3 December 1705, during Bach's famous four-month journey to Lübeck. And, on the basis of information in the printed libretto (which, unfortunately, is all that survives), Wolff believes that the instrumental grandeur of this work served as a model for one of Bach's earliest cantatas, *Gott ist mein König*, BWV 71, for the Mühlhausen town council election in 1708. Wolff suggests that in the realm of keyboard music, too, Buxtehude's approach to composition had a decisive impact on Bach. He notes that Buxtehude's organ preludes "held the rank of *exempla classica* within the Bach circle" (p. 51) and cites Buxtehude's great Prelude in G Minor, BUXWV 149, to illustrate what Bach learned from the elder composer: "Buxtehude's expansion of the traditional multisectional prelude/toccata of the *stylus phantasticus* genre into an unprecedented large-scale and thematically controlled format suggests a general path that Bach later pursued as well. … With respect to the extraordinarily expansive tendencies of prelude and fugue as separate entities, Buxtehude's synthesis unquestionably provided the point of departure for Bach" (p. 54).

"Vivaldi's Compositional Art, Bach, and the Process of 'Musical Thinking' " is one of Wolff's most recent and original contributions. He tackles the important but difficult task of determining exactly what Bach learned from his studies of Vivaldi's music. His point of departure is the famous remark in Johann Nicolaus Forkel's Bach biography (1802) that Bach's keyboard transcriptions of Vivaldi's violin concertos taught the composer "how to think musically." Wolff sheds light on the meaning of this provocative phrase by attempting to reconstruct Bach's process of analysis as he transformed Vivaldi's Concerto in G Major, op. 3, no. 3, into the Concerto in F Major, BWV 978. Though Wolff's conclusions cannot be easily summarized – indeed, much of the essay's interest is in the analytical details – the essence of Vivaldi's compositional method, identified by Forkel (and Bach) as a process of genuine "musical thinking," involves the elaboration of a musical idea by means of "the closely interrelated categories of Ordnung [order/organization], and Zusammenhang [connection/continuity], and Verhältnis [relation/proportion] that provide the functional framework for developing, organizing, and unifying a piece" (p. 78). Only by continuing to pursue similar lines of inquiry will we gradually move toward the elusive goal of defining more precisely the Italian component of Bach's musical language.[13]

BACH'S EARLY WORKS

Wolff has devoted much of his attention to the chronological extremes of Bach's career: the works composed during his last decade (to be discussed later) and his earliest compositions. In "The Neumeister Collection of Chorale Preludes from the Bach Circle," Wolff documents what is arguably his most spectacular accomplishment: the discovery of thirty-three previously unknown chorale preludes by Bach in a late-eighteenth-century manuscript at Yale University. Since this event was reported widely in both musical publications and the general media, the story need not be recounted here.[14] It is worth pondering the implications of this find, however, for it has significantly illuminated Bach's early compositional activities, a notoriously obscure corner of Bach studies.

Wolff provides a richly detailed description of the manuscript; an overview of its repertory; biographical information on its compiler, Johann Gottfried Neumeister (1756–1840); and brief discussions of the works of each of the composers represented in the volume. As for the chorale preludes by Bach, Wolff believes that they are among his earliest extant compositions, dating from his adolescence (ca.1695–1705).

A particularly intriguing feature of the Neumeister Collection is the presence of two pieces from the Weimar *Orgelbüchlein* (BWV 601 and 639) that "most likely belong to the earliest layer of the Orgel-Büchlein and therefore provide an important link with its hitherto unknown prehistory" (p.117). In a related essay, "Chronology and Style in the Early Works: A Background for the Orgel-Büchlein," Wolff goes a step further, proposing an earlier date for the *Orgelbüchlein* than has previously been assumed. While Georg von Dadelsen had thought that the work dated largely from ca.1713–14,[15] Wolff suggests that it may have been started as early as 1708–9, the beginning of Bach's tenure in Weimar. With this earlier date in mind, he explores the relationship between the repertory of the Neumeister Chorales and the *Orgelbüch-*

13. Two valuable recent studies are Jean-Claude Zehnder, "Giuseppe Torelli und Johann Sebastian Bach: Zu Bachs Weimarer Konzertform," *Bach-Jahrbuch* 77 (1991): 33–95; and Gregory Butler, "J. S. Bach's Reception of Tomaso Albinoni's Late Instrumental Works" (paper read at the meeting of the American Bach and American Schütz Societies, New York, 24 April 1992).

14. See the excellent résumé in Russell Stinson's review of Wolff's editions of the Neumeister Chorales and the Yale manuscript, in the *Journal of the American Musicological Society* 40 (1987): 352–61.

15. Georg von Dadelsen, "Zur Entstehung des Bachschen Orgelbüchleins," in *Festschrift Friedrich Blume zum 70. Geburtstag*, ed. Anna Amalie Abert and Wilhelm Pfannkuch (Kassel: Bärenreiter, 1963), 74–79.

lein. Through examination of selected examples, Wolff illustrates how certain stylistic traits of the chorales in the Neumeister Collection (e.g., bold harmonic progressions and relatively dense contrapuntal textures) mark these pieces as precursors of the settings in the *Orgelbüchlein*.[16]

With regard to formative influences on Bach, Wolff points to the famous north German organists Reinken, Buxtehude, and Georg Böhm as the "decisive mentors of the young Bach" (p.56). Wolff's article on the Bach-Buxtehude connection was discussed earlier, and the relationship between Bach and Böhm is the subject of a recent, extensive essay by Jean-Claude Zehnder.[17] Another contribution by Wolff, "Bach and Johann Adam Reinken: A Context for the Early Works," completes the trilogy. Although Spitta downplayed his influence, Wolff argues that "Reinken represents a major, perhaps even *the* major, figure in young Bach's life" (p.57). This essay is important not only for what it reports about the Bach-Reinken association specifically but also because it contains an excellent synopsis of the current state of knowledge about Bach's early years.

In this essay, Wolff explores Johann Sebastian's relationship with his elder brother Johann Christoph more thoroughly than has been done in the past.[18] Johann Christoph had studied with Pachelbel in Erfurt and "must have wished, above all, to pass on to his brother what had been suggested to him by his own training" (p.60). Although the book "full of keyboard pieces by the most famous masters of the day, Froberger, Kerll, and Pachelbel," that Sebastian copied out "by moonlight" and that was confiscated by his brother (according to the account in the obituary) has not survived, Wolff suggests that its repertory must have been similar to that preserved in the 1692 tablature book of Johann Valentin Eckelt, a contemporary of Johann Christoph Bach, who was also a pupil of Pachelbel. The book, most of which is in Pachelbel's hand, contains works by Pachelbel, Johann Jacob Froberger, Philipp Heinrich Erlebach, Andreas Nicolaus Vetter, Johann Caspar Kerll, Johann Philipp Krieger, and Eckelt himself. Wolff contends that "the 'core' of the volume – espe-

16. The interrelations between these two collections are explored further in Russell Stinson, "Some Thoughts on Bach's Neumeister Chorales," *Journal of Musicology* 11 (1993): 455–77; and in Stinson's forthcoming book on the *Orgelbüchlein*. See also Werner Breig, "Textbezug und Werkidee in Johann Sebastian Bachs frühen Orgelchorälen," in *Musikkulturgeschichte: Festschrift für Constantin Floros zum 60. Geburtstag*, ed. Peter Petersen (Wiesbaden: Breitkopf & Härtel, 1990), 167–82.

17. Jean-Claude Zehnder, "Georg Böhm und Johann Sebastian Bach: Zur Chronologie der Bachschen Stilentwicklung," *Bach-Jahrbuch* 74 (1988): 73–110.

18. An important complementary study is Hans-Joachim Schulze, "Johann Christoph Bach (1671–1721), 'Organist und Schul Collega in Ohrdruf,' Johann Sebastian Bachs erster Lehrer," *Bach-Jahrbuch* 71 (1985): 55–81.

cially the pieces by Pachelbel and Froberger – is probably roughly the same as the repertoire entrusted to Johann Christoph Bach. ... It offers welcome insights into the knowledge of contemporary keyboard literature, the level of technical skill, and the rudiments of composition that Johann Sebastian might have possessed by the time he departed for Lüneburg" (pp. 60–61).[19]

Wolff also advances several ideas that run contrary to traditional views about Bach's youth. For instance, he thinks it more likely that Johann Christoph was introduced to north German keyboard music by his younger brother than vice versa. He believes, too, that "Böhm's direct influence on the young Bach was less in the area of the specifically North German manner of pedal playing than in the sphere of French-derived manual repertoire" (p. 62). He supports this notion by observing (1) that the pedals on Böhm's organ were in a state of disrepair in the early years of the eighteenth century; (2) that almost all the works by Böhm in the Möller Manuscript and the Andreas Bach Book (two large keyboard collections assembled by Johann Christoph Bach) are clavier suites; and (3) that the Braunschweig-Lüneburg court was dominated by the "Frantzösischer Geschmack." Wolff also argues that the purpose of Bach's visit to Lübeck in 1705–6 was to gain knowledge of Buxtehude's *Abendmusik* rather than his organ music. According to this view, Bach established ties with Reinken during his Lüneburg years, and Reinken introduced Bach to the organ works of Buxtehude: "The Lübeck trip of 1705–1706 would then be viewed as the culmination, not the beginning, of a long, intensive involvement with matters of organ writing" (p. 64).[20] Finally, Wolff redates Bach's arrangements of movements from Reinken's *Hortus musicus* (BWV 954, 965, and 966) from 1720 (Spitta's dating) to sometime before 1710. He considers these works to be related to Bach's fugues after Italian trio sonatas (by Corelli, Albinoni, and Legrenzi), which also date from his early years. At the end of this essay, Wolff issues a plea for a reevaluation of Bach's early period,

19. Wolff has discussed this source more fully in "Johann Valentin Eckelts Tabulaturbuch von 1692," in *Festschrift Martin Ruhnke zum 65. Geburtstag*, ed. Mitarbeitern des Instituts für Musikwissenschaft der Universität Erlangen-Nürnberg (Neuhausen-Stuttgart: Hänssler, 1986), 374–86. See also Robert Hill, " 'Der Himmel weiss, wo diese Sachen hingekommen sind': Reconstructing the Lost Keyboard Notebooks of the Young Bach and Handel," in *Bach, Handel, Scarlatti: Tercentenary Essays*, ed. Peter Williams (Cambridge: Cambridge University Press, 1985), 161–72.

20. The existence of a manuscript of Buxtehude's Prelude in G Minor, BUXWV 148, in the hand of Johann Christoph Bach from the time his younger brother was living with him in Ohrdruf (1695–1700) suggests that Sebastian may have been acquainted with Buxtehude's music even before he arrived in Lüneburg (see Hans-Joachim Schulze, "Bach und Buxtehude: Ein wenig beachtete Quelle in der Carnegie Library zu Pittsburgh/PA," *Bach-Jahrbuch* 77 [1991]: 177–81; and Don O. Franklin, "The Carnegie Manuscript and J. S. Bach," *Bach: The Journal of the Riemenschneider Bach Institute* 22, no.1 [Spring/Summer 1991]: 5–15).

concluding that we "must grant the young Bach a greater measure of compositional craft and artistic discipline than has been done in the past" (pp. 70–71).[21]

BACH'S PUBLISHED WORKS

Wolff has made significant contributions to our knowledge of several major publications dating from the last phase of Bach's life. The essay "The Clavier-Übung Series," a reprint of Wolff's commentary to a facsimile edition of these prints, includes fundamental information about earlier works with similar titles (by Bach's predecessor in Leipzig, Johann Kuhnau, and others); the rationale governing the succession of keys in the six Partitas of Part I; and the overall plan of the work, "in which Bach exhibited an encyclopedic survey of his artistry in the field of keyboard music" (p. 191). An important section on the technical aspects of printing concludes that, despite frequent reports to the contrary in the secondary literature, "there is no documentary evidence ... to support the claim that Johann Sebastian ever engraved any part of his works" (p. 194).[22] On the other hand, it is clear (e.g., from the autograph corrections in the single issue of the Second Partita) that Bach participated in other ways in the preparation of his printed compositions.

The balance of the article consists of sections on each of the parts of the *Clavier-übung*. We learn that the original prints of this work were not produced entirely in Nuremberg, as previously assumed. For the collected edition (1731) of Part I (the six Partitas) the Leipzig engraver Johann Gottfried Krügner prepared the title page as well as the individual titles of the partitas and their pagination; in addition, he

21. Several scholars have already rallied to the call, including two Wolff protégés, Robert Hill and Daniel Melamed. In addition to the studies cited in nn. 16–20 above, see Andreas Glöckner, "Zur Echtheit und Datierung der Kantate BWV 150 'Nach dir, Herr, verlanget mich,'" *Bach-Jahrbuch* 74 (1988): 195–203; Karl Heller, "Norddeutsche Musikkultur als Traditionsraum des jungen Bach," *Bach-Jahrbuch* 75 (1989): 7–19; Robert Hill, "*Echtheit angezweifelt*: Style and Authenticity in Two Suites Attributed to Bach," *Early Music* 13 (1985): 248–55, and "The Möller Manuscript and the Andreas Bach Book: Two Keyboard Manuscripts from the Circle of the Young Johann Sebastian Bach" (Ph.D. diss., Harvard University, 1987); Robert Hill, ed., *Keyboard Music from the Andreas Bach Book and the Möller Manuscript*, Harvard Publications in Music, vol. 16 (Cambridge, Mass.: Department of Music, Harvard University, 1991); Friedhelm Krummacher, "Bachs frühe Kantaten im Kontext der Tradition," *Die Musikforschung* 44 (1991): 9–32; Daniel R. Melamed, "The Authorship of the Motet 'Ich lasse dich nicht' BWV Anh. 159," *Journal of the American Musicological Society* 41 (1988): 491–526; Russell Stinson, "Bach's Earliest Autograph," *Musical Quarterly* 71 (1985): 235–63, and *The Bach Manuscripts of Johann Peter Kellner and His Circle: A Case Study in Reception History* (Durham, N.C.: Duke University Press, 1989), 122–30.

22. In this respect Bach differed from Telemann, who routinely engraved his own compositions (see Werner Menke, "Die zeitgenössischen Text- und Notendrucke Telemanns," in *Georg Philipp Telemann: Leben, Werk und Umwelt in Bilddokumenten* [Wilhelmshaven: Florian Noetzel, 1987], 137–46).

engraved the movement headings for the last three single issues. Indeed, it seems likely that "all the printing work of the partitas was carried out in Krügner's Leipzig workshop" (p. 198).[23] A tantalizing detail in the discussion of Part II is mention of a pre-1762 manuscript in the Boston Public Library containing an early version of the Italian Concerto. As for Part III, Wolff reports the results of Gregory Butler's research, which again indicate a greater role for Krügner (over half the print was engraved in Leipzig before it was turned over to Balthasar Schmidt in Nuremberg) and an earlier date (though it did not appear until 1739, the work may have been composed as early as 1736–37) than formerly believed.[24] In the section on Part IV (the Goldberg Variations), Wolff rejects the notion that, because it appears in the second *Clavierbüchlein* for Anna Magdalena Bach (1725), the Aria must have been composed by someone other than Bach and written down during the 1720s. On the contrary, "no firm argument against the authenticity of the Aria from the Goldberg Variations can be put forth,"[25] and the characteristics of Anna Magdalena's script reveal that it "could hardly have been entered before 1740" (pp. 212, 209). Wolff is also skeptical of the traditional view that the Goldberg Variations were commissioned by Count Keyserlingk, a story that originated in Forkel's biography of Bach. He thinks that "after the publication of the work Bach may have dedicated a freshly printed copy of the work to his patron, the count, from which [his house harpsichordist Johann Gottlieb] Goldberg later may frequently have played to while away the sleepless nights of his master. It can be proven that Bach stayed at Keyserlingk's Dresden house in November 1741, and it seems highly plausible that Bach gave him on that occasion a presentation copy of the last part of the Clavier-Übung hot from the press" (p. 213).

In addition to the highly informative general essay, there are two articles on more specialized aspects of the *Clavierübung*. In "Text-Critical Comments on the Origi-

---

23. Here, Wolff relies heavily on the work of Gregory Butler, a participant in his graduate seminar at the University of Toronto in 1968–69, who has since become a leading authority on Bach's original prints. Butler's publications in this area include "Leipziger Stecher in Bachs Originaldrucken," *Bach-Jahrbuch* 66 (1980): 9–26; "Ordering Problems in J. S. Bach's Art of Fugue Resolved," *Musical Quarterly* 69 (1983): 44–81; "J. S. Bach and the Schemelli Gesangbuch Revisited," *Studi Musicali* 13 (1984): 241–57; "The Engraving of J. S. Bach's *Six Partitas*," *Journal of Musicological Research* 7 (1986): 3–27; "Neues zur Datierung der Goldberg-Variationen," *Bach-Jahrbuch* 74 (1988): 219–23; and "The Engravers of Bach's Clavier-Übung II," in *A Bach Tribute: Essays in Honor of William H. Scheide*, ed. Paul Brainard and Ray Robinson (Kassel: Bärenreiter; Chapel Hill, N.C.: Hinshaw, 1993), 57–69.

24. See Gregory Butler, *Bach's Clavier-Übung III: The Making of a Print: With a Companion Study of the Canonic Variations on "Vom Himmel Hoch."* BWV 769 (Durham, N.C.: Duke University Press, 1990).

25. Compare the defense of Bach's authorship of the Aria in Marshall, *The Music of Johann Sebastian Bach*, 57–58.

nal Print of the Partitas," Wolff takes to task the editor of the partitas for the Neue Bach-Ausgabe, Richard D. Jones. The general lesson here concerns the importance of collating *all* extant copies of printed works, in order to take into account variant readings from one printing to the next and important manuscript entries in some sources. Wolff's specific complaint is that Jones relied too heavily on the copy in the British Library while neglecting important information in the other three that are extant (Staatsbibliothek zu Berlin-Preussischer Kulturbesitz; Library of Congress; and the University of Illinois Library). By giving inadequate attention to the readings in the Library of Congress copy in particular, Jones missed a number of important details – added tempo markings and embellishments, rhythmic revisions, and even changes of specific pitches – in the Second and Third Partitas.[26]

"The Handexemplar of the Goldberg Variations" offers a thorough examination of this newly located source and details another of Wolff's more sensational discoveries. This print is more important than the other personal copies because it contains not only handwritten revisions for the Goldberg Variations but also a set of fourteen enigmatic circle canons in Bach's hand on the inner side of the back cover.

Shortly after the discovery of Bach's copy of the Goldberg Variations, the *Handexemplar* of the Schübler Chorales unexpectedly resurfaced. This source had been used by Friedrich Conrad Griepenkerl and Wilhelm Rust for their editions of Bach's organ works, but it vanished in the 1850s and was considered lost until 1975, when it was purchased by William H. Scheide (Princeton NJ) from Albi Rosenthal, a British book dealer. In "Bach's Personal Copy of the Schübler Chorales," Wolff explores the provenance of this document on the basis of two letters from Spitta that still accompany it today. Sometime between 1852 and his death in 1858 the Berlin librarian Siegfried Wilhelm Dehn apparently gave this copy of the print to Henri Eugène Philippe Louis d'Orléans, duke of Aumale (1822–97), who, in turn, gave it to Chopin's student, the celebrated pianist Marcelline Czartoryska, née Princess Radziwill (1817–94). She passed it on to her student, the pianist and music historian Franciszek Bylicki, who was the recipient of Spitta's letters.[27] The early history of the source is more straightforward: it was inherited by Carl Philipp Emanuel Bach after his father's death in 1750; Emanuel sold it to Forkel in 1774; Griepenkerl procured it from Forkel's estate in 1819; and after Griepenkerl's death in 1849 it went to Dehn. Perhaps the most significant result of these investigations is the correct identification of Bach's personal copy of a different work. It has long been thought that the copy of *Clavierübung* III in the Berlin Staatsbibliothek is Bach's *Handexemplar*. But a faded

---

26. Jones is (dutifully) preparing a revised edition of the partitas for the NBA.

27. See Christoph Wolff, "From Berlin to Lódz: The Spitta Collection Resurfaces," *Notes* 46 (1989): 319.

ink notation in Griepenkerl's hand that matches a description in the 1819 catalog of Forkel's estate proves that the print in the Musikbibliothek der Stadt Leipzig, actually was the composer's personal copy.

In an influential essay on the published works as a whole, "Principles of Design and Order in Bach's Original Editions," Wolff illuminates the rationale governing the order of the individual components in Bach's major publications. This is an exceptionally rich contribution, only a fraction of which can be summarized here. Wolff notes that Bach's works are ordered according to two principal criteria: "On the one hand, there is the composer's wish to design his works in a manner of lucid exposition governed by discernible principles as model collections. On the other hand, didactic aims – especially in the keyboard works – guide the composer" (p.343). *Clavierübung* I (the six Partitas) and the Schübler Chorales are both based on the principle of variety, "that is, a joining of works of similar kind and rank that differ merely as to their musical character" (p.344). *Clavierübung* II (the Italian Concerto and the French Overture) stresses the principle of opposition: contrasting genres (concerto and overture), contrasting national styles (Italian and French), and the contrasting tonalities of F major and B minor (opposite modes separated by the distance of a tritone). *Clavierübung* III is the first truly cyclic work. Its complex structure is "a summation encompassing various principles of disposition: pivotal arrangement; arrangements in groups of corresponding or contrasting pairs; arrangement in intensifying the symmetrical sequence. These are all joined in an overall framework of architectonic conception in which smaller groupings follow their own respective orders. The manifold combinations arising from purely musical considerations are enhanced by extramusical ones, namely the distinction of Mass and Catechism settings. The duets form again a distinct group" (p.346). The design of the Goldberg Variations (*Clavierübung* IV) involves ten groups of three movements, "each concluding with a canonic variation. The canons themselves are written at intervals arranged in rising order" (p.347), and the entire complex is framed by the Aria at the beginning and end. The Canonic Variations on "Vom Himmel hoch" are preserved in two versions, with the movements in different orders: "The order of the engraved version [published in 1747] reflects a gradual increase in contrapuntal complexity. ... In contrast to the printed version ... the autograph – the authentic version emanating directly from the composer – shows a symmetric form" (pp.349–50). As for the disposition of the individual components of the Musical Offering, "it seems equally feasible to employ the principle of increasing contrapuntal complexity [i.e., *Ricercar à 3, Ricercar à 6*, five contrapuntal canons, five thematic canons, *Sonata*] or the principle of axial symmetry [i.e., *Ricercar à 3*, five contrapuntal canons, *Sonata*, five thematic canons, *Ricercar à 6*]" (p.352). In the Art of Fugue, if one disregards several questionable additions in the engraved version, it is possible to "identify a tangible structure based on the principle of grouping sections by fugal techniques and placing them in the order of intricacy. Apparent also are smaller structural gestures, such as the pairing of fugues on single themes, the growing complexity in the sequence of counterfugues as well as their symmetrical arrangement (obtained by placing the movement in French style in the center), the symmetrical arrangement of the double and triple fugues, and the pairing of contrasting mirror fugues" (p. 354). On the other hand, the version preserved in the autograph "does not suggest any patterned sequence, ... the order of movements being largely arbitrary" (p. 356).

BACH'S LATE WORKS

Wolff established his scholarly reputation through his studies of Bach's late works. Indeed, most of his publications before 1975 concern aspects of works composed during Bach's last decade.

The pair of essays on the Musical Offering provides a wealth of insights. While previous investigations have been hindered by inadequate studies of the sources, Wolff's research is based on examination and collation of all seventeen extant copies of the original print in connection with the editing of the Musical Offering for the Neue Bach-Ausgabe.

In "New Research on the Musical Offering," Wolff tackles the most difficult, controversial, and central questions about this work. He shows that the unusual use of double and single leaves in oblong and upright position, which has puzzled many scholars, simply amounts to three fascicles with separate title covers, "an admirable solution to the difficult assignment of finding an appropriate way to publish a work which represents a mixed repertoire of keyboard and ensemble pieces" (p. 250). The layout of the print speaks against the notion of the Musical Offering as a cyclic structure; its unity does not extend beyond the use of the royal theme throughout the work. From various signs of haste in the engraving process, coupled with a newly discovered document (an announcement in a supplement to the *Leipziger Zeitungen* for 30 September 1747), Wolff concludes that the Musical Offering was not published in installments over an extended period of time (Spitta's hypothesis); rather it was composed and printed within a few months after Bach's May 1747 visit to the court of Frederick the Great in Potsdam. With regard to instrumentation, Wolff notes that the entire work can be played with only the instruments specified in the trio sonata and the canon no. 2 (*à 2 Violini in unisono*): flute, two violins, and continuo. In view of the stylistic elements of *Empfindsamkeit* that pervade the three-part ricercar and documentary evidence that late in life Bach acted as a sales agent for Silbermann fortepianos in Leipzig, Wolff reaches the novel conclusion that "the three-part ricercar may be considered a composition inspired by and conceived for the fortepiano and its new sound effects" (p. 255).[28]

In "Apropos the Musical Offering: The Thema Regium and the Term *Ricercar*," Wolff considers two other central issues. First, he examines the "royal theme," arguing that Bach reworked the melody given by Frederick, which was, in turn, derived from two "conventional soggetto motifs, as they are frequently found in imitative keyboard pieces of the seventeenth century" (p. 326). Second, he explores the question of why Bach chose the same heading for two works so radically different as the three- and six-part ricercars. He finds the key in the twofold definition of *ricercare* in Johann Gottfried Walther's *Musicalisches Lexicon* (1732). In the *Ricercar à 3* the term refers to a "Prelude, or a kind of Fantasy," stressing its improvisational qualities. The six-part ricercar, on the other hand, is "the prototype of an 'elaborate fugue.' ... In its conception one recognizes clearly the model of the seventeenth-century imitative ricercar in the manner of Frescobaldi" (p. 331).

Wolff's book also includes three seminal essays on the Art of Fugue.[29] In "The Compositional History of the Art of Fugue," Wolff shows that this work was composed in stages; he distinguishes between two distinct versions. The first is preserved in the oldest extant source, an autograph fair copy dating for the most part from ca. 1742, which must have been preceded by a working copy (now lost) from the late 1730s. The work was originally conceived "according to the principles of contrapuntal types, in an order of progressive complexity" (p. 279): three fugues in simple counterpoint; six fugues in double counterpoint; three fugues in triple counterpoint; a perpetual canon in augmentation; two mirror fugues.[30] The more familiar printed version represents a thorough revision that proceeded in phases beginning around 1747. Here "the determining principle of design becomes that of fugal manners": four fugues in simple counterpoint but duplicity of theme formation (*rectus* and *inversus*); three counterfugues in which the expositions of *rectus* and *inversus* forms of the theme are combined; four double fugues with from two to four themes

---

28. This line of research is explored more fully in Christoph Wolff, "Bach und das Pianoforte," in *Bach und die italienische Musik – Bach e la musica italiana*, ed. Wolfgang Osthoff and Reinhard Wiesend, Centro Tedesco di Studi Veneziani – Quaderni, vol. 36 (Venice: Centro Tedesco di Studi Veneziani, 1987), 197–210.

29. Wolff's work on the Art of Fugue also served as the catalyst for a seminar report by his students at Columbia University ("Bach's 'Art of Fugue': An Examination of the Sources," *Current Musicology* 19 [1975]: 47–77) and resulted as well in his two-volume critical edition (Frankfurt: C. F. Peters, 1987).

30. The early version of the Art of Fugue was recorded by Robert Hill (harpsichord) in 1987 for Music and Arts Programs of America, Inc. (Berkeley, Calif.), CD-279.

and four canons; quadruple fugue (p. 278). This new perspective on the origins of the Art of Fugue suggests that it "was not the utmost and final goal representing Bach's concept of the monothematic cycle of instrumental music," as it has traditionally been regarded, "but rather its point of departure" (p. 279).[31]

In "Bach's Last Fugue: Unfinished?" Wolff takes issue with the conventional view that the last movement of the Art of Fugue is incomplete because Bach's illness and subsequent death prevented him from finishing it. Instead he argues that the composer stopped writing precisely at the point of the retransition from the dominant to the tonic because the continuation of the piece was already written down on a lost fragmentary manuscript, originally drafted in order to try out the combinatorial possibilities of the four subjects of the quadruple fugue. He concludes that "the last fugue was not left unfinished as it appears today and, in fact, the Art of Fugue must have been a nearly completed work when Bach died" (p. 263).

"The Deathbed Chorale: Exposing a Myth" traces the emergence of the idea that on his deathbed the blind Bach dictated a chorale "on the spur of the moment." Beginning with a brief statement in the original edition of the Art of Fugue (published shortly after Bach's death), Wolff reviews the relevant accounts in Forkel's and Spitta's biographies and in the critical commentary to Rust's edition for the Bachgesellschaft, showing how each embroidered the story and thereby contributed to the legend of a "deathbed chorale." He notes that the four-part organ chorale "Wenn wir in höchsten Nöten sein," BWV 668a, was joined to the original edition of the Art of Fugue not because of any essential connections between the two works but as "a pious gesture to offset the lack of a conclusion for the final fugue" (p. 282). Through a detailed reexamination of the original musical sources and their relationship to one another, Wolff concludes that "this so-called deathbed chorale was never 'dictated ... on the spur of the moment,' but that Bach dictated in his blindness revisions for an existing composition" (p. 292).

There are also two important essays on aspects of the B Minor Mass. In "Origins of the Kyrie of the B Minor Mass," Wolff calls attention to stylistic parallels between the Kyrie of a Mass in G minor by Johann Hugo von Wilderer (1670–1724), the Palatine electoral court composer who was a student of Giovanni Legrenzi, and the Kyrie of the B Minor Mass. Wolff surmises that this work, which is preserved

---

31. At the end of his important "Zur Chronologie der Spätwerke Johann Sebastian Bachs: Kompositions- und Aufführungstätigkeit von 1736 bis 1750" (*Bach-Jahrbuch* 74 [1988]: 7–72), Yoshitake Kobayashi notes that the net effect of Wolff's earlier dating of the Art of Fugue and his own later dating of the B Minor Mass is to reverse the traditional chronological relationship between these two works: "From now on not the Art of Fugue but the B Minor Mass is to be regarded as Bach's *opus ultimum*" (p. 66).

in a manuscript copy in Bach's hand, was obtained through his connections with the Dresden court.

"The Agnus Dei of the B Minor Mass: Parody and New Composition Reconciled" offers a detailed comparison of the Agnus Dei with "Ach, bleibe doch, mein liebstes Leben," BWV 11/4, and the movement that served as the model for them both, "Entfernet euch, ihr kalten Herzen!" from the Wedding Serenata, BWV ANH.196 (text by Johann Christoph Gottsched; music lost). A companion piece, of sorts, to an article by Alfred Dürr,[32] Wolff's essay reaches beyond the material at hand to provide insight into Bach's parody procedure more generally. For instance, in seeking to understand why Bach went to such lengths to rework an old composition when it would surely have been much easier to compose a new one, he remarks that "one reason … must have been his declared desire to preserve a particularly exquisite piece, to elaborate and improve on it" (p.337). Wolff's critical comparison of the two movements leads to the conclusion that "in general, the Agnus Dei is a much more thematically controlled piece of music than its parody model" (p.338). He views the increased "contrapuntal sophistication and canonic technique" of the material that was added as evidence of "a deliberate aesthetic rapprochement and musical integration of the Agnus Dei in the large-scale structure of the B Minor Mass" (p.338). Not surprisingly, the adjustments that Bach made in the process of integrating this movement into the B Minor Mass both affected and were affected by the larger context of the entire new work.

The articles on the Musical Offering, the Art of Fugue, and the B Minor Mass are rounded out by a general essay, "Toward a Definition of the Last Period of Bach's Work." This wide-ranging contribution, which mentions virtually all relevant compositions and biographical details, provides an excellent overview of the terrain. Wolff identifies the following characteristics as typical of Bach's late works: "a theoretical component, a tendency toward melodic writing in cantabile style (without abandoning harmonic-contrapuntal elaboration), an integral stylistic plurality, and a historically-oriented dimension" (p.365). Moreover, in his last decade Bach's "musical intuition and his mastery of composition enabled him to blend tradition and modernism. What emerges is a quasi-historical attitude that leads Bach into the musical past (to Palestrina and the forebears of the Bach family) as well as bestowing upon him, especially through the exchange with his students and sons, a foretaste of future developments" (p.367).

---

32. Alfred Dürr, " 'Entfernet euch, ihr kalten Herzen': Möglichkeiten und Grenzen der Rekonstruktion einer Bach-Arie," *Die Musikforschung* 39 (1986): 32–36.

INSIGHTS ON INDIVIDUAL COMPOSITIONS AND REPERTORIES

Wolff's book includes five miscellaneous essays on aspects of particular works or groups of works. His article on "The Architecture of the Passacaglia" is a detailed analysis of the structure of this famous organ composition (BWV 582). Wolff views earlier accounts as unsatisfactory because they are either "rigidly systematic" or "arbitrary." His attempt to let the work "speak in all its fine details" (p. 307) leads to the conclusion that the first part of the work, the twenty ostinato variations, has a remarkably symmetrical structure: a central pair of variations (vars. 10–11) is framed by groups of four (6–9, 12–15), three (3–5, 16–18), and two (1–2, 19–20).

Though it originally appeared over fifteen years ago, the essay "Bach's Audition for the St. Thomas Cantorate: The Cantata 'Du wahrer Gott and Davids Sohn'" grew out of Wolff's work on a volume of the Neue Bach-Ausgabe that has recently been released. The article was occasioned by the unexpected reappearance of three original performing parts for the cantata (BWV 23): an autograph part for *Violoncello* as well as a continuo part in A minor and a part for *Basson è Cembalo* (both written by copyists).[33] One particularly interesting item that emerges from Wolff's examination of the continuo parts is the likelihood that organ and harpsichord were used simultaneously in the continuo section.[34] In addition to clarifying many other details about the performance history of the cantata, Wolff convincingly argues that "the final version [dating from between 1728 and 1732] reverts to the original conception of the work, both in the choice of key (C minor) and sonority (regular oboes)" (p. 140), after having been performed several times in B minor with oboes d'amore.

"The Reformation Cantata 'Ein feste Burg'" focuses on three specific issues in Bach's famous Cantata 80, which have important ramifications for its history and performance. (1) It has long been known that the work is a revision of the Weimar cantata *Alles, was von Gott geboren*, BWV 80a, although only the text of the Weimar version (1715) survives. Cantata 80 probably dates from 1730 (the two hundredth anniversary of the Augsburg Confession), but we cannot know for sure because no original manuscripts have been preserved (the earliest source is a manuscript copy by Johann Christoph Altnikol, Bach's son-in-law). Wolff calls attention to a previously unknown intermediate version (BWV 80b), documented by three fragments of the first leaf of the autograph score. This page (reproduced in a composite facsimile on p. 153) can be dated to 31 October 1723 on the basis of the watermark and the inscrip-

33. See Hans-Joachim Schulze, "Zur Rückkehr einiger autographer Kantatenfragmente in die Bach-Sammlung der Deutschen Staatsbibliothek Berlin," *Bach-Jahrbuch* 63 (1977): 130–34.

34. Another Wolff protégé, Laurence Dreyfus, has been the leading proponent of the theory of dual accompaniment in certain vocal works of Bach (see *Bach's Continuo Group: Players and Practices in His Vocal Works* [Cambridge, Mass.: Harvard University Press, 1987], esp. 38–40).

tion *Festo Reformationis*. While the beginning of the second movement, at the bottom of the leaf, is identical with the second aria of Cantata 80, "the first movement is a hitherto unknown piece, surprisingly a straightforward four-part chorale harmonization – a highly unusual cantata opening" (p. 155). Since Bach took the trouble to "write a new score rather than merely inserting the new chorale into the score of the Weimar version," Wolff believes that "the revision of movements contained in the Weimar version ... was more thorough than has been guessed so far. Thus the version BWV 80a would be less easily reconstructed than has been assumed" (p. 155). (2) Wolff points out the incongruity of the trumpet and timpani parts in the version of mvts. 1 and 5 in the Bachgesellschaft edition, which is still used for most performances and recordings. These can be traced back to Wilhelm Friedemann Bach's reorchestrated parodies with the Latin texts "Gaudete omnes populi" (mvt. 1) and "Manebit verbum Domini" (mvt. 5). Not only are the trumpet and timpani parts inauthentic, but close inspection of the Altnikol copy also reveals that three oboes should be used for the opening movement (instead of two oboes in unison, the Bachgesellschaft reading). (3) Wolff discusses the unusual twofold bass part – cantus firmus and continuo – of the opening movement. In Altnikol's score "the next-to-last line, the actual continuo part, is designated *Violoncello e Cembalo* and the bottom line (the canonic part), *Violone e Organo*. Thus the *Cembalo* continuo is intended to sound in 8′ register, the organ bass in 16′ register" (p. 161).

"Bach's Leipzig Chamber Music" is one of the most important essays in the book. Here Wolff proposes "to replace the deep-rooted dichotomy between cantor and capellmeister with more varied relationships between the many facets of Bach's rich personality" (p. 224). Specifically, he takes issue with the traditional view that most, if not all, of Bach's chamber music was composed during the period in which he served as Kapellmeister at the court of Prince Leopold of Anhalt-Cöthen (1717–23). Wolff argues persuasively that the size of Bach's chamber music repertory must originally have been much larger than it is today: "It does not seem plausible that the transverse flute, which became important in Germany only from around 1720, should alone have represented the wind instruments in Bach's chamber sonatas. ... In addition to the flute, the oboe and recorder hold such an important place in the scoring of Bach's vocal works that their absence from his sonatas is simply inconceivable. ... The losses must have exceeded by far those in ... Bach's vocal music" (pp. 224–25). In addition, he demonstrates that during his Leipzig years Bach had many opportunities to pursue the composition and performance of chamber music, "through the Collegium Musicum, the circle of family, students, and friends, and ... through involvements outside Leipzig" (p. 231). Finally, Wolff discusses five works (the Sonata in B Minor for Flute and Harpsichord, BWV 1030; the Sonata in G Major for Viola da Gamba and Harpsichord, BWV 1027; the Concerto in A Minor for Violin, BWV

1041; the Concerto in D Minor for Two Violins, BWV 1043; and the Suite in B Minor for Orchestra, BWV 1067) "which are traditionally regarded as Cöthen works but for which we possess strong source- and style-critical evidence that suggests an origin in the 1730s" (p.234).

The essay "The Organ in Bach's Cantatas" provides basic information about the role of the organ in the performance of Bach's cantatas, including questions of registration. Wolff draws particular attention to a group of cantatas (BWV 146, 170, 35, 169, 49, 188, 120a, 29) with virtuoso organ parts, in which the organ is used as a solo instrument "in a manner which was otherwise completely unknown at that time" (pp.319–20).[35]

BACH'S REPUTATION

In recent years there has been renewed interest in the reception of Bach's music, both during his lifetime and after his death.[36] Wolff has been an active participant in this arena, too. "On the Original Editions of Bach's Works" contains much of the same information as the individual essays on the composer's published works, but it emphasizes their role in the development of Bach's reputation, both during his lifetime and in the century after his death. It also casts a glance at the publications of Bach's predecessors and contemporaries, from which several important points emerge. By comparison with composers like Palestrina, Monteverdi, Praetorius, and Schütz, Bach published relatively little. The reasons for this include "the decline of the music trade in central Germany after the Thirty Years War," the high cost of printing polyphonic keyboard music, and the difficulty of Bach's music, which limited its commercial appeal (pp.372–73). Wolff notes that "an orientation toward the tastes and needs of a wider public seems to have been entirely foreign to Bach." This is seen in the complexity and relative inaccessibility of the Leipzig cantatas, none of which were published during his lifetime: "In this conscious exclusiveness Bach's work is clearly distinguished from that of his contemporaries [e.g., Telemann]." It is also evident in the compilation of the Brandenburg Concertos – "six pieces of radically different texture and scoring, to say nothing of their exacting demands on performers" – which also remained unpublished (p.374). In view of his apparent indifference to commer-

35. These compositions are explored more thoroughly in Laurence Dreyfus, "The Metaphorical Soloist: Concerted Organ Parts in Bach's Cantatas," *Early Music* 13 (1985): 237–47.

36. Among the more influential studies are Günther Wagner, "J. A. Scheibe–J. S. Bach: Versuch einer Bewertung," *Bach-Jahrbuch* 68 (1982): 33–49; Martin Zenck, "Stadien der Bach-Deutung in der Musikkritik, Musikästhetik und Musikgeschichtsschreibung zwischen 1750 und 1800," *Bach-Jahrbuch* 68 (1982): 7–32, and *Die Bach-Rezeption des späten Beethoven: Zum Verhältnis von Musikhistoriographie und Rezeptionsgeschichtsschreibung der "Klassik"* (Stuttgart: Franz Steiner, 1986); and Ludwig Finscher, "Bach in the Eighteenth Century," in *Bach Studies*, ed. Don O. Franklin (Cambridge: Cambridge University Press, 1989), 281–96.

cial considerations, "it seems almost miraculous that Bach managed to market more than a dozen large and ambitious publications" (p.375).

The intricacy of Bach's musical idiom is also the focus of the essay "Bach's Vocal Music and Early Music Criticism." Apparently the reason that Bach's works were rarely discussed in music journals during his lifetime is that "the complexity of his manner of composing was beyond the reach of contemporary critics in as much as it did not provide them with adequate standards of values" (p.377). On the basis of passages in Mattheson's *Critica Musica* and Scheibe's *Critischer Musicus* (particularly the famous debate between Scheibe and Birnbaum), Wolff documents the collision between the expressive ideals of Bach's vocal music and the aesthetic values of the age.

In another notable essay, "On the Recognition of Bach and 'the Bach Chorale': Eighteenth-Century Perspectives," Wolff calls attention to "the 'latent' rise of Bach's fame, initially restricted to the sphere of professionals" (p.384), in the second half of the eighteenth century, as opposed to the more familiar "public" Bach movement of the nineteenth century. Because they united the archetypal and the individual elements of Bach's art, the publication of the four-part chorales played a central role in spreading his fame: "To impart the stamp of originality upon the norm was Bach's aim, and this goal forms his challenge to later generations. ... 'The Bach chorale' is the abstraction and essence of this creative ability in its most impressive form, and its influence abides in unbroken tradition until our day" (pp.389–90).

The final essay in the book, "'The Extraordinary Perfections of the Hon. Court Composer': An Inquiry into the Individuality of Bach's Music," is one of Wolff's most profound and ambitious contributions, a fitting conclusion to a most distinguished collection. Its goal is nothing less than an attempt to define the unique qualities of Bach's art, that which sets it apart from the music of his contemporaries. Beyond his "uncompromising professional attitude" and "infinite thirst for knowledge ... regarding all facets of the art of composition" (p.392), Wolff points to "the principle of elaboration of given ideas in the sense of deeper penetration" (p.395), which manifests itself in such diverse contexts as "Bach's technique of arrangement and transcription ... , his practice of parody, ... successive different settings or harmonizations of a *cantus firmus*, ... [and] the probing of an idea in multiformity and diversity of execution (the Orgel-Büchlein, harpsichord concertos, Well-Tempered Clavier, chorale cantata cycle)" (p.396). He views this as "originating in [Bach's] quest for perfection, the constant impetus for elaboration" (p.397).[37] While Wolff does not allege that other composers were content merely to replicate countless un-

---

37. A similar point of view was articulated by Spitta, who noted "the fact, which may be observed throughout Bach's works, that when he essays the employment of a new form, he never contents himself with a single attempt, but endeavors to exhaust it as far as possible by repeating the experiment" (*Johann Sebastian Bach*, 1:434).

differentiated examples of particular genres, his remarks do imply that the degree of variety within any part of Bach's œuvre outstrips by far the norm for music in the first half of the eighteenth century. Accordingly, Wolff's summation is a useful model for understanding the essential distinctions between Bach's art and that of, say, Vivaldi, Handel, or Telemann.[38]

OUTLOOK

From the breadth and depth of these essays, it is obvious that Wolff's book will be consulted by scholars and students for many years to come. Indeed, recent recognition of its pivotal significance came when it was granted an ASCAP–Deems Taylor Award. It is all the more regrettable, therefore, that the first edition contains a large number of misprints, ranging from typographical errors to inaccurate bibliographic citations. Although many of them will be evident to the careful reader, others are likely to elude detection and will be perpetuated in the Bach literature. For this reason, it is essential that the requisite corrections be made in future editions.

Half the essays appear here for the first time in English, and Alfred Mann's translations are consistently of the highest caliber. Unfortunately, the same cannot be said of chapters 2–4, 15, 24, and 30 (apparently reprints of earlier translations), which would have benefited from Professor Mann's sure editorial hand.

Not to be overlooked are the valuable "postscripts" that appear with the notes at the end of the volume. These contain a wealth of new information – explanatory notes, comments, corrections, and references to recent research – including an important discussion of Johann Balthasar Denner's portrait (ca.1730), possibly depicting Bach and three of his sons (pp.400–401), and Wolff's long-awaited response (pp.421–23) to Ursula Kirkendale's assault on his research on the Musical Offering.[39]

Despite a few deficiencies in its production, the overall impact of this book is powerful, even monolithic. The collective weight of these essays is astonishing, as is their quantity and diversity. Through bold questioning of entrenched views, buttressed by intimate acquaintance with the musical style as well as the manuscript and printed sources of this repertory, Wolff has made major contributions to our present-day picture of Bach. At the same time, by signaling new directions and uncovering fresh areas of inquiry, he has given us reason to believe that the deep well of Bach research will not soon run dry.

Stephen A. Crist

38. This paradigm informs the investigation of one especially prevalent movement type in my forthcoming book on the forms of Bach's arias.

39. Ursula Kirkendale, "The Source for Bach's *Musical Offering*: The *Institutio Oratoria* of Quintilian," *Journal of the American Musicological Society* 33 (1980): 88–141.

Keyboard Music from the Andreas Bach Book and the Möller Manuscript. Edited by Robert Hill. With a foreword by Christoph Wolff. Harvard Publications in Music, vol.16. Cambridge, Mass.: Department of Music, Harvard University (distributed by Harvard University Press), 1991. xlvii, 210 pp.

Music editing is at once the highest and lowliest calling of our profession. While few Bach scholars need to be reminded of the fundamental importance of scholarly editing to our understanding of Bach and his music, the musical community at large tends to disparage scholarly editing as a tedious, uncreative task, and performers generally assume that any self-proclaimed "Urtext" edition is a guarantor, or at least a major step in the direction of, authenticity. Not everyone recognizes that editing is a demanding task best undertaken by seasoned musician-scholars who take an active interest in current methods and philosophies of both editing and performing. Even Bach scholars may need to be reminded that the formats, methodologies, and underlying philosophies of critical editions are constantly changing. Publishers may need to be shown that tried and true house styles and procedures sometimes fail to meet the needs and concerns of contemporary users of their editions.

Procedures and policies now customary for the editing of works preserved in eighteenth-century fair-copy autographs may provide little guidance to editors faced with conflicting, error-full copies of uncertain provenance of seventeenth-century works. Traditional engraving practices that evolved in response to the needs of nineteenth-century music and printing technology may be irrelevant to and may even obscure important aspects of older music. Even the supposedly inessential minutiae of the original notation, such as the beaming of small note values and the placement of so-called cautionary accidentals, may convey significant information to the player or editor willing to take them into consideration. Particularly in an age when computer-generated music typography permits greater flexibility than before, and when performers as well as scholars are increasingly accustomed to notation departing from nineteenth-century standards – in both old and new music – editors must constantly reassess their working procedures if these are to present an acceptable and accurate text.

These thoughts occur in examining Robert Hill's recent edition of keyboard pieces from two large manuscripts compiled by J. S. Bach's older brother and teacher Johann Christoph Bach of Ohrdruf (1671–1721). Well known as a harpsichordist and Bach scholar, Hill meets all the criteria one might reasonably seek in an editor. He has given us a number of fine recordings and articles as well as a valuable dissertation on the two manuscripts in question.[1] Here he presents an edition of just under half the 111 entries in those two manuscripts (hereafter referred to as ABB and MM), including sixteen previously unpublished works.

Long underrated because of their uncertain provenance (and because of the loss of MM during the nineteenth century), the manuscripts and their music have been undergoing a reevaluation since Hans-Joachim Schulze's identification of the principal copyist.[2] In a brief foreword Christoph Wolff places the manuscripts in their historical context and points out their importance: not only are they the earliest and most authoritative sources for many of the young Bach's keyboard works, but they provide good and in many cases unique sources for music by Pachelbel, Buxtehude, Böhm, and Reinken as well as a number of lesser composers.

Hill's introduction summarizes the most important findings of his dissertation on the dating of the manuscripts, the identities of the secondary copyists, and other codicological matters. A comprehensive inventory follows as well as critical notes on the musical text. Hill, probably wisely, refrains from speculating on performance issues in this repertory, notably on the question of keyboard medium, which with one exception the sources leave unspecified.[3]

The selection of works ranges from the earnest post-Froberger suites of Reinken and Böhm to lively transcriptions of contemporary theatrical music. Among the hitherto unpublished works are Heydorn's fugue on a theme by Reinken and anonymous arrangements of orchestral pieces by Lully, Marais, and Steffani. Also included are works unavailable in dependable recent editions: suites by Ritter and Zachow; Buxtehude's A-major organ prelude BUXWV 151; J. S. Bach's *pedaliter* fantasy on "Wie schön leuchtet der Morgenstern," BWV 739; and the early version of Bach's Toccata in D Major, BWV 912a. Hill also edits works whose transmission in these manuscripts is of particular interest – for example, the six pieces by Pachelbel, Johann Christoph's

1. Robert Stephen Hill, "The Möller Manuscript and the Andreas Bach Book: Two Keyboard Anthologies from the Circle of the Young Johann Sebastian Bach" (Ph.D. diss., Harvard University, 1987).

2. Hans-Joachim Schulze, *Studien zur Bach-Überlieferung im 18. Jahrhundert* (Leipzig: Edition Peters, 1984), 52–54.

3. The exception is Bach's fantasy "pour le Clavessin" BWV 944/1. Titles in the manuscripts sometimes include the terms *manualiter* and *pedaliter*, but, as the former is confined to the three toccatas by J. S. Bach (BWV 910, 911, and 916), these sources add nothing to the discussion begun in Robert L. Marshall, "Organ or 'Klavier'? Instrumental Prescriptions in the Sources of Bach's Keyboard Works," in *J. S. Bach as Organist: His Instruments, Music, and Performance Practices*, ed. George Stauffer and Ernest May (Bloomington: Indiana University Press, 1986), 212–39; reprinted as "Organ or 'Klavier'? Instrumental Prescriptions in the Sources of the Keyboard Works," in Robert L. Marshall, *The Music of Johann Sebastian Bach: The Sources, the Style, the Significance* (New York: Schirmer Books, 1989), 271–93.

teacher. The decision to include as a work of J. S. Bach the anonymous Fantasy in C Minor, BWV ANH.205, is liable to raise eyebrows. But the copy in ABB (in tablature) is an autograph, and it ends with a type of cadence that Russell Stinson has pointed to as a possible J. S. Bach fingerprint.[4]

The richness of the collection is such that no one seriously interested in Baroque keyboard music will wish to be without it. While the Bach works are clearly the most significant in the volume, the anonymous transcriptions from Marais's opera *Alcide* and the suite by Ritter on the "departure" of his patron Charles XI of Sweden are notable additions to the literature.[5] Equally welcome are the new editions of the excellent suites by (or formerly attributed to) Böhm and Zachow, of Ritter's F♯-minor suite, and of Telemann's ("Mr. Melante's") *Ouverture* in E♭ Major. The arrangement of the great chaconne from Lully's *Phaeton* is of considerable interest since, as Hill notes, it is independent of the one published by D'Anglebert. It is, however, less idiomatic than the Marais transcriptions, in which the French rubrics and ornament signs and the polished harpsichord style more strongly suggest a French origin.[6]

Also noteworthy are the E-minor fugue by Buttstedt, with its obsessively "repercussive" motivic material, and two curiously disparate capriccios both attributed to "Polaroli" (who may or may not be identical to the opera composer Carlo Francesco Polarollo, as Hill presumes). An attractive D-major toccata by Edelmann that bears a generic resemblance to Bach's early organ fantasies BWV 563 and 570 is unfortunately a fragment; an anonymous courante in B♭ major contains a turn of phrase (mm. 4–5) reminiscent of the sarabande from the doubtful suite BWV 821, also in B♭ major. A number of items, such as the bumbling fugue by Coberg and the banal preludes by Küchenthal and Buttstedt, are little more than curiosities. But so little of this repertory survives that one is grateful for the inclusion of these works, as for that of the three ornament tables, which have been frequently cited in the Bach literature.

---

4. Russell Stinson, "The Authenticity of Bach's Neumeister Chorales" (paper read at the meeting of the American Bach and American Schütz Societies, New York, 25 April 1992).

5. Actually, only the *allemanda* of Ritter's suite bears the heading *in discessum Caroli xi Regis Speciae* [*sic*]. Charles XI died in 1697; *discessum* presumably means "death," but the allemande lacks the obvious representational elements of earlier memorial allemandes and *tombeaux*.

6. Hill's table of contents and inventory identify the Marais transcription as an "overture suite," but unlike the Telemann *Ouverture* this is a series of opera excerpts, not unified by key; hence the term used is inappropriate. In addition, the movement here designated "Marche" is actually a minuet in rondeau form; perhaps the title belongs with the preceding "Air de Trompette." The latter does not share a "motto" theme with the "Aire pour les trompettes" in Bach's suite BWV 832, as claimed in Hartwig Eichberg and Thomas Kohlhase, eds., NBA v/10 (*Einzeln überlieferte Klavierwerke II und Kompositionen für Lauteninstrumente*), KB, 71.

Unfortunately, users of the edition must overcome a number of obstacles. The musical typography is sometimes amateurish, and no thought whatever seems to have been given to creating good page turns. The introduction and textual commentary have been poorly proofread (among other things, a line needs to be transposed from p. xxiv to p. xxv), and what appear to be instructions to the music autographer have found their way into the critical notes, which contain an unsettling number of further errors.

Sadly, the musical text also contains substantial errors. Particularly disappointing are the editions of BWV 739, 832, 833, 896, 912a, 917, and 967, and BUXWV 151 – works to which Hill pointed in his dissertation as needing new editions. The most serious errors in these works are listed below.

Some of these errors, such as those listed for BWV 739 (m. 33) or for the prelude of the partita BWV 833 (m. 27), may reflect hasty proofreading. Others appear to be by-products of the venerable procedure of creating a new edition by marking up an existing one. Thus errors or faulty emendations going back at least to the old *Bachgesamtausgabe* (BG) live on (see, e.g., both readings given below for the fugue BWV 896/2). Many readings from late sources (containing the revised version) persist in BWV 912a. Some editorial emendations given in small type in the Neue Bach-Ausgabe appear here in large type (e.g., the top fermata at the end of BWV 549a; the *dal segno* sign at the beginning of the aria of BWV 833).

Other problems raise questions of the type alluded to at the opening of this review. Is this volume meant to be a diplomatic transcription of the sources, a critical edition of selected works, or something else? Hill notes the possibility of using variants in the ABB and MM texts to distinguish "layers of compositional revision" and to reconstruct aspects of the copyist's exemplar for each piece – that is, whether it was a manuscript score, a print, or a "tablature autograph" (p. xxv). The critical apparatus is too meager to carry this plan to fruition or even to serve as an adequate textual commentary in the usual sense; readings from concordances are rarely reported. Clearly, however, the volume is more than a diplomatic facsimile, for otherwise Hill would not have carried out so many of the now-customary modernizations of the notation – changes in clefs, accidentals, etc. – or corrected some erroneous readings.

One must also ask whether sufficient thought has been given to the details of the musical notation. Many of the notational details in question are generally regarded as inessentials – "accidentals," in the jargon of textual criticism. Yet, especially in the light of recent publications in the area of early keyboard music, one must reconsider which details are truly inessential and therefore subject to tacit editorial alteration. This is one of the most important points made in Alexander Silbiger's review entitled "Recent Editions of Early Keyboard Music," which should be required reading for anyone contemplating or editing keyboard music before 1800.[7] It may well be time to extend considerations now customary in the editing of sixteenth- and seventeenth-century music to keyboard works copied or composed during Bach's lifetime and even beyond.

The introduction to the present volume states that editorial accidentals are given in small type or mentioned in the textual notes and that the edition preserves the readings and notation of the sources save for some revisions of stem direction to clarify voice leading (p.xxvii). In fact, editorial accidentals are often supplied silently in regular type, as are rests. Stemming – both the directions of stems and the grouping of note heads onto stems – has frequently been altered, but not according to any consistent pattern; the same is true of the beaming of small note values. Ornament signs often differ substantially from those in the manuscripts, especially the arpeggio signs, which the edition generally gives in the form specifying upward arpeggiation, although this is rarely clear in the sources.[8]

Such details, perhaps insignificant individually, grow in importance when they are systematically altered throughout a large volume of music. Heinrich Schenker long ago showed that beaming often reflects distinctions between motives,[9] and performers now recognize its possible relevance to articulation.[10] In attempting to clarify voice leading an editor imposes the notational style of the mature Bach onto earlier music, imputing to it a contrapuntal rigor that may in fact be absent, thereby discouraging certain freedoms in performance. Even the mature Bach was less rigorous than is the present edition when, for example, it reverses upward and downward stems in the fugue BWV 949 (m. 28) in order to show the putative alto entering with the subject above the soprano (this reading, incidentally, stems from the BG). Here, as in many other keyboard fugues of the period, it is simply not possible to trace each voice from beginning to end; indeed, this remains true in the C♯-minor and B♭-minor fugues from Book 1 of the Well-Tempered Clavier.

Such departures from the original notation can encourage questionable interpretations. For example, in BUXWV 151, m.16, the original beaming and stemming clearly

---

7. Alexander Silbiger, "Recent Editions of Early Keyboard Music," *Journal of the American Musicological Society* 42 (1989): 172–88. Silbiger extends his considerations of early notation to works of J. S. Bach in his "Is the Italian Keyboard *intavolatura* a Tablature?" *Recercare* 3 (1991): 91–92.

8. The singular ornament signs in the Capriccio by Witt are also altered and occasionally given wrongly; the proper readings can be ascertained by comparison with the facsimile on p. xlvii.

9. Heinrich Schenker, "Weg mit dem Phrasierungsbogen," in *Das Meisterwerk in der Musik*, vol.3 (Munich: Drei Masken, 1925; reprint, Hildesheim: Georg Olms, 1974), 43–60.

10. See, e.g., Silbiger, "Recent Editions of Early Keyboard Music," 175.

distinguish the last three sixteenths (e'–f♯'–g♯') from the one on the fourth beat (e', tied to the previous note). German theorists of the period refer to the last three notes as a *suspirans* figure,[11] a point obscured by the edition's beaming together all four notes. Two measures later both the *Ped.* indication and the separate flags on the first two eighth notes in the bass – which are beamed together in the manuscript – are editorial. Thus, although Hill follows the source in not placing the pedal part on a separate staff, he still distinguishes the pedal notes as a polyphonic part separate from the lowest voice in the *manualiter* sections – a distinction that is far from clear in this repertory, as this example shows.

Conventions governing accidentals are also less clear in this repertory than some editors may be willing to acknowledge. By failing to distinguish so many added accidentals from original ones, this edition leaves the reader unable to determine where an alternate interpretation is possible. For example, in the A-minor sonata BWV 967, m. 65, instead of Hill's natural on g'' one might supply a sharp on f''.

Although departing from the manuscripts at these points, the edition retains all their ornament signs, many of which have long been recognized as later additions. Assertions that these are "clearly in the appropriate taste of the day" and that they "will lead to a highly articulated style" (p.xxviii) perhaps represent only one modern school of keyboard interpretation. Some of these signs appear to be contrary to the usage of J. S. Bach and his better French and German contemporaries (see, e.g., the trills in BWV 833, allemande, m. 5, and courante, m. 36, which may be errors for mordents).

The treatment of ornaments raises the vexed question of how "to achieve a text," as Philip Brett puts it in his indispensible survey of early music editing.[12] It is well known that modern musical text editing descends from the literary text criticism of the nineteenth century. What is less well known is that there are radically differing philosophies of text editing. Furthermore, the most-discussed literary texts, such as the Bible, are preserved in hundreds if not thousands of sources that fall into more or less clearly delineated source families. Procedures for determining text filiation and choice of copy text under such circumstances can hardly be carried over unaltered to musical works that are preserved in only one or two unrelated sources, which may be of equally dubious authority. Music editors must carefully choose a method appropriate to their repertory and purpose.

Since Hill worked primarily from a single manuscript for each piece, the solution

11. See John Butt, *Bach Interpretation: Articulation Marks in Primary Sources of J. S. Bach* (Cambridge: Cambridge University Press, 1990), 21.

12. Philip Brett, "Text, Context, and the Early Music Editor," in *Authenticity and Early Music: A Symposium*, ed. Nicholas Kenyon (Oxford: Oxford University Press, 1988), 99.

may seem obvious: reproduce the text of ABB and MM except in cases where they transmit an obviously ungrammatical or impracticable reading, in which case emend on the basis of another source or make an editorial conjecture. Unfortunately, the fact that ornaments were entered at various times means that each state of the manuscript – before, during, and after the entry of ornaments – needs to be considered as a separate source for philological purposes.[13] In addition, the fact that Hill has failed to emend or take note of many questionable readings suggests that errors are often far from obvious.

Not only doubtful ornaments but some doubtful pitches are retained, as in earlier editions. Thus a natural is omitted from bass B in BWV 833, allemande, m. 4, despite its presence at the corresponding point in the courante, which is a variation of the allemande. In the suite BWV 832 and the fugue BWV 949, both in A major, one is faced with puzzling G♯'s that one suspects are there only because the copyist forgot that they had to be canceled (they are in the key signature). Hill does emend a considerable number of notes placed in the wrong register through apparent misreadings of tablature. But other notes are simply missing; for example, in the sarabande of the Reinken suite in C major (MM no. 6), mm. 12 and 13, notes have clearly been omitted in the tenor and alto, respectively. One therefore wonders how often the odd voice leading, strange chords, and occasional puzzles involving accidentals in other works stem from misreadings – either Hill's or the copyist's.[14]

An attentive editor would have noted these things in the critical apparatus and might have supplemented the text – in brackets or in small type, of course. Editors have grown reluctant to do the latter out of veneration for the fair-copy autographs and authorized prints of the mature J. S. Bach and other master composers. But apparent lacunae and other errors suggest that many of the texts in ABB and MM are less sound than has been thought.[15] If a critical edition is to be more than a diplomatic facsimile – if it is to be usable by students and nonspecialists – it must take a genuinely critical attitude toward the text. Given a seemingly faulty text that is probably several copies removed from the autograph or that may have been inaccurately tran-

13. This is the procedure adopted by, e.g., Alfred Dürr, in editing such works as Book 1 of the Well-Tempered Clavier and the French Suites (see Alfred Dürr, ed., NBA v/6, pt. 1 [*Das Wohltemperierte Klavier I*] and NBA v/8 [*Die sechs Französischen Suiten*]).

14. For example, in the E-minor fugue by Buttstedt, one must question the parallel octaves (leading to an open fifth) in m. 19, the irregular seventh chord in m. 22, and the D-major chord (error for a diminished triad on D♯?) in m. 43.

15. Hill speaks of the "newly confirmed authority of the MM/ABB transmission of Bach texts" (p. xxv) and the "newly affirmed reliability of the earliest J. S. Bach copies in MM and ABB" (p. xxvi). But these remarks do not necessarily apply to every work in the volume or even to all of Bach's (e.g., BWV 967).

scribed from a tablature exemplar, a responsible editor may have no choice but to collate and emend.

Thus, even though ABB and MM are the sole sources for many of the works edited here, it may be impossible to proceed mechanically from the principle – all too often taken for granted by modern editors – that a single "principal" source can automatically provide the main text for each work. As in ancient Greek lyric poetry and other poorly transmitted literary texts, substantial emendation, amounting to reconstruction, may occasionally be needed to produce a comprehensible text.[16] Less substantial but nevertheless significant emendation may be necessary to preserve the cogency of less obviously defective texts, such as those for the suites by Bach and Reinken mentioned above.

Hill indicates that the main end of the volume is to help us "come to terms with the new picture of the young Bach's keyboard composition presented by" the two sources (p. xxvi). But the picture is far from clear. For one thing, it remains impossible to say whether the non-Bach works in the two manuscripts represent J. S. Bach's repertory or that of his brother. In either case it is uncertain that these are works that J. S. Bach would have studied during his student years, which ended effectively with his appointment at Arnstadt in 1703, well before the completion of either manuscript. On the whole, the repertory in ABB and MM is conservative; the transcriptions as well as the original works tend to belong to the previous generation, unlike most of Bach's own surviving copies, which favor up-to-date works by his contemporaries. Thus the selection here may reflect more the taste of Johann Christoph than of J. S. Bach, who, although fourteen years younger, was already better traveled and presumably more cosmopolitan by the time the manuscripts were made.

Second, the volume does not provide much insight into how the young Bach achieved his very exceptional personal style. Little in the works of the other composers represented here closely resembles either the modulatory fantasy of pieces like the early G-minor *Ouverture* BWV 822 or the rigorous yet imaginative keyboard counterpoint of early fugues like BWV 896 or the fantasy BWV 917. Fabricius's *Gigue belle* modulates from C minor to as far as A♭ minor and D♭ major but is clumsily composed and unidiomatic for the keyboard. Heydorn's fugue – really a multisectional canzona – on what the title declares to be a Reinken theme (the model is unidentified) is earlier in style and much less assured technically than Bach's works after Reinken. Heydorn's other fugue in the volume, in G minor, does show parallels thematically

16. Music editors may find it instructive to examine critical editions of writers such as Sappho and Alcaeus or of Aeschylus's *Libation Bearers*, whose opening is largely a modern reconstruction (see Denys Page, ed., *Aeschyli septem quae supersunt tragoedias* [Oxford: Clarendon Press, 1972], 201). Knowledge of these works would be limited to specialists if editors feared to offer their own coherent readings.

and structurally to Bach's C-minor fugue after Legrenzi BWV 574.[17] Still, the fact that some of Bach's early works show vague parallels to these, or to the suites by Flor and Pestel, may indicate nothing more than a common interest in certain types of composition then in the air. Before the later of the two sources, ABB, had been completed, Bach's concerns had gone far beyond the genres and styles evident in these manuscripts, particularly in the areas of Italian instrumental music and German chorale elaboration, which are barely represented. The fact is that neither ABB nor MM, nor any other source, tells us as much as we would like to know about the really young Bach, that is, Bach the precocious student or Bach the unbridled virtuoso improviser.

Thus the greatest value of the present volume lies in the repertory itself and in the broad view that it opens onto the little-known musical world of early eighteenth-century Germany. Reissued with corrections, or provided with a thorough and accurate list of errata, the volume would be even more valuable to performers and historians.

SELECTED EMENDATIONS

Readings given are those of ABB or MM unless otherwise noted. I have examined both sources in microfilm copies at the Isham Memorial Library, Harvard University.

BWV 739: m.33, tenor, last note, add (editorial) ♮; m.43, add inner voices on downbeat – g/d' (eighths); m.56, soprano, notes 15–16, g″–a″ instead of d♯″–f♯″; mm.70–71, add tie on c″ (present in MM and in the autograph, SBB MUS. MS BACH P 488).

BWV 820, overture: m.4, right hand, first chord, add downward arpeggio; left hand, note 3, trill instead of mordent. Entrec: m.18, left hand, note 7, no ♯ on c′; m.19, right hand, note 9, no ♯ on f; m.24, right hand, note 3, no ♭ (late addition in MS).

BWV 832, air: m.12, soprano, note 8, d″ instead of c♯″; m.15, left hand, note 1, delete g (only a blot [?] in MS – g leads to parallel octaves); m.16, soprano, note 2, ♯ is editorial (♯ is in key signature, but ♮ is possible); m.22, left hand, a, upward stem is editorial; m.24, 4th beat, e, upward stem is editorial.

BWV 833, praeludium: m.27, delete c″, d″, fermata. Allemande: m.2, bass, note 3, d instead of B♭; m.4, bass, last note, add editorial ♮. Courante: m.1, possibly downward instead of upward arpeggio. Sarabande: m.7, bass, last note, g instead of a.

BWV 896, fugue: m.16, soprano, note 5, e″ instead of g♯″; m.47, alto, note 4, d′ instead of d♯′.

BWV 912a: m.16, third beat, tenor, c♯″ instead of a′; m.30, second beat, f♯′ belongs to tenor, e′ to alto; m.44, soprano, note 5, c♯″ instead of b′; m.52, soprano,

---

17. Both are double fugues in which the two subjects are introduced separately. Heydorn's first subject resembles Bach's second one – more closely than the latter resembles the subject of the fugue by Legrenzi discussed by Hill in "Die Herkunft von Bachs 'Thema Legrenzianum,'" *Bach-Jahrbuch* 72 (1986): 105–7.

note 5, b′ instead of a♯′; m. 54, second beat, d″ belongs to soprano, a″ to inner voice; m. 55, last beat, a′ belongs to tenor, g′ to alto; mm. 61 and 62, bass, notes 5–6, G♯–g♯ instead of G–g; mm. 69 and 70, *tr.* should be italic instead of boldface (= *trem.* in m. 68); m. 86, bass, notes 4–6, eighth and two sixteenths instead of three eighths; m. 105, bass, notes 3–4, f♯ (eighth) instead of f♯–A (sixteenths); m. 105, alto, second beat, f♯′–e♯′ (eighths) instead of f♯′–f♯′–e♯′ (two sixteenths, eighth); m. 107, bass, note 6, g♯ instead of g; m. 109, soprano, no accidental on final e″; mm. 112–14, right hand, inner voices editorial; m. 119, ♮ on c″ is editorial; mm. 153 and 157, alto, quarters [*sic*] instead of eighths (rests are editorial); mm. 167 and 169, right hand, note 1, d″/f♯′ instead of b′/d′; m. 204, ♯ (middle part, c″) is editorial; m. 205, ♮ on c″ instead of d″; m. 232, tenor, add editorial ♮; m. 236, left hand, middle part, doubles f♯ instead of a; m. 242, second beat, right hand, add middle part e♯′ (dotted eighth) and tie tenor b–b; m. 244, soprano, a′ instead of a♯′; mm. 260 and 264, bass, note 4, f instead of g; mm. 263 and 267, last chord, add d′.

BWV 917: m. 7, e♭″ instead of e″; m. 37, MM has whole note a on downbeat (in addition to rest).

BWV 967: m. 21, accidentals on g″ editorial – both might be ♮; mm. 36 and 37, soprano, last 3 notes, b‴–b″–d″ instead of c‴–c‴–f″ ([?]add editorial figures 6/4/2); m. 40, bass, note 6, ♮ is editorial – could be ♯; m. 40, bass, note 7, f♯ instead of f; m. 42, bass, note 8, could be g instead of g♯; m. 57, soprano, note 5, b′ instead of b♭′ (sign not fully drawn in MS); mm. 65 and 71, all naturals editorial, other readings possible; mm. 76–77, tenor, tie may be stray mark in MS.

BUXWV 151: m. 6, beats 1–2, alto, stems up (dictates division of figure between hands); m. 17, tenor, last note, a instead of b; m. 18, bass, notes 1–2, eighths (e–E) beamed together, "Ped." is editorial.

David Schulenberg

CONTRIBUTORS

JAMES A. BROKAW II received his doctorate from the University of Chicago with a dissertation on Bach's procedures of formal expansion in the preludes and fugues. His work has appeared in *Bach Studies, Bach, Notes*, the *Journal of Musicological Research*, and the *Newsletter of the American Bach Society*. He is a volunteer fireman in Ogden Dunes, Indiana, and a computer programmer in Chicago.

ERIC T. CHAFE is a professor of music at Brandeis University. He is the author of *Tonal Allegory in the Vocal Music of J. S. Bach* (University of California Press) and *Monteverdi's Tonal Language* (Schirmer Books), for which he received the American Musicological Society's Otto Kinkeldey Award. He is currently completing a book on Bach's church cantatas.

STEPHEN A. CRIST is an assistant professor of music at Emory University. His recent and forthcoming publications include essays on Bach in *The Cambridge Companion to Bach*, the *College Music Symposium*, and a *Festschrift* for Paul Brainard; two articles on Hugo Wolf in *The International Dictionary of Opera*; and an introductory study and facsimile edition of *Enchiridion Geistliker Leder vnde Psalmen*, the unique copy of a Low German hymnal that originally appeared in Magdeburg in 1536. He is currently writing a book on the Bach arias, with the support of a Fellowship for University Teachers from the National Endowment for the Humanities.

MICHAEL MARISSEN is an assistant professor of music at Swarthmore College and has also taught as a visiting professor at Princeton University. He has published articles on Bach's instrumental and vocal music in various journals and recently completed *The Social and Religious Designs of J. S. Bach's Brandenburg Concertos* (Princeton University Press). He is currently working with Daniel Melamed on a guide to Bach research, to be published by Garland.

DAVID SCHULENBERG is the author of *The Keyboard Music of J. S. Bach* (Schirmer Books) and *The Instrumental Music of Carl Philipp Emanuel Bach* (UMI Research Press). He performs on harpsichord and other early keyboard instruments and is director of the collegium musicum at the University of North

Carolina at Chapel Hill, where he is an assistant professor of music. He is currently working on problems of meaning and interpretation in Baroque music. Forthcoming publications include a study of attribution problems in the keyboard music of William Byrd and a critical edition of seven keyboard sonatas by C. P. E. Bach.

RUSSELL STINSON is an associate professor of music and college organist at Lyon College (formerly Arkansas College). His research on Bach's instrumental music has led to numerous publications, including *The Bach Manuscripts of Johann Peter Kellner and His Circle: A Case Study in Reception History* (Duke University Press) and *Keyboard Transcriptions from the Bach Circle* (A-R Editions). He is currently completing a book on Bach's *Orgelbüchlein*, to be published by Schirmer Books in its forthcoming series Monuments of Western Music.

GENERAL INDEX

Page numbers in italics refer to music examples.

Adami, Johann Christian (*Güldene Aepffel*), 122

Albinoni, Tomaso, 3

Altnikol, Johann Christoph, 200

Andreas Bach Book (Bach, Johann Christoph), 8, 191, 205–14

Anonymous 303, 29

Arfken, Ernst, 57 n.31

August the Strong, 138, 159

Bach, Carl Philipp Emanuel, 1 n.1, 2, 13, 25–26, 28, 33, 194
   H.24 (w.48/1): Prussian Sonata no.1, 35, 37
   H.46 (w.65/16): Sonata in C Major, 26 n.58
   H.47 (w.65/17): Sonata in G Minor, 37, *38*
   H.75/3 (w.63/6/3): Fantasy in C Minor, 35 n.90, 36
   H.76 (w.119/1): *Duo in contrapuncto*, 4 n.12
   H.101 (w.119/4): Fugue in A Major, 4 n.12
   H.102 (w.119/6): Fugue in E♭ Major, 4 n.12
   H.150 (w.51/1): Sonata in C Major, 28 n.66
   H.156 (w.65/35): Sonata in C Major, 28 n.66
   H.157 (w.65/36): Sonata in C Major, 28 n.66
   H.160 (w.117/14): Fantasy in D Major, 28, 29
   H.340: Polonoise in G Major, 11 n.33
   H.348: Fantasy in E♭ Major, 22–23, 36, 37, *38*
   H.484: Concerto in D Minor (bwv 1052a), 24–25
   H.772 (w.215): Magnificat, 4 n.12, 10–11
   H.867 (w.121): *Miscellanea musica*, 26 n.58

"Ich ruf zu dir, Herr Jesu Christ" (bwv anh.73), 29

Bach, Johann Christoph (1642–1703; organist in Eisenach), 11
   Sarabanda con 12 variazioni, 11, *12*

Bach, Johann Christoph (1671–1721; Johann Sebastian's brother), 2, 8, 190, 191 n.20, 205, 212
   See also *Andreas Bach Book*; *Möller Manuscript*

Bach, Johann Nicolaus, 8 n.22, 13

Bach, Wilhelm Friedemann, 4, 26, 33, 44 n.1, 93 n.21, 201
   F.14: Fantasy in C Major, *22, 23*
   F.21: Fantasy in E Minor, *24*, 35

Bach Compendium, 184

Bach-Jahrbuch, 184

Bassani, Giovanni Battista (*Acroama Missale*), 187

Bernhard, Christoph, 187

Böhm, Georg, 58 n.33, 190, 206, 207

Bonporti, Francesco Antonio (*Inventioni*), 34 n.88

Brandenburg, Margrave of, 82, 185

Buelow, George, 25

Bülow, Hans von, 34

Busoni, Ferruccio, 163

Butler, Gregory, 193

Buttstedt, Johann Heinrich, 207, 211 n.14

Buxtehude, Dietrich, 9, 58 n.33, 65 n.46, 166, 187–88, 190, 191 n.20
   Abendmusik, 191
   buxwv 123: *Canon duplex per augmentationem*, 188
   buxwv 124: *Divertisons nous aujourd'hui* (canon), 188

217

INDEX OF BACH'S COMPOSITIONS

Page numbers in italics refer to music examples.

Index of Bach's Compositions